RETRIEVAL & RENEWAL

Ressourcement

IN CATHOLIC THOUGHT

Volumes available

In the Beginning:
A Catholic Understanding of the Story of Creation and the Fall
by Cardinal Joseph Ratzinger

Hans Urs von Balthasar: A Theological Style
by Angelo Scola

Prayer: The Mission of the Church
Jean Daniélou

The Discovery of God
Henri de Lubac

Medieval Exegesis, *volume 1:*
The Four Senses of Scripture
Henri de Lubac

The Heroic Face of Innocence:
Three Stories by Georges Bernanos
Georges Bernanos

On Pilgrimage
Dorothy Day

On Pilgrimage

DOROTHY DAY

WILLIAM B. EERDMANS PUBLISHING COMPANY
GRAND RAPIDS, MICHIGAN

T&T CLARK
EDINBURGH

Originally published 1948 by Catholic Worker Books

Introduction first published in *Communio*, 24 (Fall 1997).
© 1997 *Communio: International Catholic Review.*

Foreword © 1999 by Wm. B. Eerdmans Publishing Co.

This edition published jointly 1999 by
Wm. B. Eerdmans Publishing Co.
255 Jefferson Ave. S.E., Grand Rapids, Michigan 49503
and by
T&T Clark Ltd
59 George Street, Edinburgh EH2 2LQ Scotland

Printed in the United States of America

04 03 02 01 00 99   7 6 5 4 3 2 1

Library of Congress Cataloging-in-Publication Data

Day, Dorothy, 1897-1980.
On pilgrimage / Dorothy Day.
p.   cm.
Originally published: New York: Curtis Books, c1972.
Includes bibliographical references.
ISBN 0-8028-4629-7 (pbk.: alk. paper)
1. Day, Dorothy, 1897-1980 Diaries.
2. Catholic Worker Movement. I. Title.
BX4705.D283A36
267'.182'092 — dc21

[B]   99-23525
                                             CIP

British Library Cataloguing-in-Publication Data

A catalogue record for this book is available from the British Library

ISBN 0 567 08691 7

Contents

Foreword

While to be a saint is always to be a paradox, the reverse is not necessarily true. Dorothy Day, who had a healthy respect for paradoxes and a ferocious devotion to saints, famously evaded an embarrassing invitation to speculate on her own sanctity with the retort, "I don't want to be dismissed that easily." But whether or not she ought to be considered a saint, as I believe she should, she is undeniably a paradox, and whether or not she is ever canonized, as I believe she will be, she will never be easily dismissed.

In this rambling account of her doings during the year of 1948, Dorothy, as most of her admirers familiarly presume to call her, speaks frequently and casually about saints. (This is true of her other writings and of her conversation and public speaking as well. It is one of the delightful anomalies of our time that when the Federal Bureau of Investigation began keeping its file on her, its agents felt obliged to furnish explanatory footnotes with brief biographies of Francis of Assisi, Vincent de Paul, and others.) Dorothy managed to write only nine journal entries in January of 1948, having moved into a chaotic West Virginia farmhouse to help her expectant daughter and son-in-law run the farm, raise their two toddlers, and prepare for the new arrival. But even in these few pages, St. Angela of Foligno, St. John of the Cross, St. Teresa of Ávila, St. Agnes, St. Francis, St. Catherine of Siena, St. Paul, St. Martin, and St. John Bosco all make appearances, along with the Brontë sisters, Charles Dickens'

Mrs. Jellyby, Reverend Reginald Garrigou-Lagrange, O.P., Ignatio Silone, Hilaire Belloc, G. K. Chesterton, Arthur Koestler, Aldous Huxley, and Martin Buber. Anecdotes from the lives of the saints came as naturally to her mind and lips and pen as quotations from Kropotkin, legends of the I.W.W., gossip from the Catholic Worker House on Mott Street, the Collect from last Sunday's Mass, speculations on the death of a billy goat, denunciations of corporate capitalism, grocery lists, a paean to "one of those wonderful dustpans with long handles," and meditations on the will of God.

An advertent enemy of the state, Dorothy liked to describe herself unreservedly as a daughter of the Church, and that filial relationship was no mere metaphor for her. As a convert freshly arrived in the household of the Faith, she sought to make the saints her daily companions. And she succeeded. Her own soul, the soul of an ardent American revolutionary, resounded with those celebrated in the liturgical calendar, the souls of astonishing characters, agitators for the Kingdom produced by the ultimate revolution fought out in a million peculiar times and places.

When a terrorized grade-schooler finally stands up to a playground bully, when a Rosa Parks refuses to move to the back of the bus, when a Franz Jägerstätter declines his local bishop's well-meant advice to enlist in Hitler's army, when a tragically pregnant young woman declines the proffered RU 486, when a conscientious college graduate turns down a potentially lucrative career with Planned Parenthood or the Central Intelligence Agency, something akin if not identical to the revolution of the saints is underway. By 1948, according to the available evidence, Dorothy Day, a treasonous, muckraking, anarchistic jailbird, was a principal partisan and theoretician in just such a revolution.

It was a revolution that Jacques Maritain splendidly describes in "The Peasant of the Garonne," at the root of which "there is something so profound in the soul that one does not know how to express it — let us say that it is a simple refusal, a total, stable, supremely active refusal to accept things as they are. This act has to do with a fact, an existential fact: things as they are are intolerable. In the reality of existence, the world is infected with lying, injustice, wickedness, distress, and misery; creation has been corrupted by sin to such an extent that in the very marrow of his soul, the saint refuses to accept it as it is. Evil — I mean by that the power of sin, and the universal suffering which it drags in its wake — evil is such that the only thing the saint has immediately at hand to oppose it totally, and that intoxicates the saint with liberty, exultation, and love, is to give everything, to abandon everything, the sweetness of the world, and what is good, and what is better, and what is delectable and permitted, and more than anything, himself, in order to be free to be with God. To do this is to be totally stripped and given over in order to seize the power of the cross: it is to die for those he loves. This is a flash of intuition and will above any order of human morality. Once the soul has been touched in flight by this burning wing, it becomes a stranger everywhere. It can fall in love with things; never will it take repose in them."

Dorothy's life and writings abound in heartening examples of the richness, profundity, and durability of the revolution of the saints. In these pages particularly can be seen a specifically American reading of the *Letter to Diognetus,* whose author observed that Christians "live in poverty, but enrich many; they are totally destitute, but possess an abundance of everything." Like the soul described by Maritain, Dorothy could indeed fall in love with things without taking repose in them. Of renunciation, she wrote, "One can get by if one's wants are modest. One can withdraw from the factory, refuse to make munitions, airplanes, atom bombs. In sections like this [of West Virginia] rent is ten dollars a month, sometimes even five dollars, and there are empty houses. But city people are afraid, afraid of the country, afraid of the dark, afraid to be alone, afraid of the silence."

If Dorothy Day were writing that passage today — some fifty years later — I think she might replace the term "city people" with "suburbanites." In any event, her impatience with such bourgeois fear certainly arose from her kinship with the saints and her participation in their common life. For a different sort of convert, a different sort of revolutionary, the Gospel's call to renunciation might become merely another convenient way to taunt the Wonder Bread lifestyle of fatuous middle-class North Americans. Not so for the woman who could write this passage, from an entry on a hot day in mid-September, something which St. Francis might have written, and which is fairly reverberative throughout the journal:

> Yesterday we canned sixteen quarts of peaches and today twenty quarts of tomatoes. In the afternoon we went down to the brook and bathed. Today we saw three large turtles swimming under water and any number of striped fish about eight inches long. While we sat on a gravelly bank collecting pieces of stone with the imprint of shells and leaves on them, of which the brook bed is full, Susie caught sight of a slim little garter snake the color of a twig, coiled out on a branch sunning himself. No matter how close the pebbles we threw came to him, he would not move. Now we will be adding more verses to our "all ye works of the Lord" song.

This agreeable evocation of what Pope John Paul II has recently called "the culture of life" springs from the heart, mind, soul, and pen of a woman who could also vividly perceive the culture of death ascendant in the nation's customary ways of making do. That culture's idolatrous worship of individual autonomy, its reliance on usury, its fetishizing of corporate power, its nonchalance about sexuality, its neglect of the poor, its murderous addiction to increasingly apocalyptic weaponry to underwrite a spurious notion of security — all are instances of an intolerable situation in which acquiescence has become indistinguishable from sin. "Our problems stem," she used to say, "from our acceptance of this filthy, rotten system."

Dorothy Day's thorough renunciation of our filthy, rotten system has made her, at the very least, a challenging heroine. What makes her something more, what shines through this journal particularly, is her distinctive announcement that the one true antidote for the system is the Church. As a young man, John Cort, one of the first Catholic Workers, heard the announcement this way:

> I remember sitting in that dingy hall and saying to myself, "This woman is getting a lot of fun out of life, and I would like to get some of that for myself, so maybe I'd better try the same kind of

life." As much as anything it was a quality of humor and laughter that seemed to reach down to the secret, hidden places of the soul, promising at any minute to explain the mysteries of life and human striving.

The world needs more revolutionaries like her.

MICHAEL O. GARVEY

INTRODUCTION

Dorothy Day and the Catholic Worker Movement

MARK *and* LOUISE ZWICK

I have been disillusioned, however, this long, long time in the means used by any but the saints to live in this world God has made for us.

DOROTHY DAY

The year 1997 was the one-hundredth anniversary of Dorothy Day's birth and the seventieth anniversary of her entrance into the Catholic Church. On the occasion of her death in 1980, Dorothy was described by Catholic historian David O'Brien as "the most significant, interesting, and influential person in the history of American Catholicism." On her eightieth birthday, New York's Cardinal Terence Cook presented Dorothy with a special greeting from Pope Paul VI. Her picture and articles about her appeared in *Time*, *Newsweek*, and *Life* magazines. The *New York Times* said she was a "nonviolent social radical of luminous personality." For Sister Brigid O'Shea Merriman, O.S.F., she was "foremost among the witnesses of the incomprehensible Goodness who is God."[1]

---

1. Brigid O'Shea Merriman, *Searching for Christ: The Spirituality of Dorothy Day,*

In 1972 Dorothy was given the Laetare Medal by the University of Notre Dame. After her death, Father John Hugo said at a talk at Marquette University, "Dorothy Day has been in our time a luminous example of the twofold love of God and neighbor fused into one in the furnace of divine love." The December 1996 issue of the *Catholic World Report* celebrated her sanctity and her commitment to Christ in the poor. Today she is featured in many textbooks for religious education as a model for Catholic youth. She has been proposed for sainthood by the Claretian Fathers and Brothers.

Daniel Berrigan, S.J., credits her in his introduction to her autobiography, *The Long Loneliness:*

Without Dorothy, without that exemplary patience, courage, moral modesty, without this woman pounding at the locked door behind which the powerful mock the powerless with games of triage, without her, the resistance we offered would have been simply unthinkable. She urged our consciences off the beaten track; she made the impossible (in our case) probable and then actual. She did this first of all by living as though the Truth were true.[2]

What made Dorothy Day great? What was the truth that made her life so distinct, her witness so powerful? What was it that sustained her during a lifetime of commitment to the poor and to nonviolence in the face of criticism?

Robert Ellsberg, in the introduction to her *Selected Writings,* said of her, "It was not what Dorothy Day wrote that was extraordinary, nor even what she believed, but the fact that there was absolutely no distinction between what she believed, what she wrote, and the manner in which she lived."[3]

Dorothy was always open to the religious spirit. Her search for

---

Notre Dame Studies in American Catholicism (Notre Dame: University of Notre Dame Press, 1994), p. vii.

2. Dorothy Day, *The Long Loneliness: The Autobiography of Dorothy Day* (San Francisco: Harper & Row, 1952, 1981), p. xxiii.

3. *Dorothy Day: Selected Writings: By Little and By Little,* ed. Robert Ellsberg (Maryknoll, N.Y.: Orbis Books, 1993), p. xv.

the Absolute throughout her life was even in childhood and youth accompanied by her concern for the poor and a just social order.

The event that had the greatest impact on Dorothy Day's life occurred in 1927, when she became a Catholic at the age of thirty, not long after giving birth to her daughter. Her decision to enter the Church marked a dramatic conversion from a bohemian, worldly lifestyle to total commitment to Christ, to the Church, to the poor, to peace.

However, years before, even as a child, Dorothy had experienced a spiritual awakening. Although her family members were not active churchgoers, neighbors and ministers at different times invited the children to go to Protestant churches. Dorothy was baptized and confirmed in the Episcopal Church at age twelve, and the Psalms, the formal prayer of the church, became a part of her childhood.

Dorothy grew up in a household in which lightweight literature was forbidden. Her adolescent reading included the New Testament, John Wesley's *Sermons,* the works of St. Augustine, and William James's *Varieties of Religious Experience,* in which she discovered St. Teresa of Ávila and St. John of the Cross. In addition, she read and cherished Thomas à Kempis's *Imitation of Christ,* which became a lifelong favorite; the works of Dostoyevsky, which were also significant throughout her life; and the works of Tolstoy and other classics.

Dorothy reflected on these writings, especially the Gospel, even in her childhood, and wondered how they could be implemented in reality. In *The Long Loneliness* she wrote,

Children look at things very directly and simply. I did not see anyone taking off his coat and giving it to the poor. I didn't see anyone having a banquet and calling in the lame, the halt, and the blind. And those who were doing it, like the Salvation Army, did not appeal to me. I wanted, though I did not know it then, a synthesis. I wanted life and I wanted the abundant life. I wanted it for others too. I did not want just the few, the missionary-minded people like the Salvation Army, to be kind to the poor as the poor. I wanted everyone to be kind. I wanted every home to be open to the lame, the halt, and the blind. . . . Only then did people really live, really love their brothers. In such love was the abundant life, and I did not have the slightest idea how to find it.[4]

In the university she came across novelists Upton Sinclair and Jack London, whose social commentary encouraged in her a radical concern for the urban poor. She had been reading Prince Peter Kropotkin, who also brought to her attention the plight of the poor, the workers. She asked herself, "Why was so much done in remedying social evils instead of avoiding them in the first place? Where were the saints to try to change the social order, not just to minister to the slaves but to do away with the slavery?"[5] With the encouragement of professors, Dorothy questioned the role of religion in life. She remembered that in her community, the destitute had always been looked upon as shiftless, worthless, without talent of any kind, all because of their own fault. She read that workers were exploited in the stockyards and observed that the rich were smiled at and fawned upon by churchgoers. She longed for a synthesis, a way of life that would help to resolve these problems.

In her searching, Dorothy joined the Socialist Party in college and wrote for the student paper of the University of Illinois. After attending college for two years, she moved with her family to New York when her father, a newspaperman, began to work for the *Morning Telegraph*. There Dorothy wrote for the socialist papers *The Call, The Masses,* and *The Liberator*.

Dorothy was very much a part of the socialist antiwar movement before World War I. She participated in demonstrations against U.S. involvement organized by socialists, and she was clubbed, albeit accidentally, by police. *The Masses,* for which she wrote at the time, took a pacifist stand. For all practical purposes it was closed down by the local postmaster, who refused to send it bulk rate, since he considered it treasonous. In their book *American Catholic Pacifism: The Influence of Dorothy Day and the Catholic Worker Movement,* Anne Klejment and Nancy L. Roberts document the influence of wartime

4. Day, *The Long Loneliness,* p. 39.
5. Day, *The Long Loneliness,* p. 45.

repression on Dorothy Day and demonstrate how it was "absorbed into her religious pacifism."[6]

Later, after joining in protest against treatment of other protestors, Dorothy found herself in jail for the first time in Washington, D.C., at Occoquan. Placed in solitary confinement, she asked for a Bible. Having read the Psalms many times in the past, she turned to them. She said she read them there with a "sense of coming back to something I had lost." In *From Union Square to Rome,* she described her time in solitary confinement, telling of her spiritual search and the suffering that bound her to others:

> All through those weary first days in jail when I was in solitary confinement, the only thoughts that brought comfort to my soul were those lines in the Psalms that expressed the terror and misery of man suddenly stricken and abandoned. Solitude and hunger and weariness of spirit — those sharpened my perceptions so that I suffered not only my own sorrow but the sorrows of those about me. I was no longer a young girl, part of a radical movement seeking justice for those oppressed; I was the oppressed. I was that drug addict, screaming and tossing in her cell, beating her head against the wall.[7]

In *The Long Loneliness* she continued her description of her time in Occoquan, at the end of which she turned away from the religion that had initially comforted her:

> I lost all feeling of my own identity. I reflected on the desolation of poverty, of destitution, of sickness and sin. That I would be free after thirty days meant nothing to me. I would never be free again, never free when I knew that behind bars all over the world there were women and men, young girls and boys, suffering constraint, punishment, isolation, and hardship for crimes of which all of us were guilty. The mother who had murdered her child, the drug ad-

6. *American Catholic Pacifism: The Influence of Dorothy Day and the Catholic Worker Movement,* ed. Anne Klejment and Nancy L. Roberts (Westport, Conn.: Praeger, 1996), p. 18.

7. Dorothy Day, *From Union Square to Rome* (Silver Spring, Md.: Preservation of the Faith Press, 1938), p. 6.

dict — who were the mad and who the sane? Why were prostitutes prosecuted in some cases and in others respected and fawned on? People sold themselves for jobs, for the paycheck, and if they only received a high enough price, they were honored. If their cheating, their theft, their lie were of colossal proportions, if it were successful, they met with praise, not blame. Why were some caught, not others? Why were some termed criminals and others good businessmen? What was right and wrong? What was good and evil? I lay there in utter confusion and misery. . . .

The thirty days stretched out before me interminably. I would be utterly crushed by misery before I was released. Never would I recover from this wound, this ugly knowledge I had gained of what men were capable [of] in their treatment of each other. It was one thing to be writing about these things, to have the theoretical knowledge of sweatshops and injustice and hunger, but it was quite another to experience it in one's own flesh. . . .

I had no thought of religion these last days [out of solitary confinement]. I was very much in the world again, talking with others, reading and writing letters, and I no longer thought of the depths I had been in. To be so degraded was to be shamed and humbled, but I rejected the humiliation. I had seen myself too weak to stand alone, too weak to face the darkness of that punishment cell without crying out, and I was ashamed and again rejected religion that had helped me when I had been brought to my knees by my suffering.[8]

It was later, in Chicago, that Dorothy discovered the trilogy of novels by Joris-Karl Huysmans that helped her in her search for God. She read *En Route, The Oblate,* and *The Cathedral,* and she later said that these books had made her feel that she could be at home in the Catholic Church. They acquainted her with what went on there, and she was drawn to it: "I felt the age, the antiquity of the Mass, and here to find in Huysmans detailed instructions in regard to rubrics, all the complicated ritual, was a great joy to me."[9] Huysmans

8. Day, *The Long Loneliness,* pp. 78, 79, 83.
9. Day, *The Long Loneliness,* p. 107.

introduced her to the liturgy, to monasticism, and particularly to the Benedictines, who had such a great influence on the Catholic Worker movement. Many years later, Dorothy followed in the footsteps of the oblate in the novel when she herself became a Benedictine lay oblate. In describing her study in preparation for becoming a Catholic, Dorothy credited both Dostoyevsky and Huysmans: "Dostoyevsky, Huysmans (what different men!) had given me desire and background. Huysmans had made me at home in the Church."[10]

It was around this same time that she got to know other Catholic families. They reminded her of Mrs. Barrett, a Catholic whom she had known as a child. She remembered her childhood visit to Mrs. Barrett's home vividly:

It was around ten o'clock in the morning that I went up to Kathryn's to call for her to come out and play. There was no one on the porch or in the kitchen. The breakfast dishes had all been washed. . . . Thinking the children must be in the front room, I burst in and ran through the bedrooms.

In the front bedroom Mrs. Barrett was on her knees, saying her prayers. She turned to tell me that Kathryn and the children had all gone to the store and went on with her praying. I felt a burst of love toward Mrs. Barrett that I have never forgotten, a feeling of gratitude and happiness that warmed my heart. She had God, and there was beauty and joy in her life.

All through my life what she was doing remained with me. And though I became oppressed with the problem of poverty and injustice, though I groaned at the hideous sordidness of man's lot, though there were years when I clung to the philosophy of economic determinism as an explanation of man's fate, still there were moments when in the midst of misery and class strife, life was shot through with glory. Mrs. Barrett in her sordid little tenement flat finished her breakfast dishes at ten o'clock in the morning and got down on her knees and prayed to God.[11]

10. Day, *The Long Loneliness*, p. 142.
11. Day, *From Union Square to Rome*, p. 10.

Watching these families unashamedly kneeling in prayer in their homes affected her powerfully: "This posture, this gesture convinced me that worship, adoration, thanksgiving, supplication — these were the noblest acts of which men were capable in this life."[12]

Later, in New York, after spending long nights in Greenwich Village talking with artists and writers like Eugene O'Neill (he once read Francis Thompson's poem "The Hound of Heaven" to her), Dorothy would walk home and see the immigrant women who cleaned offices during the night going to early-morning Mass. The Catholic Church was visibly the church of the poor in its incarnation of the Gospel, not just the Church of the middle or upper classes.

Dorothy's years of flirting with the intellectual and devotional aspects of Catholicism culminated in her seeking baptism, first for her child to be born and later for herself, although she was in a common-law marriage (not her first) with Forster Batterham. This relationship dissolved rather quickly, albeit very painfully, as Forster did not believe in religion, marriage, or having children! It was the birth of her daughter, Tamar, at which time "love overflowed," that led her to want to do something definite about her faith. She felt that belonging to a church would bring the order into her daughter's life that her own life had lacked. In *From Union Square to Rome,* Dorothy described her motivation in coming to the Church:

> But always the glimpses of God came most when I was alone. Objectors cannot say that it was fear of loneliness and solitude and pain that made me turn to Him. It was in those few years when I was alone and most happy that I found Him. I found Him at last through joy and thanksgiving, not through sorrow.
>
> Yet how can I say that either? Better let it be said that I found Him through His poor, and in a moment of joy I turned to Him.[13]

In a sense, Dorothy felt that she was betraying her socialist background by becoming Catholic. In socialist circles it had been em-

---

12. Day, *The Long Loneliness,* p. 107.
13. Day, *From Union Square to Rome,* p. 10.

phasized again and again that the Church was the opiate of the people, that "the Church was lined up with property, with the wealthy, with the state, with capitalism, with all the forces of reaction." But she had made her decision. She was baptized conditionally, made her confession, and received Communion. In *The Long Loneliness* she reflected on this criticism of the Church, which she believed, and why she, who was as much against capitalism and imperialism as ever, was "going over to the opposition." In spite of what she had been taught in radical movements, she said,

> I wanted to be poor, chaste, and obedient. I wanted to die in order to live, to put off the old man and put on Christ. I loved, in other words, and like all women in love, I wanted to be united to my love. Why should not Forster be jealous? Any man who did not participate in this love would, of course, realize my infidelity, my adultery. In the eyes of God, any turning toward creatures to the exclusion of Him is adultery, and so it is termed over and over again in Scripture.[14]

The nun who instructed Dorothy in Catholicism gave her the *Baltimore Catechism* as her study guide, as well as copies of the *Sacred Heart Messenger*. Dorothy also continued reading *The Imitation of Christ*, St. Augustine, and the New Testament.

She continued studying after her conversion, reading Karl Adam's *Spirit of Catholicism* and books by and about St. Teresa of Ávila. Later, a priest taught her to say the Little Office of the Blessed Virgin and gave her a St. Andrew's Missal, where she read the many introductory passages from the Church Fathers and began to live by the Church calendar.

The turning point in Dorothy Day's transition from Catholic convert to founder of a great lay movement and a lifetime of action and contemplation began on the Feast of the Immaculate Conception in 1932. She was covering the Hunger March in Washington, D.C., for *Commonweal*, regretting every minute of being an observer rather than a participant, remembering the protests of her pre-Catholic days. In

14. Day, *The Long Loneliness*, p. 149.

despair she went to the crypt of the unfinished Basilica of the Immaculate Conception to pour out her heart to the Lord.

"As I knelt there," Dorothy remembered, "I realized that after three years of Catholicism my only contact with active Catholics had been through articles I had written for one of the Catholic magazines. Those contacts had been brief, casual. I still did not know personally one Catholic layman." She prayed with tears and some anguish "that some way would open up for me to use what talents I possessed for my fellow workers, for the poor. And when I returned to New York, I found Peter Maurin — Peter the French peasant, whose spirit and ideas will dominate the rest of my life."[15]

Peter had read her articles in several Catholic magazines and was waiting for her at her home in New York. He was convinced that she was the person who could implement his program, which involved his ideas about "cult, culture, and cultivation," opening houses of hospitality, and especially starting a newspaper. He began immediately on her Catholic education, which included a Catholic outline of history and the social teachings of the Church (he wanted to make the encyclicals take root), as well as instruction about personalism, the common good, liturgy, and hospitality. Each day when he returned to continue his teaching, he brought up the idea of a newspaper and kept harping on it, according to Dorothy.

In her humility, she credited Peter with teaching her everything she knew. That is not correct. While she did say that she knew nothing of Catholic social teaching at the time she met Peter, both her life experience and a lifetime of reading prepared her for the founding of the Catholic Worker movement. As she listened to Peter, she was most interested at first in his idea for the newspaper: "Of course it was getting out a labor paper which caught my imagination, popularizing the teachings of the Church in regard to social matters, bringing to the man in the street a Christian solution of unemployment, a way of rebuilding the social order."[16]

15. Day, *The Long Loneliness*, p. 166.

16. Dorothy Day, *House of Hospitality* (New York and London: Sheed & Ward, 1939), p. xvii.

When Dorothy asked Peter where they were going to get the money to start the paper, he told her, "In the history of the saints, capital was raised by prayer — God sends you what you need when you need it. You will be able to pay the printer. Just read the lives of the saints."[17] Dorothy had been reading about the life of Rose Hawthorne, Nathaniel's daughter, who had started a hospice in New York for the poor who had cancer. Her method of raising money simply by telling people what she was going to do appealed to Dorothy. Perhaps she could start in a small way.

She began the paper with two small checks she had received for articles written for Catholic magazines. Peter wanted to call the paper *The Catholic Radical,* but Dorothy insisted on *The Catholic Worker.* It was a unique response to the Communist *Daily Worker.*

The first issue of *The Catholic Worker* appeared in May 1933; 2,500 copies were printed. Within three years the circulation rose to one hundred thousand. This was no accident. Dorothy actively sought bulk subscriptions: many parishes received five hundred copies; one Catholic high school, three thousand. Copies were sold on the streets and put in public places.

Soon afterward came the first house of hospitality, which the initial issue of *The Catholic Worker* had described. People in need had quickly found the paper's editors, taking them at their word that they would help the poor with works of mercy. Bread and soup lines for the hungry soon became a reality. First there was only Peter Maurin, Dorothy's brother John, and Dorothy herself to do the work. Soon others came to help, and more houses were opened.

Along with houses of hospitality, other components of the Catholic Worker program were developed during those early years. Peter Maurin began his lecture series for what he called "the clarification of thought," and Jesuit and Benedictine priests and prominent professors from Columbia came to speak at Peter's invitation, a tradition that continues to this day. And they brought their students to help out in the house of hospitality in New York and to learn about the idea of scholars and workers sharing and working together.

In 1936 a twenty-eight-acre farm was found, and the first farm-

17. Day, *The Long Loneliness,* p. 173.

11

ing commune began. This farm and the others that later began to dot the country were a big challenge because many of the families and single people who came to live and work on the farms actually knew little about farming. There are still several Catholic Worker farms in existence today. The agronomic universities were perhaps the least successful of the Catholic Worker projects, but they put flesh on the Distributist economics embraced by the movement. In the thirties, the Catholic Worker also founded Maternity Guilds. The paper featured these and encouraged parishes to help poor mothers and families. In the early issues of the paper, as she did much later in her life, Dorothy supported Church teaching on birth control, divorce and remarriage, and abortion.

Understanding Dorothy Day's Catholicism

Dorothy Day lived with the pain of knowing that she had not lived according to Catholic morality during the years before she became a convert. She had always had tremendous concern and sympathy for the poor and had somehow known God's presence among them. She had read the Scriptures and searched for God. In college, however, as sometimes happens, she set aside her childhood faith. During this period of her life she made certain choices that would cause her great regret after her conversion. She was involved in more than one romantic liaison, in addition to one formal marriage, and had an abortion. Juli Loesch Wiley, a pro-life social activist, has suggested that she might be the patron saint for women who are struggling with the grief of having had an abortion.

When Dorothy became a Catholic, she became one with her whole heart, soul, and mind. Her life was changed forever. Dorothy was a full-fledged Catholic. She accepted the Roman Catholic Church in all its aspects:

> Now the creed to which I subscribe is like a battle cry, engraved on my heart — the *Credo* of the Holy Roman Catholic Church. Before, in those former times, I could say, "I shall sleep in the dust: and if thou seek me in the morning, I shall not be" (Job

7:21). Now I can say, "I know that my Redeemer liveth, and the last day I shall rise out of the earth. And I shall be clothed again with my skin, and in my flesh I shall see God. Whom I myself shall see and my eyes shall behold, and not another: this my hope is laid up in my bosom" (Job 19:25-27).

I had a conversation with John Spivak, the Communist writer, a few years ago, and he said to me, "How *can* you believe? How can you believe in the Immaculate Conception, in the Virgin birth, in the Resurrection?" I could only say that I believe in the Roman Catholic Church and all she teaches. I have accepted Her authority with my whole heart. At the same time I want to point out to you that we are taught to pray for final persever-ance. We are taught that faith is a gift, and sometimes I wonder why some have it and some do not. I feel my own unworthiness and can never be grateful enough to God for His gift of faith. St. Paul tells us that if we do not correspond to the graces we re-ceive, they will be withdrawn. So I believe also that we should walk in fear, "work out our salvation in fear and trembling."

As for those two other tenets to which the Communists sub-scribe, I still believe that our social order must be changed, that it is not right for property to be concentrated in the hands of the few. But I believe now with St. Thomas Aquinas that a certain amount of property is necessary for a man to lead a good life. I believe that we should work to restore the communal aspects of Christianity as well as some measure of private property for all.

I still believe that revolution is inevitable, leaving out Divine Providence. But with the help of God and by resorting to His sacraments and accepting the leadership of Christ, I believe we can overcome revolution by a Christian revolution of our own, without the use of force.[18]

Dorothy loved the Church; it was her new home as a convert — and she was not about to be homeless. It is impossible to under-stand her without understanding her great love for the Church. But this does not mean that she accepted the neglect of the poor. She

18. Day, *From Union Square to Rome*, pp. 144-45.

loved the Church so much that she felt free to criticize it as an institution. Neglect of the poor is *not* Catholic teaching, she insisted:

> The scandal of businesslike priests, of collective wealth, the lack of a sense of responsibility for the poor, the worker . . . and even the oppression of these, and the consenting to the oppression of them by our industrialist-capitalist order . . . these made me feel often that priests were more like Cain than Abel. "Am I my brother's keeper?" they seem to say in respect to the social order.[19]

Dorothy's outspoken commitment to the poor brought accusations of subversiveness. The Catholic Workers often lived in great discomfort because of voluntary poverty, sometimes in houses without central heating or even indoor plumbing. Some who came to visit one house insisted that it could not be a Catholic place; it was too poor. They insisted the Workers must be Communists. Dorothy explained how hard it was to hear such criticisms from Catholics who were "quite content with the present in this world," who were content to give to the poor but "did not feel called upon to work for the things of this life for others. . . . Our insistence on worker-ownership, on the right of private property, on the need to de-proletarize the worker, all points which had been emphasized by the Popes in their social encyclicals, made many Catholics think we were Communists in disguise, wolves in sheep's clothing."[20]

There were times when Dorothy was frustrated with the hierarchy or with fellow Catholics. She went so far as to say, "I loved the Church for Christ made visible. Not for itself, because it was so often a scandal to me. Romano Guardini said that the Church is the Cross on which Christ was crucified; one could not separate Christ from His Cross, and one must live in a state of permanent dissatisfaction with the Church."[21]

Dorothy was uncomfortable with Pope-bashing, the kind of crit-

19. Day, *The Long Loneliness,* p. 150.
20. Day, *The Long Loneliness,* pp. 186-87.
21. Day, *The Long Loneliness,* pp. 149-50.

icism that is common in much journalism today. She did not hesitate to criticize the Church for its neglect of the poor or on the subject of war, but she was honest and felt it was important to be fair, even to Popes. Writing in Rome at the time of the Second Vatican Council, she defended Paul VI against his detractors. In her "On Pilgrimage" column in the November 1965 issue of *The Catholic Worker*, she commented on a biography of Pope Paul, *Apostle for Our Times*, by Reverend John Clancy:

> It is a fascinating book, which shows the wide experience our present Pope had in dealing with the practical affairs of the huge diocese of Milan, and tells how he said Mass in the factories and helped rebuild the working-class sections. I felt that *Time* magazine had treated him unfairly indeed by giving the impression that he was a man at home only in the State Department of the Vatican, protected from the life of the real world about him by his desk and paperwork. With all the talk of reforming the seminaries today, it was interesting to find that Pope Paul had never lived in a seminary, but carried on all his studies while living at home in the midst of a family where the father and brothers were engaged in journalistic and political work. Both by his reading and his work he kept in contact with and took part in the work of his times.[22]

Dorothy was a great model for the modern Catholic activist. When talking about reformation, she put herself first on the list. For her, charity and reformation began at home. She always emphasized and was drawn to the call to holiness, which in the Gospels so clearly applies to oneself. Dorothy often spoke of a revolution of the heart, an interior conversion that would impel someone as a Catholic to an active engagement with the world.

For Dorothy, priests were most important. She saw the clergy as "the dispensers of the Sacraments, bringing Christ to all men, enabling us to put on Christ and to achieve more nearly in the world a

---

22. Dorothy Day, *On Pilgrimage: The Sixties* (New York: Curtis Books, 1972), p. 247.

sense of peace and unity." She knew that it is Christ himself, the eternal high priest of the New Covenant, who, acting through the ministry of the priests, offers the Eucharistic sacrifice, and that the grace of the Sacrament comes not on account of the particular priest but perhaps in spite of him.

Dorothy's criticism of clerics tempered over time. Referring to her comment above about businesslike priests, she said, "With all the knowledge I have gained these twenty-one years I have been a Catholic, I could write many a story of priests who were poor, chaste, and obedient, who gave their lives daily for their fellows, but I am writing of how I felt at the time of my baptism."[23] She received a number of priests at the Catholic Worker who were in trouble with their bishops — alcoholics, for example — who really didn't have a place to go. The authors met some of these priests on a visit to the Staten Island farm with Dorothy Day.

Dorothy was not a cafeteria Catholic (so popular today), not a pick-and-choose believer. If it was Church teaching, it was her credo. This commitment and active participation in Catholicism brought Dorothy into the mainstream of a large organization together with the masses, which she called the Mystical Body of Christ. She realized the spiritual impact that all members of the Mystical Body throughout the world had on one another as they strove to live out their faith wherever they were. She referred constantly to this membership, but she also acknowledged solidarity with those who were not formally members, referring to them (sometimes she quoted St. Augustine as the source for this doctrine, sometimes St. Thomas Aquinas) as potential members of the Body of Christ.

Stanley Vishnewski, who came to the Catholic Worker in New York at age eighteen, not knowing how long he would stay, spent his entire life there. In his book entitled *Wings of the Dawn,* he tells of the excitement at the Worker over the talks given about the Mystical Body by the Benedictine priests who spoke there:

> The doctrine of the Mystical Body of Christ made our Faith a living reality. The Church was not just a brick building that stood

23. Day, *The Long Loneliness,* p. 150.

on the corner. The Church was not Father Paulauskas or Sister Perpetua. It was we who were the Church! It was the union of all the Faithful! The Church was all of us united under the Kingship of Christ. It was Christ who was our King. It was Christ, our Brother, who acted as our Mediator with God the Father.

If one of us suffered, then everyone suffered. If one of us was happy and rejoiced, then everyone was happy and shared, in a mystical manner, in the rejoicing. It was indeed consoling to know that I was not alone and that the Mystical Body of Christ both rejoiced and suffered with me. I would wake up in the middle of the night and know that at that particular moment I was sharing in the fruits of the Holy Sacrifice of the Mass that was being offered up throughout the world. What a consolation it was to know that as I slept choirs of contemplative nuns and monks were chanting the Divine Office and that I as a member of the Mystical Body was sharing in their prayers.

I began to realize how important my actions and prayers were to the health and well-being of the Church. For the first time I understood what Dorothy had meant, that cold morning, when she told me that by missing [daily] Mass I was hurting the work.

I became aware that my prayers, my sacrifices, would and could contribute the necessary graces to keep alive the Faith of some poor prisoner locked away in a Communist or Fascist concentration camp. My prayers and good works also had the power to convert his captors.[24]

Dorothy's commitment to the Body of Christ and the profound influence of this understanding of the Church from St. Paul was something she expressed in many of her writings. She emphasized it in the "Aims and Purposes of the Catholic Worker Movement," published in *The Catholic Worker* of February 1940:

Together with the works of mercy, feeding, sheltering, and clothing our brothers, we must indoctrinate. We must "give reason

---

24. Stanley Vishnewski, *Wings of the Dawn* (New York: The Catholic Worker, n.d.), pp. 56-57.

for the faith that is in us." Otherwise we are scattered members of the Body of Christ; we are not "all members one of another." Otherwise our religion is an opiate for ourselves alone, for our comfort or for our individual safety or indifferent custom.

We cannot live alone. We cannot go to heaven alone. Otherwise, as Péguy said, God will say to us, "Where are the others?"

If we do not keep indoctrinating, we lose the vision. And if we lose the vision, we become merely philanthropists, doling out palliatives.

Dorothy was not an isolated Catholic, sitting on the edge or margin of mainline Catholicism, or part of a sectarian group that lives content in the discovery of its own little truths that it keeps under a bushel, as some theologians have recently suggested (cf. *Houston Catholic Worker*, vol. 17, nos. 1 and 2). Her radicalism, her commitment to the poor, to a just social order, to peace — all were rooted in her Catholicism.

In her great article on Holy Obedience, commenting on the whole question of obedience to God and to the Church, Dorothy made it clear that her commitment, her hopes, and her obedience were to Christ the King, to the Church, and to her conscience; she eschewed mindless obedience to the modern state. Speaking about people who have not yet come to a conversion or second conversion, which "binds them with a more profound, a more mature love and obedience to the Church," she noted that they may rebel against Church authority or resent it without realizing their great freedom. In her view, many Catholics did not seem to know they possessed such tremendous freedom to do good in living out the Gospel. After observing the unswerving, unquestioning obedience of many people that was an expression of an overblown patriotism to the modern state, Dorothy pointed out, with Simone Weil, that this was a strange modern phenomenon: "Every new development of the last three centuries has brought men closer to the state of affairs in which absolutely nothing would be recognized in the whole world as possessing a claim to obedience except the authority of the State," with its militarism, centralization, bureaucracy, and totalitarianism. The same people who question obedience to the Church in spiritual matters often give unquestioning obedience to what Dorothy called "Holy Mother the State."[25]

By contrast, Dorothy insisted that as one grows in Christian faith and prayer, these things will be put in their proper perspective: "Often we comfort ourselves only with words, but if we pray enough, the conviction will come too that Christ is our King, not Stalin, Bevins, or Truman. That He has all things in His hands, that 'all things work together for good for those that love Him.'"[26]

She knew that even for bishops and clergy, the temptation to be overly influenced by the state was very real. In *The Catholic Worker* of July-August 1962, she spoke of how religious persecution in Mexico, where there were myriad martyrs, was overcome by nonviolence and civil disobedience. She declared with great faith that "The Church cannot be destroyed, the gates of hell cannot prevail against it," but at the same time pointed out that in certain historical circumstances it can almost be wiped out, citing England at the time of Henry VIII: "All the Bishops but one went with the State at that time."

Dorothy took the Catholic truths to the world, to every bishop and to parishes and high schools throughout the land. The early *Catholic Worker* was even shared with Cardinal Ottaviani, secretary of the dreaded Holy Office, now called the Congregation for the Doctrine of the Faith. Dorothy Day and Cardinal Ottaviani were both pacifists; the cardinal's views were cited in *The Catholic Worker*.[27]

Dorothy's mainstream Catholicism was bolstered by her knowledge of history and the great traditions of the Church. She integrated into her life the charisms of the Benedictines (e.g., hospitality, liturgy, divine office) and the Franciscans (works of mercy, voluntary poverty, pacifism), which brought her not only into the lives of the saints but also into the lives of the many men and women of her day who were attempting to live out the Gospel. For this great activist who was also a contemplative, the Benedictine and

25. *Dorothy Day,* ed. Robert Ellsberg, p. 172.

26. Dorothy Day, *On Pilgrimage* (New York: Catholic Worker Books, 1948), p. 18.

27. Day, *On Pilgrimage: The Sixties,* p. 32.

Franciscan visions were complemented by her deep roots in the Carmelite spirituality of St. Teresa of Ávila and St. John of the Cross. Later in life, Dorothy became attracted to the Little Way of another Carmelite, St. Thérèse of Lisieux, and wrote a book about her. As usual, Dorothy brought her own reflections to the saint's ideas, emphasizing that everyone should study the Little Way, "which is all that is available to the poor, and the only alternative to the mass approach of the state."[28]

Here again, she applied the insights of the lives of these saints to her own life and those of the Catholic Workers, encouraging all to follow in their footsteps:

> We should look to St. Thérèse the Little Flower, to walk her little way, her way of love. We should look to St. Teresa of Ávila, who was not content to be like those people who proceeded with the pace of hens about God's business, but like those people who on their own account were greatly daring in what they wished to do for God. It is we ourselves that we have to think about, no one else. That is the way the saints worked. They paid attention to what they were doing, and if others were attracted to them by their enterprise, why, well and good. But they looked to themselves first of all.[29]

Dorothy's Catholicism was at the core of her existence. It was her lifeblood. She not only participated in daily Mass, visited the Blessed Sacrament daily, prayed the Liturgy of the Hours, recited the rosary, and went to weekly Confession, but also — no Scholastic dualism for her — viewed the world through a Catholic lens and made decisions from a Catholic theological perspective. If there was anyone more Catholic than the Pope, it was Dorothy Day. Yet Dorothy and Peter Maurin were both very ecumenical, working with people of various backgrounds. They brought to their relationships with those of other faiths the profound perspective of their own faith, as is true of the best ecumenism. For example, Fritz

28. *Dorothy Day,* ed. Robert Ellsberg, p. 335.
29. Day, *House of Hospitality,* p. 74.

Eichenberg, whose woodcuts appeared often in the pages of *The Catholic Worker,* was a Quaker. Dorothy said that while the leaders of the movement were Catholics, not all participants were.

The Catholic Worker Movement

The Catholic Worker movement has philosophical, spiritual, and theological roots in the rich tradition of the Church and in the work of some of the leading philosophers and theologians of the day. It was and is a Catholic lay movement without official status in the Church and without leadership formally defined. In 1962, Cardinal Leger asked Dorothy about the position of the Catholic Worker in the Church, and she subsequently wrote about their exchange:

> I replied that we were a group of Catholics, engaged in writing and editing a paper dealing with the great problems of the day — the role of the State in man's life, war and peace, means and ends. That we had no chaplains, were in no way an organization included in Catholic Action, that we were under no bishop, and that we were therefore free to explore all possibilities of reform and restoration without committing the hierarchy to dangerous positions, and to try to rebuild the social order to make a better society "where it is easier for men to be good." To be good men, to be holy men is to be whole men, living a full life, developing all their capacities for good, using the talents God has given them.
>
> The Cardinal had been looking at me from under his heavy brows, his deep-set eyes scarcely visible. But when he lifted his head he smiled and commented, "St. John the Baptist." We are among those who go ahead and prepare the way.[30]

A number of significant themes and emphases have marked the Catholic Worker movement throughout its history, including personalism (lived out through the spiritual and corporal Works of

---

30. Day, *On Pilgrimage: The Sixties,* p. 92.

Mercy and the tenets of Matthew 25), the clarification of thought (through *The Catholic Worker,* roundtable discussions, and the bringing together of scholars and workers), voluntary poverty, pacifism, support of workers, agronomy, the importance of the retreat, the centrality of the Eucharist, and the liturgy of the Church. The Worker also critiqued both capitalism and socialism, and endorsed instead the economics of Distributism.

Dorothy was introduced to the great personalist authors such as Emmanuel Mounier, Nicholas Berdyaev, and Jacques Maritain by Peter Maurin. Peter, a French immigrant, was the first to bring these people and their ideas to the Catholic Worker. (Jacques Maritain required a translator for years.) Mounier's emphasis on a "maximum of initiative, responsibility, and spiritual life" and the affirmation of the value of the human person permeated the life and thought of Dorothy Day and the CW movement. Dorothy differentiated clearly between personalism, individualism, and collectivism. She spelled this out in her column in *The Catholic Worker* of September 1936:

> We are working for the Communitarian revolution to oppose both the rugged individualism of the capitalist era and the collectivism of the Communist revolution. We are working for the Personalist revolution because we believe in the dignity of man, the temple of the Holy Ghost, so beloved by God that He sent His son to take upon Himself our sins and die an ignominious and disgraceful death for us. We are Personalists because we believe that man, a person, a creature of body and soul, is greater than the State, of which as an individual he is a part. We are Personalists because we oppose the vesting of all authority in the hands of the state instead of in the hands of Christ the King. We are Personalists because we believe in free will, and not in the economic determinism of the Communist philosophy.

According to Brigid Merriman, the personalists who influenced Dorothy Day spoke primarily "of the dignity of the human person, who is in relationship with God and the world about him or her, and secondarily of the institutions in which he or she is to be engaged or engulfed." The personalist view was positive, with an anthropology "envisioning humankind collectively and individually as made in God's image." This positive anthropology, and the emphasis that God's grace is everywhere, encouraged the ecumenical spirit of Peter and Dorothy. The personalists called upon the laity to be leaven for good in the world. Along with them Dorothy Day always emphasized the primacy of the spiritual.[31]

She described the manner in which a personalist or a Catholic Worker must work, insisting that one must depend completely on God while working with all one's might, and quoted St. Ignatius on this: "Work as though everything depended on ourselves, and pray as though everything depended on God."[32]

The Catholic Worker movement integrated these personalist ideas with the practical living out of the great traditions of the Church and the Scriptures, emphasizing works of mercy and hospitality. *The Catholic Worker* tried to convince its readers to join the editors in this undertaking. The hope and stated purpose was that each parish would have a house of hospitality, and each home, a "Christ room." A talk by Peter Maurin on how a fifth-century Church council had required all parishes to have houses of hospitality was featured in the October 1933 issue and sent to all the bishops of the United States.

Over the years Dorothy continued to write about this subject, both in the newspaper and in her books. In *House of Hospitality,* she wrote,

> When we succeed in persuading our readers to take the homeless into their homes, having a Christ room in the house as St. Jerome said, then we will be known as Christians because of the way we love one another. We should have hospices in all the poor parishes. We should have coffee lines to take care of the transients; we should have this help we give sweetened by mutual forbearance and Christian Charity. But we need more Christian homes where the poor are sheltered and cared for. . . .
>
> So we do not cease to urge more personal responsibility on the part of those readers who can help in this way. Too often we

31. Merriman, *Searching for Christ,* p. 53.
32. Day, *House of Hospitality,* p. 75.

are afraid of the poor or the worker. We do not realize that we know him, and Christ through him, in the breaking of the bread.[33]

Dorothy and the other Catholic Workers had additional hopes for their readers — the transformation of their lives and work in a Christian personalist fashion. They suggested that some jobs were not compatible with Christianity. In November 1946, Dorothy wrote an article in *Integrity* magazine entitled "The Catholic Worker," in which she spelled this out:

We hope that those who come to us, as well as those who read the paper, will be led to examine their consciences on their work — whether or not it contributes to the evil of the world, to wars — and then to have the courage and resolution to embrace voluntary poverty and give up their jobs, lower their standard of living, and raise their standard of thinking and loving.

Dorothy spoke out about sins against the poor and judged some specific employment to be inappropriate or even sinful for Christians. She always spoke against work that produced bombs or other instruments of war, and included advertising in her critique:

So many sins against the poor cry out to high heaven! One of the most deadly sins is to deprive the laborer of his hire. There is another: to instill in him paltry desires so compulsive that he is willing to sell his liberty and his honor to satisfy them. We are all guilty of concupiscence, but newspapers, radio, television, and battalions of advertising men (woe to that generation) deliberately stimulate our desires, the satisfaction of which so often means the deterioration of the family. Whatever we can do to combat these widespread social evils by combating their causes we must do. But above all the responsibility is a personal one. The message we have been given comes from the Cross.[34]

33. Day, *House of Hospitality,* p. 241.
34. *Dorothy Day,* ed. Robert Ellsberg, p. 111.

In *House of Hospitality,* Dorothy spoke strongly — rather shockingly so for a pacifist — about advertisers, including in her condemnation those who make movies and corrupt the young:

> One young fellow wants to get out and demonstrate. Wants United Front with the Communists because so many of our aims of social justice are the same. Wants action, shouting, brandishing of placards, clubs, a fight, in other words. Demands, not appeals. Class war again. Hate your enemies. Which is all wrong.
>
> After all, we are not working for the dictatorship of the proletariat, so why work with the Communists? We believe not in acquisitive classes but functional classes. But we are not going to achieve any reform by going out and shooting all the capitalists even though we do not believe in the capitalists' system. (Personally, I'd rather shoot all the advertising men, all the moving picture men who have corrupted the minds and the desires of the youth of the country.)[35]

Throughout her years at the Catholic Worker, from 1933 until the years just before her death, when her health deteriorated, Dorothy traveled around the United States, giving talks to assist people in this transformation and helping to form new Catholic Worker groups and houses of hospitality. She later changed the name of her regular column in *The Catholic Worker* from "Day by Day" to "On Pilgrimage," which reflected these travels. As these houses of hospitality developed, she wrote about them in *The Catholic Worker* and in her books, remarking in *Loaves and Fishes* that "the houses of hospitality have remained from the start one of the cornerstones of the Catholic Worker movement."[36]

The Catholic Worker movement broadened the concept of the spiritual works of mercy (e.g., instructing the ignorant, counseling the doubtful, rebuking the sinner) to include putting out a newspaper, turning out leaflets, protesting against injustice, and always placing the works of mercy in opposition to the works of war. Doro-

---

35. Day, *House of Hospitality,* p. 75.
36. Dorothy Day, *Loaves and Fishes* (San Francisco: Harper & Row, 1963), p. 192.

thy spoke of the Catholic Worker method of "working toward a new heaven and a new earth wherein justice dwelleth" in terms of the works of mercy. Peter had drawn up a simple yet comprehensive program of action to reach people and to build a new society in the shell of the old. This became the program and ideas of the Catholic Worker movement, applied for the first time during the Great Depression, when eleven million workers were unemployed. Dorothy later described Peter's ideas in *House of Hospitality*:

> Peter feels it is not enough merely to bring the workers propaganda by way of a newspaper, pamphlets, and leaflets. One must combine this with the direct action of the works of mercy, feeding the hungry, clothing the naked, sheltering the homeless, in order that one may instruct the ignorant, counsel the doubtful, and comfort the afflicted. The corporal and spiritual works, according to Peter, must go hand in hand, and getting out *The Catholic Worker* and distributing literature were to Peter performing spiritual works of mercy.
>
> In order to carry on this work, he said, we needed hospices such as they had in the Middle Ages, and he always referred to these hospices as "Houses of Hospitality."[37]

Dorothy, who spent so much of her life responding to the needs of Christ in the poor, was criticized by many for picketing and protesting injustice and going to jail. Many sympathized with helping the poor but could not understand her protests. (Others criticized her help of the poor, either despising the poor for being lazy or calling her efforts "Band-Aid work.") She viewed all of these experiences as works of mercy, and her comments made it clear that, for her, protesting was not a lark of publicity-seeking but the result of a decision she struggled with:

> To go on picket lines to protest discrimination in housing, to protest the draft, is one of the works of mercy, which include "rebuking the sinner, enlightening the ignorant, counseling the

---

37. Day, *House of Hospitality,* pp. xix, xx.

doubtful." But I confess I always do these things with fear and trembling. I loathe the use of force. . . . On a picket line there is always the threat of violence. A picket line may be called the use of force, compelling others to hear your point of view through the medium of the poster and the placard, but I prefer to list it as a work of mercy.[38]

Dorothy wrote and spoke beautifully about the possibilities of joy and transformation through love, but she was also conscious of the Cross and the tremendous challenge of giving hospitality, of living out the Sermon on the Mount. In the houses of hospitality there were constant demands — babies being born, conflicts among the guests, threats of violence. Reality continually confronted her dreams. In *On Pilgrimage* she told the story of a difficult alcoholic that one of the Workers had been trying to help for several months:

Last week a woman came in with a policeman. She was a very difficult alcoholic whom Irene, who has charge of the women's house, had tried to help for the past six months. Over and over again she had cleaned Ann up, had tried to get her on her feet, had helped her to jobs, had forgiven her seventy times seven rather than put her out on the streets. The last time she was drunk, she had lost ten dollars in the house, and we found it. Tom has charge of the money of the house, and it was turned over to him and used for "flop money" for others, for beans for the soup, or whatnot. When she next came in, sober, with a job, and asked for her money, we told her that we had found it but used it. We live often from day to day, so there was nothing at that moment in the house to give her. We did not say that she owed us far more for her six months' stay with us. And now here she was, coming in threateningly with a policeman, demanding we give her the ten dollars.

"Give her your cloak, too," Bob said.

How to love! How to turn the other cheek, how to give your

cloak and your trousers and your shoes and then, when you are left naked, you are beaten and reviled besides.[39]

Dorothy accepted responsibility for the lack of conversion of the poor, who had often suffered much and been mistreated. At the time of this incident, she said, "I cannot get over the feeling that if we loved enough, if we were patient enough, if we were saintly enough, if we prayed enough, we would move hearts, effect conversions, and would save the lost, in other words."[40]

Sometimes communities in which the houses of hospitality were located resented the presence of poor people and tried to have them removed. Dorothy told of how the Baltimore house was closed after being declared a public nuisance because it was interracial at a time when it was against the law to have both blacks and whites under the same roof in a hostel. She stated that "civil disobedience began for us then,"[41] and emphasized that all through the years there was never any criticism from the chancery office in New York about the Catholic Worker philosophy whenever there were demonstrations about race or war.

From the earliest years, being a Catholic Worker was not necessarily a permanent vocation. Many came to to join in the work for a few days, a few weeks, a few months, or a few years. The Catholic Worker became a kind of training ground for living the Gospel. In speaking of Jacques Travers, who offered hospitality on a small scale all his life, Dorothy commented,

Such unspectacular hospitality is not for the very young ones who like to make the grand but not lasting gesture. However, if they had a true vocation for this work of love, sharing what they had very simply, they would have persevered through hell and high water, as the saying is. Meanwhile, it is a school for them, an exercise, and they can only learn by doing. They have yet to

39. Day, *On Pilgrimage*, pp. 123-24.
40. Day, *On Pilgrimage*, p. 125.
41. Day, *On Pilgrimage: The Sixties*, p. 187.

find their true vocation. Even so, as an act of love, it is of incalculable value.[42]

Living in community with those who came to be Catholic Workers and those in need of hospitality in mutual charity, giving to those most in need, seeing Christ in the poor who were served — these things were inspiring and gave authenticity to Dorothy's writings. However, community living also presented a tremendous challenge, and Dorothy wrote about it on several occasions:

The difficulty for me is not in not seeing the other person's faults, but in seeing and developing his virtues. A community of lay people is entirely different from a religious community like the Benedictines. We must imitate them by thinking in terms of work and prayer. But we must always remember that those who come to us are not here voluntarily, many of them, but because of economic circumstances. They have taken refuge with us. There is the choice of being on the streets, taking city care such as it is, or staying with us. Even many of the young "leaders" who give up home and position to come to help us in the work are the rebel type and often undisciplined. Their great virtues often mean correspondingly great faults.

Yet those who are interested in the movement fail to see why it does not run as smoothly as a religious movement. They expect our houses and farms to be governed as a religious community is ruled, and in general they take the attitude that I am the one in authority who should rule with an iron hand, the others accepting this willingly. Truly the position of authority is the difficult one.

One of the difficulties of the work is to find those who are willing to assume authority. Leaders are hard to find. The very best in our groups, members of unions, for instance, are steadfast, humble, filled with the love of God and their fellows, and their very virtues make it hard for them to assume leadership. Often, then, they leave it to the articulate ones who are often

42. Day, *On Pilgrimage: The Sixties*, p. 212.

most articulate about the wrongdoings of others. They leave the foremost positions to those who like to talk rather than do, to those who are aggressive and pugnacious and who do the movement harm rather than good. . . .

On a visit to a group, there are always a half-dozen who are filled with complaints. If you try to turn their criticisms so as to change their attitude of mind, you are "refusing to listen" to them. You don't give them a chance to show you how wrong everything is. You don't know what is going on. It is in vain that you assure them you do know what is going on, just how faulty different ones have been. "You are going to let him get away with that?" is the cry, when you try with courtesy and sympathy and respect to draw people together and induce cooperation.

Even the best of human love is filled with self-seeking. To work to increase our love for God and for our fellow man (and the two must go hand in hand) — this is a lifetime job. We are never going to be finished. Love and ever more love is the only solution to every problem that comes up. If we love each other enough, we will bear with each other's faults and burdens. If we love enough, we are going to light that fire in the hearts of others. And it is love that will burn out the sins and hatreds that sadden us. It is love that will make us want to do great things for each other. No sacrifice and no suffering will then seem too much.[43]

Community, an ideal of the Catholic Worker, often failed. In *Loaves and Fishes* Dorothy contrasted the dreams and ideals of love with the sometimes harsh and disappointing realities, saying, "Sometimes we did feel sad indeed when our houses seemed to be filled more with hate and angry words than with the love we were seeking."[44]

Throughout her life and long before her conversion, Dorothy read Dostoyevsky's works and was influenced by them. If she had a favorite author, it would probably have been Dostoyevsky. One pas-

43. *Dorothy Day,* ed. Robert Ellsberg, pp. 86-88.
44. Day, *Loaves and Fishes,* p. 38.

sage that has become closely associated with her because she quoted it so often comes from *The Brothers Karamazov*. William Miller retold the story and wrote eloquently about its influence on the CW movement in his book *A Harsh and Dreadful Love*. He begins, as the story does, with the society woman who goes to Father Zosima in the monastery to speak about her lack of faith:

> She is worried about immortality. It is such a problem; no one can prove it, "and I say to myself, 'What if I've been believing all my life, and when I come to die there's nothing but the burdocks growing on my grave?' as I read in some author. It's awful! How can I prove it? How can I convince myself?" Father Zosima responds with the Worker's radical answer, the one that Dorothy Day has repeatedly given as the substance of the Worker philosophy. To the woman's final demand of how, the monk replies: "By the experience of active love. . . . In as far as you advance in love you will grow surer of the reality of God and of the immortality of your soul."
>
> And what was meant by "active love," the woman asked. She loved humanity. Often she dreamed of a life of service to the unfortunate that filled her with warmth. She could nurse the afflicted; she would be ready to kiss their wounds. But sometimes she wondered how she would react if she were not repaid in gratitude for her service. What if the patient "began abusing you and rudely commanding you, and complaining to the superior authorities of you (which often happens when people are in great suffering) — what then?" She could not bear ingratitude. "I expect my payment at once — that is praise, and the repayment of love with love. Otherwise I am incapable of loving anyone."
>
> The radicalism that seeks to change the time-formed arrangements of values and institutions has time as its ally, but the radicalism of love ignores time, and its course for the bearer of love is the most difficult to follow. When the woman stated that she had to have gratitude as a repayment of the love she gave, Father Zosima answered in words that Dorothy Day has many times repeated: "Love in action is a harsh and dreadful thing compared to love in dreams. Love in dreams is greedy for

immediate action, rapidly performed and in the sight of all. Men will even give their lives if only the ordeal does not last long but is soon over, with all looking and applauding as though on the stage. But active love is labor and fortitude, and for some people, too, perhaps a complete science. But I predict that as you are getting further from your goal instead of nearer to it — at that very moment you will reach and behold clearly the miraculous power of the Lord, who has been all the time loving and mysteriously guiding you."[45]

This parable of Dostoyevsky was used over and over by Dorothy and many other Catholic Workers in facing the day-to-day difficulties of working with the poor and desperate, with those who had never had a success story in their lives, who came to the houses of hospitality after lives of failure. As late as May 1973, Dorothy Day wrote in *The Catholic Worker,* "I do not think I could have carried on with a loving heart all these years without Dostoyevsky's understanding of poverty, suffering, and drunkenness." Dorothy was also very interested in the work of Vladimir Solovyov, the nineteenth-century Russian theologian whom she called the systematizer of Dostoyevsky's thought. She referred to his work often — especially his book *The Meaning of Love* — and quoted him on the importance of seeking growth in love, "so that the force of love may be set loose in the world today, to combat the terrible force of hate and violence that we have unloosed."[46]

The Catholic Workers believed in voluntary poverty. There were no salaries at the Worker, and they all survived through donations and the occasional fee that Dorothy's writing for magazines brought in. The talks she gave in university Newman parishes as she traveled around the country were financed by those who invited her to speak. The Workers did not look to the government or the Community Chest or the United Way for support. When Lyndon Johnson launched the War on Poverty to solve all problems in society, an

45. William Miller, *A Harsh and Dreadful Love: Dorothy Day and the Catholic Worker Movement* (New York: Liveright, 1973), pp. 24-25.

46. Day, *On Pilgrimage,* pp. 126, 156.

interviewer asked Dorothy, "How do you think the Church can best assist the War on Poverty?" She responded, "By teaching Holy Poverty — a philosophy of poverty and a philosophy of work."[47] Peter Maurin had written an essay on St. Francis and Holy Poverty.

The workers practiced this Holy Poverty. For Dorothy Day and Peter Maurin, trying to live in Holy Poverty as the Lord Himself had done was connected to the mystery of the Lord's presence in the poor. She wrote about this in the April 1964 issue of *The Catholic Worker:* "The mystery of the poor is this: That they are Jesus, and what you do for them you do for Him. It is the only way we have of knowing and believing in our love. The mystery of poverty is that by sharing in it, making ourselves poor in giving to others, we increase our knowledge of and belief in love."

Dorothy called the Church as well to Holy Poverty, encouraging and writing about bishops and priests who followed the Lord in his poverty. In November 1965, when she was in Rome, she wrote,

> On the way I saluted the statue of Garibaldi, who was God's instrument in relieving the Papacy of those encumbrances, the Papal States, and preparing the way for the great part the Church had played in this century. Never when she was a great temporal power was the Church listened to with such attention as she is today. One might say the work of detachment has only begun. As I passed this great equestrian statue I could not help but think of the words of Bishop P. N. Geise, of Indonesia, who said that we must seek poverty, live poorly, build poor buildings, take in the poor where we are. The Bishop of Mwanza, in Tanzania, said, "The world is not divided into the East and the West but into the haves and the have-nots."[48]

From the beginning, Dorothy Day sent *The Catholic Worker* across the country and appealed for assistance for the houses of hospitality. And every year one or two appeals went out to the readers of the paper to help financially in the work. Dorothy did not set up a foun-

47. Day, *On Pilgrimage: The Sixties,* p. 207.
48. Day, *On Pilgrimage,* p. 248.

dation or amass savings. The Worker survived from day to day and year to year.

In *Loaves and Fishes,* Dorothy responded to questions about whether the official Church or Catholic charities helped them:

> Do we get much help from Catholic charities? We are often asked this question. I can say only that it is not the Church or the state to which we turn when we ask for help in these appeals. Cardinal Spellman did not ask us to undertake this work, nor did the Mayor of New York. It just happened. It is the living from day to day, taking no thought for the morrow, seeing Christ in all who come to us, trying literally to follow the Gospel, that resulted in this work. . . .
>
> We do not ask church or state for help, but we ask individuals, those who have subscribed to *The Catholic Worker* and so are evidently interested in what we are doing, presumably willing and able to help. Many a priest and bishop sends help year after year. Somehow the dollars that come in cover current bills, help us to catch up with payments on back debts, and make it possible for us to keep on going. There is never anything left over, and we always have a few debts to keep us worrying, to make us more like the very poor we are trying to help.[49]

A discussion of the works of mercy and hospitality in the Worker movement would be inadequate and incomplete without a look at Matthew 25:31-46. A key to the theology of the Worker is the biblical teaching that the poor are a profound revelation of God's presence and grace. Dorothy quoted Matthew 25 throughout her life as a central tenet of the New Testament and the Catholic Worker movement, and she wrote beautiful meditations on her day-to-day experience of knowing Christ in the poor. In the December 1945 issue of *The Catholic Worker,* she wrote a Christmas essay entitled "Room for Christ," in which she brought readers to the realization that every Catholic, every Christian, has the opportunity to serve the Lord in the poor, in the neighbor:

49. Day, *Loaves and Fishes,* p. 87.

It is no use saying that we are born two thousand years too late to give room to Christ. Nor will those who live at the end of the world have been born too late. Christ is always with us, always asking for room in our hearts.

But now it is with the voice of our contemporaries that He speaks, with the eyes of store clerks, factory workers, and children that He gazes; with the hands of office workers, slum dwellers, and suburban housewives that He gives. It is with the feet of soldiers and tramps that He walks, and with the heart of anyone in need that He longs for shelter. And giving shelter or food to anyone who asks for it, or needs it, is giving it to Christ. . . .

If we hadn't got Christ's own words for it, it would seem raving lunacy to believe that if I offer a bed and food and hospitality to some man or woman or child, I am replaying the part of Lazarus or Martha or Mary, and that my guest is Christ. There is nothing to show it, perhaps. There are no halos already glowing round their heads — at least none that human eyes can see. . . .

In Christ's human life, there were always a few who made up for the neglect of the crowd. The shepherds did it; their hurrying to the crib atoned for the people who would flee from Christ. The wise men did it; their journey across the world made up for those who refused to stir one hand's breadth from the routine of their lives to go to Christ. Even the gifts the wise men brought have in themselves an obscure recompense and atonement for what would follow later in this Child's life. For they brought gold, the king's emblem, to make up for the crown of thorns that He would wear; they offered incense, the symbol of praise, to make up for the mockery and the spitting; they gave Him myrrh, to heal and soothe, and He was wounded from head to foot, and no one bathed His wounds. The women at the foot of the Cross did it too, making up for the crowd who stood by and sneered.

We can do it too, exactly as they did. We are not born too late. We do it by seeing Christ and serving Christ in friends and strangers, in everyone we come in contact with.

All this can be proved, if proof is needed, by the doctrines of the Church. We can talk about Christ's Mystical Body, about the vine and the branches, about the Communion of Saints. But Christ Himself has proved it for us, and no one has to go further than that. For He said that a glass of water given to a beggar was given to Him. He made heaven hinge on the way we act toward Him in His disguise of commonplace, frail, ordinary humanity.

> Did you give Me food when I was hungry?
> Did you give Me to drink when I was thirsty?
> Did you give Me clothes when my own were all rags?
> Did you come to see Me when I was sick, or in prison,
>   or in trouble?

And to those who say, aghast, that they never had a chance to do such a thing, that they lived two thousand years too late, He will say again what they had the chance of knowing all their lives, that if these things were done for the very least of His brethren, they were done to Him.

Very early on, the Benedictines at St. John's Abbey responded to an appeal from the Catholic Worker with donations and also with shared ideas, materials, and friendship. They were friends who shared the commitment to Catholic social teaching and to Matthew 25, believing that the guest who receives hospitality is Christ.

Father Virgil Michel, O.S.B., of St. John's Abbey, a great leader in the liturgical movement in the United States, became a friend of both Dorothy and Peter, as well as others in the CW movement. They worked to bring together the social teaching of the Church, the liturgy, and a profound understanding of the Mystical Body of Christ. Benedictine spirituality had a natural connection with the Catholic Worker, where hospitality and the Mass were emphasized. Father Michel had the inimitable skill of connecting social consciousness with the social nature of worship, especially the liturgy of the Eucharist. He believed that our responsibility for our neighbor, believer or not, flowed from the fact that we were connected to one another in the Body of Christ and the Eucharist. The liturgical movement, before the Second Vatican Council, went back to the sources of the early Church and the Scriptures to understand the heart of the liturgy as the worship of the Body of Christ, inextricably linked with the Church's teaching on service to the poor and social justice for the suffering members of the Body of Christ.

Father Michel's writings were published in *The Catholic Worker,* and Dorothy wrote in *Orate Fratres,* edited by Father Michel. In his book *Wings of the Dawn,* Stanley Vishnewski wrote about the connection between the Catholic Worker movement and the Benedictines, suggesting that much of the heart of the movement was related to Benedictine spirituality.

The centrality of the Mass was crucial to Dorothy, and she considered it the greatest work of the day. In the early 1940s, when she addressed a group of "would-be Catholic Workers," she admonished them that "the Mass is the Work!" All their activities were first to be offered and then united frequently with the sacrifice of Christ on the Cross and on the altar, because Dorothy felt that "all life flowed from worship; only thus would their work be a success, irrespective of its external attainment."[50]

She never lost her faith in the Eucharist, in the liturgy. The liturgical movement, with its emphasis on the Body of Christ, brought a wholeness to Dorothy's faith and worship. She was in the forefront of those who wanted to bring the liturgy to the people and have them participate in it. She mentions participating in dialogue Masses in the 1930s. She rejoiced in the document on the liturgy that came out of the Second Vatican Council, but she became uncomfortable with some expressions later in the 1960s that undercut the profundity of worship by emphasizing the meal aspect; she knew that was very important, but some of the aspect of the sacrifice was lost. She was also uncomfortable with what she described as elitist, special liturgies that made people abandon their parish liturgies; this took them away from the masses, the ordinary people, what she called the "ancient lowly." For Dorothy, the Mass was the celebration of the Incarnation, bringing together all the material and spiritual aspects of our lives in the Incarnate God. (Dorothy often quoted Peter Maurin, who said that living the Mass was the way to bring the material and the spiritual together.)

In her commentary on the "New Liturgy" in her column in the

---

50. Merriman, *Searching for Christ,* pp. 97-98.

Catholic Worker of May 1967, Dorothy first quoted what she called a gem from C. S. Lewis's *Letters*:

> The advantage of a fixed form of service is that we know what is coming. Extempore public prayer has this difficulty: we don't know whether we can join in it until we've heard it — it might be phony or heretical. We are therefore called upon to carry on a critical and devotional activity at the same moment, two things hardly compatible. In a fixed form we ought to have gone through the motions before in our private prayer; the rigid form really sets our devotions free. I also find that the more rigid it is, the easier to keep our thoughts from straying. Also, it prevents getting too completely eaten up by whatever happens to be the preoccupation of the moment. . . . The permanent shape of Christianity shows through. I don't see how the extempore method can help but become provincial, and I think it has a great tendency to direct attention to the minister rather than to God.

Dorothy continued with her own reflections on the New Liturgy, recognizing that some superficiality was creeping into the implementation of liturgical reforms:

> [This] leads me into reflections on the new Masses, the intimate Masses, the colloquial Masses, the folk-song Masses, and so on. By the intimate I mean those where everyone gathers close around the altar inside the sanctuary, as close to the priest as possible. Even the young ones have a hard time standing, shifting from one leg to the other, the girls with high heels ("If I'd known it was to be like this I would have worn my sneakers," one said), the older rheumatic ones with ever-increasing pain. By the intimate I also mean those offered in small apartments before a small group. I understand that permission for this has been granted in Harlem for some time now, and priests are offering the Mass in the poorest of homes block by block in their parishes during the week — bringing Christ most literally to the people. This is wonderful.

But there is also the attempt made by some young priests to reach the young, to make the Mass meaningful to the young (the bourgeois, educated, middle-class young), where novelty is supposed to attract the attention but which, as far as I can see, has led to drawing these same young ones completely away from the "people of God," "the masses" and worship in the parish church. There is the suggestion of contempt here for the people and for the faith of the inarticulate ones of the earth, "the ancient lowly," as they have been called.

I do love the guitar Masses, and the Masses where the recorder and the flute are played, and sometimes the glorious and triumphant trumpet. But I do not want them every day, any more than we ever wanted solemn Gregorian Requiem Masses every day. They are for the occasion. They are joyful and happy Masses indeed and supposed to attract the young. But the beginning of faith is something different. The *"fear* of the Lord is the beginning of wisdom." Fear in the sense of *awe.*

The liturgical movement of the 1930s, 1940s, and 1950s, which Dorothy and Peter encouraged and in which they participated, emphasized the inseparable connection between worship and life. Father Virgil Michel had insisted strongly on the responsibility of those who ate and drank at the Table of the Lord to respond to the Gospel imperatives, to the Lord's example with the poor, and to Catholic social teaching. Catholic Workers and early liturgists alike understood that membership in the Mystical Body of Christ and participation in the liturgy brought with them social responsibility, the necessity of giving of oneself with the open generosity of Christ to help to transform the world in God. Dorothy could almost have written the statement in *Gaudium et spes* of Vatican II that says, "The artificial contrast between professional and social activity, on the one hand, and religious life, on the other hand," is one of "the more serious errors of our age."

It was natural that the Catholic Worker and the early liturgists were of one mind on the economic alternative of Distributism. In 1948 Dorothy Day wrote at length about Distributism, the economic ideas the Worker had espoused from the beginning. She insisted again, as she had in the earliest years of the movement, that capitalism and socialism were not the only economic alternatives. The Distributist movement included people like G. K. Chesterton, Hilaire Belloc, Father Vincent McNabb, O.P., Father Virgil Michel, O.S.B., and the liturgists who contributed to the early editions of *Orate Fratres* (which became *Worship* magazine). These ideas were strongly supported in the papal encyclicals. Quoting from Joseph T. Nolan in *Orate Fratres,* Dorothy insisted that these ideas were at the heart of the social teaching of the Church:

> Too long has idle talk made out Distributism as something medieval and myopic, as if four modern Popes were somehow talking nonsense when they said: the law should favor widespread ownership (Leo XIII); wages should enable a man to purchase land (Leo XIII and Pius XI); the family is most perfect when rooted in its own holding (Pius XII); and the tiller of the soil still represents the natural order of things willed by God (Pius XII).[51]

Distributism calls for a just distribution of wealth and participation in ownership and adequate wages so that workers can buy homes. Advocates of Distributism believe in private property — but private property for everyone, not just the few. There was a strong agrarian factor in Distributism and in the early Catholic Worker, but as Dorothy pointed out, "Distributism does not mean that everyone must be a farmer." It did include a right to private property, "to a home, a bit of land, and the tools with which to work, part ownership in workshops and stores and factories." It was ironic that Dorothy, often accused of being socialist, was so papal in her emphasis on private property.

After Dorothy's death in November 1980, Father John Hugo wrote about her economic theory and commitment to constructing a just social order in the *Pittsburgh Catholic*:

> Two economic systems, capitalism and socialism, strive for dominance in the world, and people generally tend to see the so-

51. Day, *On Pilgrimage*, p. 105.

lution of our socio-economic woes in one or the other of these two systems. In the West we oppose socialism and communism, which we see as a threat to our way of life. To be sure, we also recognize certain flaws in capitalist society. These we seek to cure by an endless series of Band-Aid solutions. Few in the West, even among those invoking Christian social principles, have attempted a really drastic criticism of capitalism or even admit that such a criticism is needed.

In becoming a Catholic, Dorothy Day moved away from the socialist solution, but she never fully adopted the capitalist system. She remained between them, recognizing a third possibility: a society in which the economic system is decentralized, allowing for smaller units of agriculture and business, and encouraging the independent initiative of individuals. By decentralizing the economy, ordinary people can escape an almost serf-like (with many comforts, of course) dependence on their masters, whether socialist or capitalist, and become responsible for their own destinies.

Dorothy Day was not an ideologist; she recognized her ideals in practice by promoting a tendency toward small farms and small businesses to enhance the dignity and independence of the little people. Here is the reason for the communal farms established by the Catholic Worker. These in turn would prepare individuals to live on family farms. And of course decentralism would encourage small businesses as well as small manufacturers. It is a tendency but not an ideology.

Dorothy kept up a constant struggle against all the injustices and abuses of the capitalist society in which she lived. She would help the little people in legitimate enterprise. We should not forget that the whole purpose of Catholic social action is to provide everyone with the means essential to a dignified human life. This was also very much Dorothy's goal.

Dorothy emphasized that "Distributism does not mean that we throw out the machine. The machine, Peter Maurin used to say, should be the extension of the hand of man. If we could do away with the assembly line, the slavery of the machine, and the

41

useless and harmful and destructive machines, we would be doing well."[52]

The criticism Dorothy made of the social situation in 1948, when there were so many poor who had no ownership or participation in the means of production, applies as well today in the global market, in which workers receive a pittance in assembly lines while CEOs and stockholders reap enormous profits. E. F. Schumacher embraced ideas similar to Dorothy's in his popular book *Small Is Beautiful;* his writings also appeared in *The Catholic Worker.* The wisdom of such an economics becomes clear as social critics today tell horrendous stories of environmental destruction caused by the farming methods of agribusiness and the crisis of food shortages in many countries where economic policies force countries to grow food for export instead of for their own people. Dorothy's words are as relevant today as they were in the 1930s and 1940s: "We are not expecting utopia here on earth. But God meant things to be much easier than we have made them."[53]

From the first issue, *The Catholic Worker* carried stories about labor issues, including the exploitation of men, women, and children, layoffs, strikes, and labor organizing. Peter Maurin was dismayed at some of the coverage Dorothy selected, since he had thought that the newspaper he had inspired would carry only his own ideas. He removed his name from the editorial box and announced that he would sign his writings so that authorship would be clear. "Everybody's paper is nobody's paper," he said.

Dorothy's support and sympathy for labor was strong in *The Catholic Worker* throughout the 1930s and was complemented by her picketing with the workers. Peter Maurin was not so sure about these activities, saying in his usual pithy style, "Strikes don't strike me." However, when sitdown strikes began, he gave his full support to this pacifist activity. Dorothy's support continued in the 1960s and 1970s with the United Farm Workers; once Dorothy was arrested along with Cesar Chavez. In *House of Hospitality* Dorothy re-

52. Day, *On Pilgrimage,* p. 107.
53. Day, *On Pilgrimage,* p. 102.

sponded to criticism of Catholic Worker support for labor and explained further the basis for it:

> Again and again we have helped workers on strike regardless of all talk as to whether the strike was just or unjust. We have done this for two reasons: first, it is never wrong to perform the Works of Mercy; secondly, because in a time of industrial warfare it is easy to get in touch with the workers by meetings and by widespread distribution of literature. It is a time when the workers are thinking and struggling; they are enduring hardships and making sacrifices; they are in a receptive frame of mind.[54]

Editorial support for the Child Labor amendment in 1935 cost *The Catholic Worker* many subscribers. The majority of Catholics were opposed to it for fear of government interference in the education of youth. But Dorothy, never flattened by criticism, reported that "in spite of the consistent opposition (which, as we have always pointed out, is very good for the clarification of thought), our circulation rose to 100,000 at the beginning of the third year." It is clear, however, that while Dorothy often took controversial stands in the paper, she did so with caution and judgment. This was reflected often in what *The Catholic Worker* did not publish; Dorothy once commented, "In the past six years we have had many interviews with Catholic industrialists, and many of them were not too cheering. Not wishing to increase class war attitudes, we did not publish many of them."[55]

Dorothy's support of labor activity, like all of her activity, grew out of her Christian commitment. She placed the situation of workers at the heart of the living out of Christian personalism, always in the context of Catholic social teaching. In July of 1936, *The Catholic Worker* carried an editorial entitled "Our Stand on Strikes," from which excerpts follow:

> Let us be honest, let us say that fundamentally, the stand we are taking is not on the ground of wages and hours and conditions

54. Day, *House of Hospitality*, p. 260.
55. Day, *House of Hospitality*, pp. 261-62.

of labor, but on the fundamental truth that men should be treated not as chattels, but as human beings, as "temples of the Holy Ghost." When Christ took on our human nature, when He became man, He dignified and ennobled human nature. He said, "The Kingdom of Heaven is within you." When men are striking, they are following an impulse, often blind, often uninformed, but a good impulse — one could even say an inspiration of the Holy Spirit. They are trying to uphold their right to be treated not as slaves, but as men. They are fighting for a share in the management, for their right to be considered partners in the enterprise in which they are engaged. They are fighting against the idea of the labor as a commodity to be bought and sold.

Let us be honest and confess that it is the social order which we wish to change. The workers are never going to be satisfied, no matter how much pay they get, no matter what their hours are. And it is to reconstruct the social order that we are throwing ourselves in with the workers, whether in factories or shipyards or on the sea.

The popes have hit the nail on the head. "No man may outrage with impunity that human dignity which God Himself treats with reverence."

Although Dorothy and the CW movement were often accused of "Band-Aid work," this commitment to changing the social order always accompanied works of mercy. In 1948, Dorothy herself spoke of the Catholic Worker movement as one of many Catholic lay movements active during a time of much ferment and growth of Catholic action among the laity. She mentioned the Friendship House movement, Young Christian Students, the Association of Catholic Trade Unionists, and many others. She distinguished the Catholic Worker from these others, however, by quoting Cardinal Suhard, who said, "You have to take a position on our contemporary civilization, to judge, condemn, or correct it. You must draw up an objective evaluation of our urban civilization today with its gigantic concentrations and its continual form of entertainment . . . make a gigantic synthesis of the world to come. . . . Be the leaven and the bread will rise. *But it must be bread, not factitious matter.*"

Dorothy referred to the cardinal's comment in *On Pilgrimage* w. this stark statement: "That is why we rebel against all talk of sanct. fying one's surroundings. It is not bread in the first place. It is not worth working with. We must think of these things, even if we can take only the first steps out of the morass. We may be caught up in the toils of the machine, but we do not have to think of it for our children."[56]

Dorothy spoke of the "filthy, rotten system" that made life so difficult for so many. Recently, a Catholic Worker in California commented on *Entertaining Angels,* the recent movie about Dorothy Day, criticizing it for its "weakness in depicting what Dorothy called 'the dirty rotten system.'" He felt it lacked the perceptive insight that both Dorothy and Peter had on what the economy and the war machine do to people.

In her years in socialist movements, Dorothy had known of the need to transform the unjust world. It was Peter who taught her the depth of the Catholic vision of creating a just social order, of creating a new society in the shell of the old. Peter, unfortunately, had the image of a bowery bum, whereas in fact he was an intellectual and one of the best-read men of his times. His commitment to Holy Poverty caused him to dress rather shabbily, which obscured his greatness. He attempted to gather the profound concepts that were the fruit of his many studies and express them in a free-verse form that Dorothy's brother, John, called "Easy Essays." The thoughts remained profound, but deceptively so. Dorothy collaborated closely with Peter prior to his illness and his eventual death in 1949. She quoted him often during the years they worked together, and continued to quote him later in her work and her writing at the Catholic Worker, referring to his vision. She contended that this vision, particularly in its emphasis on pacifism and Distributism, distinguished the Catholic Worker from other lay movements: "Peter Maurin's vision of the City of God included *pacifism* and *Distributism.* And that is what distinguishes us from much of the lay apostolate today. It is the talent Christ has given us, and we cannot bury it."[57]

56. Day, *On Pilgrimage,* p. 82.
57. Day, *On Pilgrimage,* p. 82.

Pacifism and Nonviolence

Both Dorothy and Peter insisted that for the Catholic Worker, pacifism and Distributism went together. Nevertheless, Dorothy Day and the Catholic Worker movement are better known for their commitment to pacifism.

In *American Catholic Pacifism. The Influence of Dorothy Day and the Catholic Worker Movement,* Charles Chatfield states, "Dorothy Day was the catalyst for the emergence, organization, and eventual recognition of Catholic pacifism in the United States."[58] One of Dorothy's great gifts to the Catholic Church and to the United States was her ability to draw together Catholic biblical, theological, and traditional resources to establish pacifism as a legitimate stance for Catholics and for Americans. The *ressourcement* accomplished by Dorothy and Peter Maurin, along with the priest-theologians who assisted them, made available teachings from the Fathers of the Church, theology and philosophy from the medieval and Renaissance periods, and stories of saints that addressed the questions of military service and the Christian's refusal to participate in violence.

Since Dorothy knew that many people viewed pacifism as passive, uninvolved, and even as a kind of appeasement, she made a point of distinguishing between true and false pacifism in *The Catholic Worker,* insisting that true pacifism must use traditional weapons of the spirit like prayer, fasting, and reception of the sacraments to resist evil. In a January 1941 article in *The Catholic Worker,* she went so far as to say, "If we are not going to use our spiritual weapons, let us by all means arm and prepare."

Nonviolence was one of the characteristic marks of the CW movement. Dorothy and Peter Maurin took the love of enemies called for in the Gospel and applied it to war at a time when it was not at all popular to do so.

During times of war, Dorothy spoke with courage and profound faith of martyrdom in loving without violence, of being willing to shed every drop of one's blood and not take the blood of one's broth-

---

58. Charles Chatfield, "The Catholic Worker in the United States Peace Tradition,'" in *American Catholic Pacifism,* ed. Klejment and Roberts, p. 1.

ers. In November 1936, during the Spanish Civil War, she wrote in an editorial, "The Catholic Church cannot be destroyed in Spain or in Mexico. But we do not believe that force of arms can save it. We believe that if Our Lord were alive today, he would say as He said to St. Peter, 'Put up thy sword.'" This neutral stand on the Spanish Civil War prompted many to criticize (sometimes very harshly) *The Catholic Worker* and Dorothy Day in particular; but others offered encouragement. In his biography of Dorothy Day, William Miller reported that Father Virgil Michel, just weeks before his death, wrote her to tell her that few things had given him "more comfort than your excellent article 'On the Use of Force'. . . . Keep up the good work, no matter what slanderous tongues may say. That is what Christ himself did." Jacques Maritain also supported her stand on the war.[59]

World War II was a difficult time for the Catholic Worker movement. Dorothy remained firm in her pacifist stance, writing in *The Catholic Worker* and publishing the writings of priests like Father John Hugo and Father Barry O'Toole, which spoke about the immorality of conscription. She was even investigated by the FBI. According to Klejment and Roberts, J. Edgar Hoover himself spent considerable time and energy "monitoring the pacifist activities of Dorothy Day and her movement." It seems incredible at this remove that before Pearl Harbor, "Director Hoover himself recommended 'custodial detention in the event of a national emergency,'" although the order was changed to restriction of activities.[60]

Most of the houses of hospitality across the country closed when the men, even though they were Catholic Workers, went off to war. Dorothy insisted that all the Catholic Worker houses distribute the New York paper during the war, even if they disagreed with its pacifist stand. This caused great pain among the Workers in the movement and decimated its ranks.

In spite of criticism, Dorothy continued to publish the rationale, gleaned from her faith, for her pacifism. In fact, she increased the pages dedicated to the Catholic basis for her stand, especially after

59. William Miller, *Dorothy Day: A Biography* (San Francisco: Harper & Row, 1982), pp. 315-16.

60. *American Catholic Pacifism*, ed. Klejment and Roberts, p. 26.

Father Hugo wrote her, "No doubt pacifism is all clear to you, but you have not tried to work it out doctrinally. If you knew no theology, it would probably be simpler to make a solution. Yet the decision must be based on doctrine. Pacifism must proceed from truth, or it cannot exist at all. And of course this attack on conscription is the most extreme form of pacifism."[61]

In January 1942 Dorothy published an editorial entitled "Our Country Passes from Undeclared to Declared War; We Continue Our Pacifist Stand," in which she wrote,

> We are still pacifists. Our manifesto is the Sermon on the Mount, which means that we will try to be peacemakers. Speaking for many of our conscientious objectors, we will not participate in armed warfare or in making munitions, or by buying government bonds to prosecute the war, or in urging others to these efforts.
>
> But neither will we be carping in our criticism. We love our country and we love our President. . . .

Dorothy Day, although a pacifist, also published arguments about just-war theology in *The Catholic Worker* before and during World War II, raising issues about the morality of war, especially in regard to obliteration bombing. Rather than abandon the just-war theory in all modern thought, Dorothy used this theory to condemn all modern war.

The February paper of 1942 carried this commentary: "Love is not the starving of whole populations. Love is not the bombardment of open cities. Love is not killing. It is the laying down of one's life for one's friends." However, when asked by the Church to modify one newspaper column in which she made specific requests of young men regarding the war, she complied, and later explained her decision to do so:

> We once went so far as to print a box in *The Catholic Worker* urging men not to register for the draft. This evidently was consid-

61. Patricia McNeal, "Catholic Peace Organizations and World War II," in *American Catholic Pacifism,* ed. Klejment and Roberts, p. 40.

ered as having gone too far, for I was called to the Chancery and told, "Dorothy, you must stand corrected." I was not quite sure what that meant, but I did assent, because I realized that one should not tell another what to do in such circumstances. We had to follow our own consciences, which later took us to jail; but our work in getting out a paper was an attempt to arouse the conscience of others, not to advise action for which they were not prepared.[62]

When a Catholic newspaper responded to the CW pacifist stand on World War II by saying that it sympathized with their sentimentality, Dorothy responded strongly, again in the February 1942 issue:

But let those who talk of softness, of sentimentality, come to live with us in cold, unheated houses in the slums. Let them come to live with the criminal, the unbalanced, the drunken, the degraded, the perverted. (It is not the decent poor, it is not the decent sinner who was the recipient of Christ's love.) Let them live with rats, with vermin, bedbugs, roaches, lice. (I could describe the several kinds of body lice.)

Let their flesh be mortified by cold, by dirt, by vermin; let their eyes be mortified by the sight of bodily excretions, diseased limbs, eyes, noses, mouths.

Let their noses be mortified by the smells of sewage, decay, and rotten flesh. Yes, and the smell of the sweat, blood, and tears spoken of so blithely by Mr. Churchill, and so widely and bravely quoted by comfortable people.

Let their taste be mortified by the constant eating of insufficient food cooked in huge quantities for hundreds of people, the coarser foods, so that these will be enough to go around; and the smell of such cooking is often foul.

Then, when they have lived with these comrades, with these sights and sounds, let our critics talk of sentimentality. As we

---

62. Day, *Loaves and Fishes,* p. 60.

have often quoted Dostoyevsky's Father Zosima, "Love in practice is a harsh and dreadful thing compared to love in dreams."

Years after the war, Dorothy was once asked how she justified her pacifism in view of the slaughter of the Jews. She replied that winning the war had not saved many Jews. Those who read *The Catholic Worker* in the late 1930s and early 1940s knew that the paper had editorialized about and campaigned for the Jews before the war when it was not yet popular. They knew that Dorothy had written early on about anti-Semitism and in defense of the Jews. "Peter," she wrote in the paper, "believes we should have more Jews than we do in this or any country. He calls them a bulwark against Nationalism. . . . Christians are followers of Christ. Because of this, says Peter, every time a Christian sees a Jew, he should be reminded of Christ and love him for being of the race that Christ was part of." Readers also knew that Dorothy and a number of her acquaintances, including writers, philosophers, artists, and a "long list of priests and nuns," had formed the Committee of Catholics to Fight Anti-Semitism. These readers had followed the editorials in 1943 urging an attempt at a negotiated peace in order to save those Jews who were still alive in concentration camps.[63] Surely Dorothy was aware of President Roosevelt's rejection of a refugee ship packed with Jewish people fleeing Nazi death camps. Fear of flooding the labor market was the reason given. The boat returned to Europe.

During the 1950s, Dorothy and other Catholic Workers were jailed for engaging in civil disobedience against compulsory nuclear civil-defense drills. As she had during previous jail stays, Dorothy used the time and the difficult circumstances as an opportunity to pray. William Miller tells us, "The Psalms were her strong spiritual fare. Jailed in the late 1950s for her refusal to take shelter during an air raid warning, she commented in her notes how some of her fellow inmates longed for a 'fix.' Her morning 'fix,' she said, was her reading of the Psalms."[64]

During the Second Vatican Council, *The Catholic Worker* prepared a special edition on peace and the moral problems of modern war

63. Miller, *Dorothy Day,* pp. 317, 319, 364-65.
64. Miller, *Dorothy Day,* p. 317.

and sent it airmail to the bishops gathered in Rome. In that issue Day wrote,

> One of our Catholic pacifists asked me to write a clear, theoretical, logical pacifist manifesto, and he added so far in these thirty-two years of *The Catholic Worker,* none had appeared from my pen.
>
> I can write no other than this: unless we use the weapons of the spirit, denying ourselves and taking up our cross and following Jesus, dying with Him and rising with Him, men will go on fighting, and often from the highest motives, believing that they are fighting defensive wars for justice and in self-defense against present or future aggression.[65]

Dorothy herself went with a group to Rome to try to influence the council fathers to include nonviolence as an essential element in living the Gospel. She met with many people, including bishops, and fasted with other women. While the council did not meet all the hopes of the pacifists, it did determine that modern nuclear war within the context of the just-war theory was immoral. The statement in chapter 5 of *Gaudium et spes* confirmed the arguments that had been published in *The Catholic Worker* over the years: "Every act of war directed to the indiscriminate destruction of whole cities or vast areas with their inhabitants is a crime against God and man, which merits firm and unequivocal condemnation." In the U.S. Catholic Bishops' Pastoral Letter on War and Peace, where conscientious objection and pacifism were understood as legitimate responses of Catholics and an expression of their faith, Dorothy was given credit.[66] However, papal statements in recent years, together with the teaching in the *Catechism of the Catholic Church* on war, bring theology and the Church teachers much closer to what Dorothy Day had hoped for.[67]

65. *The Catholic Worker,* July-August 1965, p. 7.

66. *The Challenge of Peace: God's Promise and Our Response,* The Pastoral Letter of the U.S. Bishops on War and Peace, 1983, I, C, no. 4.

67. See William L. Portier, "Are We Really Serious When We Ask God to Deliver Us from War? The *Catechism* and the Challenge of Pope John Paul II," *Communio* 23 (Spring 1996): 47-63.

Dorothy received much criticism in the sixties when she commented on Cuba and Castro. Like everyone else involved in Catholic Action in Cuba at the time when Battista was in power, she was in favor of a change in the government because of corruption and devastating poverty. Other editors of Catholic newspapers, like Dale Francis of *Our Sunday Visitor,* printed articles opposing Battista. Dorothy did not believe in violent revolution. Any hope she may have had in Castro never materialized, but quickly deteriorated in the face of his seizure of power; it was similar to what had happened in other Marxist countries, where freedom had disappeared. Dorothy responded to the criticism of her reports, which were not all negative, by speaking of an interest in historical figures like Garibaldi, Napoleon, and Castro, who make history. She asserted that "until we ourselves as followers of Christ abjure the use of war as a means of achieving justice and truth, we Catholics are going to get nowhere in criticizing men who are using war to change the social order. Too often, as Cardinal Mundelein said once, we will find ourselves on the wrong side."[68]

It was during the Vietnam War that Dorothy's fame as an activist for pacifism reached its peak; it was a time when many Catholic Workers protested the war, and some burned their draft cards. Yet even then, when there were so many massive demonstrations, she proceeded with great caution in order to avoid violence and to assure that the pacifism of the Gospel would emerge. Still, she was criticized. In the December 1965 issue of *The Catholic Worker,* she explained how a Jesuit priest from India came to visit the Catholic Worker to express his concerns, and how she answered him:

> A Jesuit priest from Madras, India, came in the office to visit us the other afternoon. When he spoke of the war in Vietnam, he spoke as one nearer to it than we were, and he reiterated the familiar argument: If Vietnam is lost to the Communists, all Asia goes too.
>
> But from the Christian point of view (and in this case from the Jesuit point of view), when he asked, "What are we to do?" I could only point to the example of St. Ignatius, who first of all

68. Day, *On Pilgrimage: The Sixties,* p. 93.

laid down his arms, then went to support himself by serving the poor in hospitals, and then went back to school to study.

Dorothy was committed to the revolution of the heart but deplored the so-called sexual revolution. For her, it was not a revolution at all but a capitulation to the bourgeois mentality that seeks comfort and pleasure, removing the Christian from the Gospel roots of real love. She viewed both war and self-seeking sex as pornographic. She had nothing good to say about war. She was able to see the real beauty of sexuality and chastity, when properly understood and lived. She spoke in glowing terms of the sweetness and beauty of love as expressed in the Canticle of Canticles and the book of Hosea, and interspersed her ideas in the September 1965 issue of *The Catholic Worker* with quotations from Pope John XXIII. She began her column with a quotation from his *Journal of a Soul*:

> While the war rages, the peoples can only turn to the Miserere and beg for the Lord's mercy, that it may outweigh His justice and with a great outpouring of grace bring the powerful men of this world to their senses and persuade them to make peace. The two great evils which are poisoning the world today are secularism and nationalism. The former is characteristic of the men in power and of lay folk in general. The latter is found even among ecclesiastics.

Continuing her column, Dorothy talked about the link between war and cheap sex. She mentioned how, while looking for a paperback in a bookstore, she was "horrified to see how sex and sadism seem to be the theme of so much of our paperback literature. Sex and war, which is the opposite of the works of mercy, are closely allied." Using an example from Scripture, Dorothy contrasted practices in modern secular society with those of the book of Maccabees, in which "young men were supposed to be in the state of grace before going into battle." She contrasted this prayerful preparation with the "preparation" of the sixties: "Nowadays, young men going on leave before battle are given contraceptives. And our country calls itself Christian. What a misuse of life forces." After more reflections on the meaning of love, she prophetically spoke of the horror of nothingness, of death toward which the world seemed to be moving, not using the phrase "the culture of death" but describing it. Again she quoted John XXIII on this theme:

> Many importunately seek rather frantically earthly pleasures, and disfigure and weaken the noblest energies of the spirit. Against this irregular way of living, which unchains often the lowest passions and brings eternal salvation into grave danger, it is necessary that Christians react with the strength of the martyrs and saints, who have always given testimony for the Catholic Church.
>
> In such a way all can contribute, according to their particular status, to the better outcome of the Second Vatican Ecumenical Council, which must bring about a reblossoming of Christian life.[69]

The Famous Retreat

From her earliest days Dorothy Day felt that the spirituality of laypeople was neglected. "So little is expected of laypeople," she said, quoting a Benedictine friend. "The moral theology we are taught is to get us into heaven with scorched behinds. What kind of an unwilling, ungenerous love of God is this," she continues. "We do little enough, and when we try to do more we are lectured on Jansenism! I don't even know what it is. I only know that I am self-indulgent."

Dorothy was criticized for holding up the counsels of perfection (poverty, chastity, and obedience) as norms of human conduct for laypeople. She thought it was sad that the minimum was always expected of laypeople. She was fond of quoting Léon Bloy: "There is only one unhappiness, and that is not to be one of the saints." To that Dorothy added, "The greatest tragedy is that not enough of us desire to be saints."[70]

69. Day, *On Pilgrimage*, pp. 238-40.
70. Day, *House of Hospitality*, pp. 266-67.

It was in 1939 that Dorothy found what she had been looking for all of her life: the retreat movement, begun by a Canadian Jesuit, Onesimus Lacouture, and spread throughout the United States by a young diocesan priest from Pittsburgh, Father John Hugo. This retreat was anything but minimalist for laypeople. Her first contact with the spirit of the retreat came via Father Pacifique Roy, a Josephite priest who visited the Catholic Worker frequently and worked there as a carpenter. Later she made the retreat with Father Hugo. He became her spiritual director and remained a tremendous influence in her life. The retreat, which was based on the first week (of four weeks) of the Ignatian Exercises stressing purification, and which consisted of a week of absolute silence (one could bring only a Bible and a writing pad), was a liberating spiritual experience for Dorothy. "This is what I was looking for in the way of an explanation of the Christian life," she exulted during a retreat with Father Hugo. "I saw things as a whole for the first time with a delight, a joy, an excitement which is hard to describe. This is what I expected when I became a Catholic."[71]

For Dorothy the retreat was another Emmaus, where the apostles recognized the Lord for the first time in the breaking of the bread. "They had to say to each other," Dorothy wrote, "WAS NOT OUR HEART BURNING WITHIN US, WHILE HE SPOKE ON THE WAY? We saw all things new. There was a freshness about everything, as though we were in love, as *indeed* we were." The retreat attempted to systematize the call to holiness, the call of the rich young man of the Gospels to give up all and follow Jesus, to guide people who made the retreat along this path.

Contrast this call with the call to be saved through keeping the precepts of the Church only — attend Sunday Mass, make the Easter duty by receiving Communion once a year, observe marriage laws, support the Church financially, raise children as Catholics — which was germane to lay Catholics in 1939.

For Father Roy, such teaching did not go far enough. He felt that every word, every thought and prayer, every action should be infused with God's love. We are saved by love, not merely by keeping

---

71. Jim Forest, *Love Is the Measure: A Biography of Dorothy Day* (Mahwah, N.J.: Paulist Press, 1986), p. 83.

the rules. "Love is the measure by which we shall be judged," he said repeatedly, quoting St. John of the Cross. This saying — *Love is the measure* — became a byword to Dorothy. She also embraced another saying of St. John: "Where there is no love, put love and you will take out love." This love was expressed in giving:

> "To give and not to take," Peter Maurin often said, "that is what makes man human." "Love," Father Roy said, "is what makes us want to give." Giving is the essence of religious life: giving space in one's life and home, giving a welcome, giving forgiveness, giving love, even giving one's life. Don't save. Don't store up "treasure which moth and rust attack." Live by the rule of giving.[72]

Father Roy challenged Christians:

> Suppose, he said, you want to go to California, and it costs a hundred dollars. You have fifteen. It is not enough. So give it away. Give it to the poor. Then you suddenly have twenty-five, and that is not enough, and so the only thing to do is to give it away too. Even seventy-five. That is not enough. Tell the Lord you need more. Throw it away recklessly. You will get it back a hundredfold. Maybe it will cover your spiritual needs, and not just your physical. But sow, sow! And as you sow, so shall you reap. He who sows sparingly, reaps sparingly.[73]

In 1940 Dorothy wrote to all the Catholic Worker houses, urging them to take part in a retreat to be led by Father Roy. Her letter was an introduction to the spirituality she hoped would become rooted in all those associated with the Catholic Worker movement.

Dorothy constantly reminded the Workers of the saying of St. Catherine of Siena, the great mystic: "All the way to heaven is heaven, because Jesus said, 'I am the Way.'" The retreat movement reinforced Dorothy's early interest in the saints and mystics. She was fascinated by the spousal relationship with Christ, and with the

72. Forest, *Love Is the Measure,* pp. 81-83.
73. Day, *The Long Loneliness,* p. 252.

presentation in the retreat of the themes from the book of Hosea in the Old Testament.

In his retreat, Father Hugo, whose writings against conscription and war were published in *The Catholic Worker*, emphasized the need for Christians to forgive. Indeed, he suggested that we forgive seventy times seven. He taught what Peter Maurin called the "shock maxims" of the Gospel, loving one's enemies (even in war), giving away your second cloak, turning the other cheek, going the second mile, being poor as Christ was poor. And he spoke of Matthew 25:31ff., pointing out that Christ was hidden in the poor, the hungry, the thirsty, the naked, the homeless.

Another great theme of the retreat was that while created goods are given to us by God and are good, we must not allow our affections to become wrapped up in them instead of God, who desires that we love with our whole hearts. Father Hugo, who cautioned against becoming stuck on the "samples" of God's glory here on earth and advocated relinquishing them in order to obtain the pearl of great price, said that "unworldliness is not an added touch to the Christian life — acceptable in the saints, who have passed from this earth," but "an essential condition for realizing the Christian life."[74]

Dorothy endorsed these ideas of the retreat and called them "the bread of the strong." She reminded the critics of the retreat that it was very much in the spirit of St. John of the Cross, whose writings she knew well, and added that when the retreat materials were shown to a prominent Vatican official, he replied offhandedly, "This is simply popularization of the great Spanish mystic and poet." Dorothy often quoted St. John on detachment, saying that we must travel lightly through the dark night.

Brigid Merriman spelled out the impact these concepts of the retreat had on Dorothy:

> It is in this dimension — her love for Christ — that the retreat contains its greatest meaning for her spirituality. Dorothy re-

---

74. *Weapons of the Spirit: Living a Holy Life in Unholy Times: Selected Writings of Father John Hugo,* ed. David Scott and Mike Aquilina (Huntington, Ind.: Our Sunday Visitor, 1997), pp. 58-60.

garded the retreat as a course in Christian living, which instructed and enabled the participant "to put on Christ" (Rom. 13:14). For her, this was no figurative expression but indicated the depth of her identification with the person of Christ. A passionate woman, she recognized that hers was a lover's quest, that her life task was the ordering and enlargement of her capacity to love. Her reading of Dostoyevsky and her own life experiences had prepared her well for the retreat teachings on love, detachment, and suffering for the sake of the Beloved. Dostoyevsky had taught her compassionate forbearance; her own experiences taught her how much she desired to love and to be loved. Her reflections on retreat teachings enabled her to place her life events in better perspective.[75]

A Canadian priest was called upon — indeed, commissioned — by a group of ten Canadian bishops to evaluate the retreat of Father Lacouture. After attending the retreat, Father Anselme Longpré gave this assessment:

> Armed with . . . the Word of God, he [Father Lacouture] swooped upon our silver idols of well-being, of comfort. He burned our Chesterfields [cigarettes], unmade our silken beds, disconnected our radios, threw in the fire our cushions and our silken fringes, preached to us to love the bare wood, because it resembled the cross of Jesus. He spoke to us of silence, solitude, a hidden life, according to the demands of our "death in Christ." During this . . . we lamented, we raged. . . . But it was necessary to pass through this: "the disciple is not greater than the Master." Is it not time that this doctrine be preached, with force, to us who are the cooperators with Christ in the work of the salvation of souls? This preaching, besides, is inspired directly by the Gospel.[76]

Since the retreat demanded so much, it was bound to have its critics. Giving up things to find a person, Jesus Christ, did not al-

---

75. Merriman, *Searching for Christ,* p. 166.
76. Merriman, *Searching for Christ,* p. 136.

ways appeal. The Gospel makes it clear that one must give up all and follow Jesus. That the retreat spelled out specific things to be given up seemed to create some of the conflict. There were those both inside and outside the Catholic Worker movement who criticized the retreat.

Dorothy issued a strong response:

> How shall we have the means to help our brother who is in need? We can do without those unnecessary things which become habits — cigarettes, liquor, coffee, tea, candy, sodas, soft drinks, and those foods at meals which only titillate the palate. We all have these habits, the youngest and the oldest. And we have to die to ourselves in order to live; we have to put off the old man and put on Christ. That it is so hard, that it arouses so much opposition, serves to show what an accumulation there is in all of us of unnecessary desires.[77]

It is not clear why such an issue was made of giving up smoking and using the car radio, but those who lived by the tenets of the retreat gave up both, especially priests. Not smoking and not having a car radio became outward signs of an inward change. Those who didn't like the retreat accused the converted of being unorthodox and borderline Catholics, almost like a sect. They were treated like outcasts, if not heretics. Never before in the history of the Church had orthodoxy been connected with not smoking or having a car radio. It is understandable that Father Hugo was vastly unpopular. He not only called a spade a spade; he called a cross a cross:

> Radical Christianity is discovered only at the cross, but who desires to be crucified? Like Peter and the other apostles — before the coming of the Holy Spirit! — we all tend to prefer a Christianity without the cross, "air-foam Christianity," as it was satirized by Ed Willock in an outrageous cartoon showing a contented Catholic snuggled down on a cross spread with that seductive cushioning. Many attempt a life of vigorous and dedi-

77. Day, *On Pilgrimage*, pp. 33-34.

cated action, while failing to realize that such action is authentically Christian and efficacious only when grafted to the Tree of Life on Calvary.[78]

The retreat challenged people powerfully and introduced them to a solid spirituality. Those who embraced it found that it changed their lives permanently. These people began to pray and meditate for the first time in their lives. Retreatants absorbed the works and thought of classical authors — St. John of the Cross, the Jesuits Lallemant and De Caussade, Chautard, Marmion, Teresa of Ávila, Thérèse of Lisieux, Newman, Faber, Thomas à Kempis.

The retreat leaders insisted on spiritual direction for retreatants to keep them on the proper path in their newfound pursuit of holiness. They quoted Teresa of Ávila, who said that "he who directs himself is directed by the Devil."

The Hugo priests went along with tough penances practiced by Carmelite nuns, but with the caution that God's hand could not be forced by spiritual acrobatics.[79] They recalled the nuns at Port Royal deep in the Jansenist heresy, who were marked as pure as angels but were proud as devils. Controversy about the retreat helped to encourage those who gave it — and Dorothy Day as well. She encouraged many to make the retreat and arranged for it to be given at the Catholic Worker farm; that way she could further study the theology of the retreat in order to assure that it had a solid theological foundation. Indications of this study are clear in Dorothy's writings. She often cited the work of Henri de Lubac, S.J., on nature and grace, as well as other theologians.[80]

Dorothy wanted everyone to be saints. This was one reason she was so drawn to the retreat. She was, however, uncomfortable with pious sentimentality and embroidered stories about saints. She was convinced that bad hagiography was a deterrent to growth and holi-

78. *Weapons of the Spirit,* ed. Scott and Aquilina, p. 137.
79. The authors remember going some years ago to a Hugo priest for spiritual direction. They were struck by how cautious he was, insisting that those he worked with get eight hours of sleep a night and eat three meals a day. They also made the retreat, which is still given in Pittsburgh and in Michigan.
80. Day, *The Long Loneliness,* p. 258.

ness. She wanted down-to-earth biographies of the saints that would help others to understand and imitate them. On one occasion she spoke of picking up two saccharine books about the Blessed Mother, closing them both with horror, and sitting down with her missal and the Scriptures instead. "No wonder no one wants to be a saint," she said. "But we are called to be saints — we are the sons of God."[81] This was a recurring theme in her writings: that the only purpose for which we were made was to become saints.

Dorothy's integration of faith and life led her to search constantly for ways to live out the retreat. Once, in a reflection during one of the retreats, she asked, "What is to be done; how is it to be done?" She answered, "Continue asking Mary that we be taught." In reflecting on voluntary poverty and giving up luxuries and unnecessary things, she noted that the saints used to walk from one end of Europe and Russia to the other. She went on to comment, "Of course, we are not all given the grace to do such things. But it is good to call to mind the vision. It is true, indeed, that until we begin to develop a few apostles along these lines, we will have no mass conversions, no justice, no peace. We need saints. God, give us saints!"

Conclusion

In 1948, in her book *On Pilgrimage,* Dorothy Day evaluated her life up to that point in the Catholic Worker movement. Even though she lived thirty more years, this is a good commentary on her life and the meaning of the Catholic Worker movement. It gives much insight into her vocation as a Catholic Christian and what sustained her in her work and prayer. Her reflections centered on love and faith, but always directly connected to the suffering of those most in need and the commitment to work for a new heaven and a new earth where justice dwells. She wrote,

> My whole life so far, my whole experience has been that our failure has been not to love enough. This conviction brought me to

---

81. Day, *On Pilgrimage,* p. 32.

a rejection of the radical movement after my early membership in the Socialist Party, the Industrial Workers of the World, and the Communist affiliates I worked with. "Youth demands the heroic," as Claudel said, so the work of these militant minorities had appealed to me. One could not read such books as Sinclair's *Jungle* and not want to do something, join with someone to do something about it. And who else was doing anything? Employers, landlords, political bosses, all professed Christians, were corrupt and rotten to the core, I felt. What was there to love in them? Certainly it seems madness to think of reforming them, converting them. Such an Augean stable was beyond cleaning up; it needed flushing out. So I reasoned. Youth certainly is always looking for a "strong conflict."

It was not that I was ever disillusioned. My conviction that there was a work to be done never wavered. Things did not need to be as bad as they were. There was a possibility of change.

Certainly, too, there was always an inward conviction that we were but dust. Alone by ourselves we could do nothing. . . .

. . . Jesus Christ knew what was in man. I was not baptized until I was twelve, but I had a conscience. I knew what was in man too. But I had too a tremendous faith in man as a temple of the Holy Ghost, in man made to the image and likeness of God, a little less than the angels. Truly I did not want to know good and evil. I wanted to know, to believe only the good. I wanted to believe that man could right wrongs, could tilt the lance, could love and espouse the cause of his brother because "an injury to one was an injury to all." I never liked the appeal to enlightened self-interest. I wanted to love my fellows; I loved the poor with compassion. I could not be happy unless I shared poverty, lived as they did, suffered as they did.

Well, now at fifty, I cannot say that I have been disillusioned. But I cannot say either that I yet share the poverty and the suffering of the poor. No matter how much I may live in a slum, I can never be poor as the mother of three, six, ten children is poor (or rich either). I can never give up enough. I have always to struggle against self. I am not disillusioned with myself either. I know my talents and abilities as well as failures. But I have done woefully little. I am fifty and more than half of my adult life is passed. Who knows how much time is left after fifty? Newman says the tragedy is never to have begun.

I have been disillusioned, however, this long, long time in the means used by *any* but the saints to live in this world God has made for us. The use of force, the use of diplomacy in foreign affairs, the use of anything but the weapons of the spirit seems to me madness. Especially now since the atom bomb. This means the weapons used by either Communist or Christian, who today seem to me in both political [and] economic life to be Marxist also.

The Communist believes in force, in espionage; so do the press and the pulpit of the Christian churches. The Communist does not believe in God; he does not see Christ in his neighbor. Nor do we, in the poor, the lame, the halt, the blind, the prodigal, the sinner, the harlot; nor in those of another race. . . .

We too have done away with property, the land, the ownership of small shop and business, with our monopolies and trusts, chain stores, hotels, gas stations, everything on a colossal scale, wiping out the dignity of man, who has hands and needs to use them, who has a body and needs shelter, food, and clothing, who needs to live in dignity with his children and enjoy the abundant life.

What should really set us apart from all other men is our love. "See how they love one another." In the Bible which is still, after all, the Book for all who have faith, the relationship between God and man is described as that between animal and master (the Good Shepherd), between servant and lord, between child and father, and between husband and wife. Right now, by our baptism, we have been made sons of God. But who does not aspire to the joys of marriage, that love which makes all things new? Who does not long to dissolve and be with Christ? The pleasures of the beatific union are described as those of a wedding banquet or an embrace. "He will overshadow me with his shoulders." "He will kiss me with the kisses of his mouth."

And strange and wonderful to think of, we should have something like this love for all creatures, for mate, for friend, for child, for enemy, too, the kind of love that makes all things new. For God first. "My heart and my flesh cry out for the living God." The love of the will, the memory, the understanding, and the love of the flesh. The tenderness of a mother for her child, the physical love and joy she feels in caressing it, contemplating it, nourishing it at the "breasts of her tenderness." "If a mother forgets her child, never will I forget you, O Jerusalem." "If a son ask of his father bread, will he give him a stone?"

How much there is to learn of love, that feeling of the body and soul, that teaches us what God is, that He is love.[82]

Toward the end of her life, when Dorothy was interviewed by William Miller, who wrote her biography, she spoke of love as the foundation of all, and especially of the Catholic Worker: "Love makes all things easy. When one loves, there is at that time a correlation between the spiritual and the material. Even the flesh is energized; the human spirit is made strong. All sacrifice, all suffering is easy for the sake of love. . . . This is the foundation stone of the Catholic Worker movement. It is on this that we build."[83]

Three weeks before Dorothy died, Sister Peter Claver, the old friend who had introduced her to the retreat, visited her in New York. Father Hugo tells of this visit and also describes Dorothy's burial:

Dorothy held on her lap a book of the retreat conferences that I had sent to her. Holding them, she turned and fondled some flowers in a little vase and said, "I am still sowing." When I heard this I rejoiced, because I realized that she was still reaching into the retreat for "the bread of the strong" as she approached the Day of the Lord, the day of harvesting. . . . Dorothy was buried in a homespun dress and laid in a plain wooden casket provided by the Trappists. Around her neck was a wooden chain holding an icon. On the casket was one flower, saying, *Resurrection.*[84]

---

82. Day, *On Pilgrimage,* pp. 126-28.
83. Quoted by Miller in *Dorothy Day,* p. 326.
84. *Weapons of the Spirit,* ed. Scott and Aquilina, pp. 148-49.

ON PILGRIMAGE

Preface

"All ye works of the Lord, bless ye the Lord." This is the refrain of the three young men who opposed (by nonviolent resistance) the ruler Nebuchadnezzar and were thrown in the fiery furnace. But the fire became as a refreshing wind, breathing upon them, and their ordeal became a time of joy, and they lifted up their hearts in exalted praise and blessed God. The song they sang is one which made an . . . appeal to me, from the time I first heard it in a little Episcopalian church in Chicago on 35th Street and Cottage Grove Avenue, until this very day.

I have spent happy hours during this last year with Becky and Susie in a wicker rocking chair, in front of a fire in the kitchen of an old farmhouse down in West Virginia, singing our morning prayers: *"All ye works of the Lord, bless ye the Lord. O ye ice and snow, O ye cold and wind, O ye winter and summer, O ye trees in the woods, O ye fire in the stove, O ye Becky and Susie and Eric, bless ye the Lord! Praise Him and exalt Him above all forever."*

It is a song with infinite variations. You can include the neighbors' cows and horses, the Hennessy goats and chickens, all the human beings for miles around. You can draw in all those in the Catholic Worker movement scattered throughout the country, all the readers of the paper, all the people on the breadlines.

I sang this song with exultation as a child, as a young mother, and now I am singing it as a grandmother. And it's in the missal, if

67

anyone wishes to sing it after Mass to himself or to children of his own.

You can make up the tune as well as add to the words, and the Lord does not mind, nor do the three youths who first composed the song. What are we here for anyway except to praise Him, to adore Him, and to thank Him?

So, dear God, let this book praise you, too, and all the work of my hands, whether it is breadbaking or writing. It is a woman's book, and for women, and I may repeat myself, but mothers always do that to be heard. I have talked about many things, and many things are implied. It is not a true journal, but written from month to month in the midst of much toil. But it deals with things of concern to us all: the family, the home, how to live, with what to live, and what we live by. There are accounts of New York, West Virginia, Pennsylvania — I have strayed no farther this past year, and it deals with the humble people of these places and the things that concern them. I pray to God to bless the book and you who read it.

January

AROUND Newburgh, New York, five miles outside of which Maryfarm is located, we had more snow than sleet, so we did not have the jeweled fairyland display of the countryside closer to New York. The wind blew the snow in drifts waist high, and Father Becker of Georgetown, who was our guest over Christmas, had plenty of manual labor helping Hans, John, Joe, and Frank get paths shoveled to and from the barns, the men's house, the road, etc. For two days the mail did not get through, though some bold truckmen kept the road open from Middletown to Newburgh.

New Year's Day, the feast of the Circumcision, we did not have a priest, but we were able to get to the nearest church before the second storm broke. Right after the nine o'clock Mass we ran into sleet for a while, and Walter, who was driving, had to get out and clean the windshield with his penknife three times in the five miles.

I hate to talk about our abundance in these times of high prices. But the peasant who has not been displaced from the land can tell the same story as we — the story of food put away for the winter. John and Frank are busy smoking eighty pounds of bacon, ten hams, and ten shoulders of pork, keeping the fire in the smoke-house going with applewood. We have an ancient orchard, so old that it has to be uprooted and replanted, so we have plenty of wood.

69

We have a barn full of apples, thanks to a neighbor, plenty of potatoes, and still some of our own cabbage and turnips, besides a few
thousand cans [of food], thanks to Dave Mason and Joe Cotter.

Our good cook Charlie, who has had a wide experience with railroad gangs and institutions, kept us supplied with pies, and that
topped the holiday meals. Neither Maureen, Marie Therese, nor I
could hold a candle to him in the kitchen. I did the bread-baking,
four pound-loaves a day, and it was the delicious unkneaded bread
of Sir Albert Howard's recommendation. Marie Therese said that
she had made it before without success, but it was because she did
not have her dough stiff enough. One should be able to pick it up
and, flouring one's hands, form it into loaves. Neighbors brought
us fruit, coffee, and cookies, and in spite of the storm we had visitors — Eileen Egan, John O'Donnell, Dave Mason, Dick Roland (of
Brooklyn Catholic Action), Stanley and Walter Vishnewski. Jane
O'Donnell was home for the holiday, and we all missed her, especially her godchild Hans.

It was a happy Christmastime, with everyone receiving Communion together. It was good to have Father Becker's informal talks every evening, in addition to homilies at Mass and discussions during
the day. It was good to get to bed early and read Dickens and listen
to the snow hit against the windowpanes in the attic, which is the
warmest part of the house.

Downstairs it was cold in spite of the furnace (our first use of
coal this winter). The walls and ceilings are unfinished, and so the
wind whistles through. The kitchen is warm, but one has to keep
coats on in the dining room. Peter Maurin, what with being so inac-
tive, found it hard to keep warm in spite of woolens, sweaters, stocking cap, and a blanket over his knees. His cough got worse, so when I
suggested a visit to Mott Street, his face lit up. He can be in my
room, next to Marjorie and Joe Hughes, and the children can run in
and out, and Peter will love that.

Johannah likes to boss him, and she softens her bossiness by
putting her pink cheek against his and hugging him. "Peter, you are
just an old man and you've got to drink your orange juice." (My
daughter used to say when she was a little girl, "When you get little
and I get big, I'll take care of you!") Peter is "little" to Johannah now.

We had to call the doctor for Peter when he went to Mott Street because his excitement at the change of scene led him to overdo it. The doctor diagnosed his cough as cardiac asthma and said otherwise all was well. So he is not trying to venture out for any walks in this weather. Kay Martin and the baby Joe are in the back room, and their stove is so roaring hot that Peter's bedroom is well heated too. And Hazen and Joe and Dave and Mike have dropped in to see him for a little conversation.

There is a skeleton staff at the farm now that the Christmas holidays are over. The next retreat will be Easter week, for women, but we hope also before then to have a Lenten retreat at the beginning of the season.

I left the farm at 8:10 in the morning, catching the bus which goes right by the door straight in to New York. That same bus returns past the farm at 9:30 every night.

I must remember to bring out the point that in describing the comfort of our Christmas on the farm, I do it to contrast the city and the country. If we who are tied to the city cannot go villageward at once, we can begin to hold it as an ideal for our children, and begin to educate them towards it.

In a few weeks I am borrowing a car and going to West Virginia, where my twenty-one-year-old daughter is now settled with husband and babies. She is expecting another, so I shall be there for several months writing about my family, which, after all, is like all families, so that when I write "I" and "mine," my readers put themselves in my place, and it is their own hopes and fears and joys and sorrows they are reading about, common to us all.

January 17, 1948
West Virginia, 5°

WHEN YOU are in the country, the temperature is important. To write I lie in bed with a hot-water bottle at my feet, a loose old coat covering me. A bathrobe would not be enough. The hot-water bottle is a pint-size whiskey bottle.

This is a typical country bedroom, one window facing north, the other west. There is a roomy closet, a door into the front hall, flanking which there are two other bedrooms, and another door to a northeast room, also two windows that get the morning sun. There is a narrow flight of stairs leading down to the summer kitchen. There are eight rooms in the house, a porch front, side, and back, a good tin roof. On this farm there is a shed, pigpen, chicken house, smokehouse, an old cannery from which the machinery has been removed, and which is used now to house goats: the four does, one buck, and two kids. There is a well and pump in the cannery, and a pump on the back porch of the house. Fifty-five acres of hilly woodland and twenty acres of fields go with this farm, for which the owners are asking twenty-five hundred dollars. We are two miles from the highway, three miles from a store, and twelve miles from town and church.

This is a good house, a good farm, in spite of the fields being far from the house beyond the woods. It is renting now for ten dollars a month.

Down the dirt road across a brook about twenty-five feet wide and a foot deep, there is another farm for sale, seventy acres, for twelve hundred dollars. Good barn and chicken coop, granary, pigpen, garage, and smokehouse, but the seven-room, low-ceilinged house is in very bad repair, and the porch on the side is caving in. Also there is a spring in the cellar, and some rainy seasons there is a foot of water under the house. Whether this can be drained and the house repaired in this era of expensive materials and scarcity of craftsmen is a question.

There are other good farms in the neighborhood for three thousand and thirty-five hundred, and everywhere the soil is good, the bottomlands fertile, the hills covered with pine and oak (no one burns coal); there is hunting and fishing.

Here on a neighboring farm, priced at six thousand, a farmer raised and educated three boys and a girl. But he operated the cannery as well as farmed. Others farm summers and work winters, leaving early and arriving home late, leaving their wives to tend to the children and the animals, wood, and water. It is a lonely life for a woman with many small children. It is a life of solitude in city and village anyway, since a young mother cannot get out, but in town neighbors and friends can at least drop in.

Spring, summer, and fall are so beautiful in the country, but the winters are hard. Life then is in two rooms, and the bedrooms are grim. The children may get out, but they soon run in with streaming eyes complaining of hands and feet, and already our two here have chilblains.

Yesterday the snow fell all day, and the children ran out getting pans of it to eat. David says it is called the poor man's manure, as it is filled with chemicals that enrich the soil. It tastes sooty, just as it does in the city. The wheat, barley, and rye in the bottomlands, green and frozen, were soon blanketed. The hills, ridges, and paths were outlined, and all was black and white, blue and gray, with a hint of lavender behind the trees, and the gorgeous fresh green of the pines. Today with the sun out, gold and blue is added to the bright, cold picture. We are indeed in the dead of winter, in the depths of winter.

Tamar's baby is due in ten days now, and we are praying the pains will not come at night or in such cold when it will be hard to start our borrowed car. The path from the house to the road is icy and hard to get down. We could not get to Mass this Sunday morning because of that path, so perilously steep and treacherous.

Our days are spent in cooking, dishwashing, clothes washing, drawing water, keeping two fires going, feeding babies, consoling babies, picking up after babies. The bending and lifting alone should take the place of all exercise. But tomorrow we are going to pretend our long porch is the deck of a ship, and we are going to take a brisk walk up and down and around, just to get out of the house and enlarge our vision a bit. It always fascinated me how the Brontë sisters paced the floor of their living room in front of the fire. It must have been a very large room. My friend Tina has a habit of pacing the floor, and in small quarters it can be nerve-wracking for non-pacers.

On my way down here I bought some supplies and I shall list the prices. Whole wheat flour from a mill, nine cents a pound; buckwheat, ten cents. And at a farm woman's store, homemade candy, seventy cents a pound; sorghum, seventy-five cents a quart; butter, ninety-five cents; beef for a stew, fifty cents a pound (there was much fat). Homemade aprons were eighty-five cents and a dollar. Patchwork quilts were twenty-eight dollars.

Thinking of cash crops to sell by mail, perhaps, there is candy, aprons, Tamar's homespun, home-woven materials, etc. It would supplement the tiny income from D's mail-order book business. (He specializes in Distributist authors, so his field is limited.)

How to live — that is the question. Daily expenses — how to meet them? The goats are not giving milk now. Skim milk is ten cents a quart (the farm wife is always contributing some sauerkraut, a piece of pork, etc.); canned milk is six-twenty a case.

January 19

LAST NIGHT it went down to four below. The water froze in the jug in the bedroom; my feet were cold all night. Susie woke up at four-thirty and cried for an hour. I could hear her even in the far room upstairs. David got up and built the fire and went himself to a camp cot, and Susie slept in with Tamar. She gets colic, so there is no telling whether she is spoiled or sick. She has been waking up in the night all winter. Becky, who will be three in April, does not mind the cold so much.

Today, as usual, dishwashing, cooking, baby tending. I wrote a few letters in time for the mailman, received a few. I could not get my borrowed car started. We need kerosene for the lamps and for the small portable bedroom heater. Five gallons for eighty-five cents. Candles, thirty-five cents a dozen. We do not read late as we are too tired, David with constant wood-chopping, water fetching, etc. Every time he comes in the house, the children clamor for his attention.

Today we found Spike, the young buck goat, a splendid animal, dead. A farm tragedy. Two of our four does are already "lined," as the local saying is, but the other two just had doe kids. Our neighbor has a three-legged buck, and a kid buck which he will now raise, though he and his wife had intended eating him. The goat heart, liver, and kidneys are very large, but there is not too much meat on the frame. They are as good as lamb if prepared right.

We do not know what killed Spike. He was eating the same as the others — corn husks, fodder, some corn, salt, and water. The others all seem to be thriving. The ground is too hard to dig a grave, and he is lying there in the end of the barn. They say there is a wildcat in the neighborhood and we should look after our stock. One year it was a pack of dogs that killed four goats.

The moon is increasing to full, and it is now the coldest time of the month. Tamar is uneasy about her time. She feels "funny," she says. We do hope and pray she is not taken in the dead of the night, when it is coldest and hard to get the car started. And so hard for her too to go out into the night and the cold. I do wish she could have it at home.

We are so far from church, and the snow kept us from getting to Mass Sunday. So we read the epistle and gospel for the day and have been doing it daily since. Sunday's epistle was about the marriage feast of Cana. When my friends are in sorrow and trouble, or even when they are just without spirit, I like to pray, "Jesus, they have no wine," or "Mary, they, have no wine." It is a good prayer for many sad hearts today.

Not much time for prayer these busy days. Only the short ones. And not much time to think of self, either; or comfort — physical, spiritual, or mental. So that is good too. "Self" is the great enemy. "Deny yourself, take up your cross, and follow Me."

In a way, of course, taking care of your own, children and grand-children, is taking care of yourself. On the other hand, there is the sacrament of duty, as Father McSorley calls it. There is great joy in being on the job, doing good works, performing the works of mercy. But when you get right down to it, a work which is started person-ally often ends up by being paperwork — writing letters, seeing visi-tors, speaking about the work while others do it. One can become a veritable Mrs. Jellyby, looking after the world and neglecting one's own, who are struggling with poverty and hard work and leading, as such families with small children do these days, ascetic lives. There are vigils, involuntary ones, fasting — due to nausea of pregnancy, for instance — but St. Angela of Foligno said that penances volun-

75

tarily undertaken are not half so meritorious as those imposed on us by the circumstances of our lives and cheerfully borne.

The Christian life is certainly a paradox. The teaching of St. John of the Cross (which was for beginners, he said) is of the necessity for detachment from creatures; of the need of traveling light through the dark night.

Most of us have not the courage to set out on this path wholeheartedly, so God arranges it for us.

It would seem to the unthinking that mothers of children, whether of one or a dozen, are intensely preoccupied with creatures: their little ones, food, clothing, shelter, matters that are down to earth and grossly material, such as dirty diapers, dishes, cooking, cramming baby mouths with food, etc. Women's bodies, heavy with children, dragged down by children, are a weight like a cross to be carried about. From morning until night they are preoccupied with cares, but it is care for others, for the duties God has given them. It is a road, once set out upon, from which there is no turning back. Every woman knows that feeling of not being able to escape, of the inevitability of her hour drawing ever nearer. This path of pain is woman's lot. It is her glory and her salvation. She must accept.

We try to escape, of course, either habitually or occasionally. But we never can. The point I want to make is that a woman can achieve the highest spirituality and union with God through her house and children, through doing her work, which leaves her no time for thought of self, for consolation, for prayer, for reading, for what she might consider development. She is being led along the path of growth inevitably. But she needs to be told these things, instructed in these things, for her hope and endurance, so that she may use what prayer she can, to cry out in the darkness of the night.

Here is her mortification of the senses:

Her eyes are affronted by disorder, confusion, the sight of human ailments and human functions. Her nose also; her ears tormented with discordant cries, her appetite failing often; her sense of touch in agony from fatigue and weakness.

Her interior senses are also mortified. She is alone with her little ones, her interest adapted to theirs; she has not even the companionship of books. She has no longer the gay companions of her youth (their nerves can't stand it). So she has solitude, and a silence from the sounds she'd like to hear — conversation, music, discussion.

Of course there are consolations and joys. Babies and small children are pure beauty, love, joy — the truest in this world. But the thorns are there — of night watches, of illnesses, of infant perversities and contrariness. There are glimpses of heaven and hell.

January 20

SIX DEGREES above zero this morning, but by afternoon it warmed up so it was like spring. The men worked out in the woods, and in the afternoon Tamar and the babies and I went to town to see the doctor. He is a nice, casual soul, assuming that if there is anything worrying you, you will tell him. No examination. Just a weekly visit, and when the pains begin, he says, go to the little hospital, and they will call him.

We had him examine Sue too as she is restless, irritable, and very wakeful at night. He finds nothing wrong, thank God.

I am trying to read some of Garrigou-Lagrange on the interior life every night. I am too dog-tired to read much. He writes, "As everyone can easily understand; the interior life is an elevated form of interior conversation which everyone has with himself as soon as he is alone, even in the tumult of a great city. From the moment he ceases to converse with his fellowmen, man converses interiorly with himself about what preoccupies him most. This conversation varies greatly according to the different ages of life; that of an old man is not that of a youth."

What kind of an interior life can a mother of three children have who is doing all her own work on a farm with wood fires to tend and water to pump? Or the grandmother either?

Here is my day. With Sue waking at all hours of the night for attention, we sleep late — that is, until seven-thirty. Then there are those shuddering hours of building fires in kitchen and living room and waiting for the water to boil for that warming, encouraging cup of coffee. The babies are not in too much of a hurry for their bottles. They are very giddy indeed first thing in the morning and talk and shout and run around in bare feet unless I get them dressed in double-quick time.

Breakfast of sausage, hotcakes, apples, and coffee. Dishes, water heating for clothes, bread-baking. That was today. Yesterday it was pumpkin pies. These things do not take all morning so I have time for writing letters. Then there is the arrival of the mail, at 11:30 in the morning, always something to look forward to in the country, with a book arriving from a friend, a package of food from my sister. Yesterday it was fish balls, cheese, baby food, candies, and two toys. Today there was the letter from a friend, asking if her boy and girl, sixteen and fifteen, could spend their vacations here, which would help pay bills nicely for a few months besides being enjoyable company. But can they put up with poverty, confusion, dirt, disorder? There is that old saying, "Order is heaven's first law." But the way people use it irritates me, reminding you that "cleanliness is next to godliness," "a place for everything, and everything in its place!"

Babies know nothing of such things, nor that "willful waste makes woeful want."

Sue is at the age when food goes in her ears, her hair, all over the floor. She will not be fed. Fortunately, there are the chickens to eat all that she tosses riotously around. Becky, aged two-and-a-half, is neat and tidy in her eating, but her toys, papers, books, anything she can lay her hands on is also flung here and there. My back aches with constant bending. We are trying to buy one of these wonderful dustpans with long handles.

Lunch next, and dishes and hanging up the wash, and today to the doctor, which meant a bath and all clean clothes for the children. Then on the way to town Becky got sick and vomited all over herself and me and the car, which means more washing and cleaning. She had insisted on helping with the bread-baking and eaten large hunks of whole-wheat dough, apples, topped by milk, potatoes, and baked cabbage for lunch.

Home just in time for supper, and more dishes and bottles and undressings and so on.

Not to speak of their innumerable rescues from imminent danger all through the day from the time they wake until the time they sleep.

How to lift the heart to God, our first beginning and last end, except to say with the soldier about to go into battle — "Lord, I'll have no time to think of Thee but do Thou think of me." Of course, there is grace at meals, a hasty grace, what with Sue trying to climb out of her high chair on the table. Becky used to fold her hands and look holy at the age of eighteen months, but now she does nothing. If you invite her participation, she says, "I won't." If you catch Sue in a quiet, un-hungry mood, she will be docile and fold her hands. But rarely. She is usually hungry, and when she starts to eat she starts to hum, which is thanks too.

But there is that lull in the morning before the mailman comes when I can take out the missal and read the epistle and gospel for the day, and the collect, which is always pertinent. That is refreshment always.

"The language of the Gospel, the style used by our Lord, lead us more directly to contemplation than the technical language of the surest and loftiest theology," Garrigou-Lagrange says. So this reading, directly from the gospels and the epistles of St. Paul, [is] the best I can have. The author of *The Cloud of the Unknowing* talks of the conscious stretching out of the soul to God. So I must try harder to pause even for a fraction of a minute over and over again throughout the day, to reach toward God. We certainly feel the need of physical stretching.

What do I talk to myself about? When I am truly alone, with no babies around, as when I am in church alone, I pray. I say the rosary, I read my psalms, make the Acts: adoration, contrition, thanksgiving, supplication. And there is time. At home, kneeling by my bed, or in the bitter cold, saying my prayers in bed, they are brief, half-conscious, and the planning, the considering, the figuring of ways of "making ends meet" goes on. Until I catch myself and turn to God again.

"All these things shall be added unto you." "He knoweth that ye have need of these things." St. Teresa of Ávila says we should not trouble our Lord with such petty trifles. We should ask great things of Him.

So I pray for Russia, for our own country, for our fellowmen, our fellow workers, for the sick, the starving, the dying, the dead.

January 21
Feast of St. Agnes

IN READING about the feast today, the custom of giving the Benedictine nuns, who have their convent at the site of the church of St. Agnes, two white lambs to raise until Good Friday, is very interesting. They are shorn, and the wool is used to make the Bishop's pallium.

Tamar was especially interested in this, as she had her sheep too, and spun the wool and wove it. Knowing how timid and stubborn sheep are, though they can become pets, and also how dirty they are, and how hard to keep clean, we wondered at the nuns and how they put up with them. When the lambs are taken to the Holy Father to be blessed, they have probably been cleaned and combed. But is Rome as sooty a city as Easton, Pennsylvania, for instance, where we kept four sheep and an angora goat? They were most distressingly dirty all the time. It was joy to wash the wool and see how creamy white it could become. The angora wool was white as snow.

It is fun to wash, tease, and card the wool — I can do all those things, though I cannot spin or weave. Tamar learned those skills in Canada, where the convent schools, *Ecoles Manageres,* all teach these crafts. The tuition is only eighteen dollars a month, or was when she went there five years ago. Then there is the cost of materials too. She spent from October until Easter in a school at St. Martine and came back with these delightful skills. While there she wove material, cut it out, and sewed it into a suit, a dress, and coat, all in two weeks! It is not the kind of a suit which will ever wear out. She has her loom now, which cost ninety-five dollars, and a spinning wheel which was purchased for her in Canada for thirteen dollars. She can spin a hank of wool in half an hour. From three sheep she got enough wool to make, when sent away to be cleaned and spun at a mill up in Maine, fifteen pounds of single-ply thread for weaving. I have heard it said that it takes nine spinners to keep one weaver busy. Weaving goes very fast, once the loom is set up right. Our friend, Mary Humphries, out in St. Joseph, Minnesota, says it takes the whole family to set up her loom — and as she has five children, she means, I suppose, that they all insist on being in on it.

When we went driving down to the fish hatcheries at Ridge today, we found in the store there some woven rag rugs for four dollars apiece. I shall get two as soon as I can to start furnishing my own bedroom, which I have decided to put under the patronage of St. Ann, as she was a grandmother. To earn some money, I must write a few more articles, and Catholic magazines pay very little indeed.

Tamar would weave some rag rugs, but her loom is set up in a beautiful plaid design (her own home-dyed wool), and she must finish the cloth she has on it. Right now it is pulling, she has some intricate job to do on it, and waiting as she is these last days for the new baby, she is letting it go for smaller jobs such as knitting socks for Susie.

Besides, weaving, she says, is not the work for pregnant women. In Ireland and in Scotland, it was the work of men, according to Father Vincent McNabb. Fishermen in their off season became weavers. It can become too heavy work for women, if they sit long at it and the muscles of stomach and thighs, as well as of the arms, shoulders, and back, are called into play.

To continue the story of Tamar's education, after her winter in Canada (which she remembers especially for its cold and the preponderance of sweets in the diet), she spent a year as an apprentice in the home of Ade de Bethune, artist in stained-glass windows, wood carving, woodcuts, lettering, etc. Ade is interested in making things in general and has, over a period of years, made everything she uses, including hats, shoes, socks, and dresses, and has raised food such as chickens and rabbits for her table.

One way of combating the system, she says, is to stop buying the products of our machine world, our capitalist industrial society. If you want a rug, make it. If you want rosary beads, or [a] crucifix, make them. The crudest samples of your own work will be better than that which you can buy very often. Ade lives in Newport, and

81

Tamar stayed with her and her family for a year. Part of her education was to shop intelligently for the family groceries. How to buy and cook cheap cuts of meat, how to bake and churn, keep a kitchen fire going, how to care for small animals in a backyard, how to letter and bind a book. For a Christmas present, Tamar lettered a chapter from Eric Gill's *What Is Christianity?* and bound it in sailcloth for me.

There were weekly evenings when one of the monks from Portsmouth Priory came and gave a course, whether it was philosophy or theology for layfolk (women layfolk at that), I do not know. There were concerts of chamber music at friends' houses, folk dances on Friday nights, evenings of visiting the marine hospital to teach crafts to the wounded sailors.

How to take care of the money you had, how to earn money by taking care of children, sitting with invalids, repainting murals in an old church — this too was part of the course.

The well-to-do know how to care for what they have, increase it, add to it, so they can help others. The poor are notoriously extravagant. They have so little, it scarcely seems worth saving. They have so little, they are always seeking compensation in spending, consoling themselves with luxuries for the necessities they cannot have, such as a home, a garden, space, security of a fashion. If I mention money often in this account, it is for a purpose. Few people know how others live, the hand-to-mouth existence that is theirs, their fear of debt, their lack of opportunity.

My mother used to say, "Them as has, gits," meaning, I suppose, that if one had capital to make a start, one could increase what he already had. Capital to start farming, or a book business, or a weaving school, or even a boardinghouse.

Say, for instance, Tamar wished to take in summer guests. She would need money to furnish three bedrooms — bedsprings, mattresses, dressers, curtains, shades, rugs, paints, calcimine, washstands, pitchers, basins — quite a little outlay.

One would need also the energy to do the cleaning or painting, or the money to pay a neighbor to do it. And would one's neighbors wish to do such paid work? Here in this independent community they come gladly to help wash, cook, and clean when there is illness, but would they come as paid help? And as Americans, we are unused to receiving help. Our America! Its faults and virtues; our fierce independence and our pride. Our generosity and our fear of making fools of ourselves. "Fools for Christ." If we were only truly Christian, "putting on Christ," putting on the life of the Holy Family, in simplicity and manual labor!

When I talk about poverty, I do not mean *destitution,* which is something quite different. Nor do I want to "talk poor mouth," as my mother used to say. I talk about the poverty of young people newly married, the girl without dowry, the young man without anything, either a team of horses, or a sum of money, or a truck, to make a start in life. Mainly because their parents were also poor, or had many children, or at any rate no tradition of the parents' duty to educate and start their children in life. I read somewhere that according to Jewish law, if a father did not give his son a trade, that son did not owe his father support in his old age. St. Paul, a scholar, was a tentmaker, a weaver of goats' hair.

Peter Maurin, founder of a movement, a man of vision, changing the course of thought of thousands, has talked for fifteen years of crafts, of manual labor. Yet how many have tried to acquire a skill, either to carpenter, lay brick, make shoes, tailor, or work at a forge? Many, thinking of the family, the need for a home and space and food, have turned to the farm. But a farmer needs capital and many skills, besides the *habit of work.* A village economy could use doctors, barbers, veterinar[ies], baker[s], launderers, canners, builders, shoemakers, tailors, etc. Not to speak of weavers. Every man, doing some particular job, could be an artist too, and from his work, beauty would overflow. As Peter always put it, there would be a synthesis of cult, culture, and cultivation.

Today it was warmer, and we went to the neighboring farm for our milk. It is an old log house with ancient boxwood in front, but all is in bad repair and unpainted. The hills rose in folds on all sides, and there was the beauty of yellow fields, green pines, and blue sky. But the fences were down, the barns decrepit, all decaying. It is this way everywhere in the country. One old woman and her son are left, the others all gone to the cities. At all the farms they sell their cream, and one can buy only skim milk, for ten cents a quart.

People lived far more substantially, far more beautifully once.

I remember Tamar saying before her marriage, "I don't care if we have no food. I am going to have flowers around my house." But paint and mended fences are needed too, and that means money, time, and strength.

It is true we have here "no lasting city," no abiding dwellings; it is true we are on pilgrimage, but, as St. Catherine of Siena said, "All the way to heaven is heaven, for He said, 'I am the Way.'" So it is our duty to take the materials God gives and take up our job of co-creator, and do the best we can.

St. Francis' first job was to clean up a church. The family's first job is the home.

January 23

HAD TO omit my writing last night, as I took over the baby tending. Susie has been wakeful every night for months, starting crying at midnight, sometimes keeping it up for hours, sometimes sleeping restlessly in bed with David and Tamar. So that Tamar can get some good nights' sleep before her time comes, I am sleeping downstairs with the children, and they take over my room upstairs at ten.

As usual, Sue woke at twelve-thirty, but she went to sleep after I took her in bed with me, though restlessly. She is spoiled, of course, but if we let her cry, Becky wakes up and cries with her — "Take Tudie in, take Tudie in" — and her distress is for her sister as well as for herself.

T. says she feels as if she could scarcely drag herself about or lift her feet from the floor. She laughs at her own ungainliness and shuffling steps. But she is not suffering from sour stomach and sickness as she was last week. This sounds over-realistic as I write, and I have remembered these last few days a book I read years ago, a supposedly realistic account of early married life with pregnancies, little babies, dirt, disorder, egg-on-the-tablecloth kind of emphasis. It was a dreary tale. There is a wonderful quotation from Stevenson in a recent review: "True realism always and everywhere is . . . to find out where joy resides, and give it voice. . . . For to miss the joy is to miss all."

Another lovely quotation from the same review is "There is an idea abroad among moral people that they should make their neighbors good. One person I have to make good: myself. But my duty to my neighbor is much more nearly expressed by saying that I have to make him happy — if I may."

The latter reminds me of Father Faber's conferences on kindness; the former, of St. Paul — "All that rings true, all that commands reverence, and all that makes for right; all that is pure, all that is lovely, all that is gracious in the telling; virtue and merit, wherever virtue and merit are found — let this be the argument of your thoughts."

There is so much fear and distraction these days over the state of the world — there is sadness in the Pope's Christmas message, in articles, in letters, in all endeavors. And yet surely, "all times," as St. Teresa said, "are dangerous times."

We may be living on the verge of eternity — but that should not make us dismal. The early Christians rejoiced to think that the end of the world was near, as they thought. Over and over again, even to the Seventh Day Adventists of our time, people have been expecting the end of the world. Are we so unready to face God? Are we so avid for joys here that we perceive so darkly those to come?

It is one of the strange paradoxes of the Christian life that we can say with St. Paul, "As dying, yet we behold we live." We can suffer with others, we can see plainly the frightful chaos, the unbelievable misery of cold and hunger and bitter misery, yet all the time there is the knowledge "that the sufferings of this time are not to be compared to the joy that is to come."

Often we comfort ourselves only with words, but if we pray enough, the conviction will come too that Christ is our King, not Stalin, Bevins, or Truman. That He has all things in His hands, that "all things work together for good to those that love Him."

Oh, but the misery of those who do not, of those who because of suffering turn from Him and curse God and die!

It is hard to think of these things. It is not to be understood; we cannot expect to understand. We must just live by faith, and the faith that God is good, that all times are in His hands, must be tried as though by fire. "I believe, Lord. Help Thou my unbelief."

THERE IS another attitude of despair which I cannot agree with — that expressed by Peter Michaels in *Integrity* last November. He writes, "It is too late for any purely economic or political nostrum, even a good one. It is interesting to speculate as to whether Belloc's and Chesterton's Distributism (which was essentially an economic scheme) might have saved England and possibly Europe, if it had been applied, in, say, the 1920s. One wonders if some correction of the ills of usury wouldn't have mended many matters once. Quite possibly so. While we were still suffering from acute mortal sin there was the possibility of turning back, and whereas it would have to be accompanied by a turning back to God also, it could possibly have started with economic reform. Chesterton's insistence that we go back to where we took the wrong road, and his insistence also that it had to be done very quickly, were probably quite correct at that time. It was the eleventh hour. We didn't turn back. Now it is midnight and we are dying!"

I don't like to use cliches, but sometimes they are wonderfully apt. Father Gillis tells the story of the preacher all puffed up with his sermon who later greets one of his parishioners in the sacristy.

"I want to tell you how wonderful your sermon was, Father," he said.

"And what, my good man, was it that especially struck you?" said the priest, hungry for praise.

"That part about 'it's never too late to turn over a new leaf.'"

When T. read this outburst of Michaels, she said, "He still must eat, he still must live!" And that is the point — we are still in the flesh. Body and soul are not separated. We still have to take care of Brother Ass, and the most of us must do it by the sweat of our brows. How are we going to feed, clothe, and shelter ourselves? By going along with big business? By continuing to work for the Gallup Poll, the Anaconda Copper, Standard Oil, Metropolitan Life Insurance, and go right on adding our little bit to the sum total of chaos?

To be a personalist does not mean to be a quietist. No matter if it seems hopeless, "we must hope against hope." "In peace is my bitterness most bitter." These are hard words to understand, but we can at least remember that all times are in the hand of God.

There are so many writers, so many who think, who talk, among us. What can we do? We can "be." In all the fifteen years Peter Maurin has talked of manual labor, how many we know have learned a trade? There are printers, stained-glass-window makers, there are a few. But so many go right on in their white-collar jobs in business offices.

A priest we know who does not like our emphasis on Distributism, decentralism, or whatever one wishes to call it, said one time, "It is too late for anything but love." That sounded good to many people. But that same priest was going about his business having his church repaired — twenty thousand dollars' worth.

No, all times are dangerous times. St. Paul said, "It behooves us all to act, if we have wives, as though we had not."

So even in those days, a holy and happy perspective on the present time was enjoined. To be aloof, to be superior to the heat or the cold, the buffetings of fortune — this holy indifference is good and to be admired. I can remember how the heroes in my girlhood romances, which I read in my teens, all had this lofty indifference.

Here is a wonderful quotation from Eric Gill:

When I consider how we Christians exhibit our Christianity — making it appear that there's not a ha'porth of difference between Christians and anyone else — neither in our daily life and behavior nor in our political and economic theory — when I consider this, I say, I don't see how we can expect to convert the world. Perhaps we don't expect to; we are quite comfortable with our manners and customs.

Communism started as a movement to overthrow capitalism. It is now, it appears, an equally bloody tyranny. I think the Christians have none but themselves to blame. So it is in many affairs. By our lukewarmness and complacency and blindness we have betrayed our own cause. I think we've got to learn our Christianity again. I think we have succumbed to the prevailing and all-pervading poison of material progress. We think we can get riches and plenty by political and scientific and mechanical trickery. Trickery, that's what it comes to. Press the button and the figure works. They call it the application of science to industry. It's not. It's the application of Science to money-making. And the Christians haven't seen through it. No, they think it's "jolly fine" and that working men ought to be grateful for the higher standard of living and the lower standard of muscular effort.

Well, the point here is not social reform or the rottenness of capitalist culture. The point is that the whole world has got it firmly fixed in its head that the object of working is to obtain as large an amount of material goods as possible, and that with the increased application of science and the increased use of machinery that amount will be very large indeed, while at the same time the amount of necessary labor will become less and less, until machines being minded by machines, it will be almost none at all. And the point is that this frame of mind is radically un-Christian and anti-Christian. And the point of that is that it is therefore contrary to Nature and contrary to God — as anti-God as any atheist could wish. And that, no doubt, is why our English industrialism is so popular among Russian Communists.

The alternative is the Cross. That's the awful fact. And it's not simply a matter of ethical behavior, as who should say, "Take up your cross and follow me." It's also a matter of intelligent behavior, as who should say, "Thou fool, this night thy soul shall be required of thee." Man is made for happiness, not for wealth, and the two are entirely independent of one another and even inimical. A moderate amount of physical health and material wealth is necessary to man, that he may maintain his life. Of course! But even so it is better to give than to receive and therefore better to be given than to take. The whole of our trouble is the secularization of our life, so that we have descended to animal conditions of continual struggle for material goods. By sin — sin, that is to say, self-will and self-worship — by sin man does not descend from the superhuman to the merely human, but from the superhuman to the sub-human. Strange fact! Man cannot live on the human plane; he must be either above or below it.

The marvelous feats of our mechanized (scientific) industrial world are not human feats. They are no more than the feats of highly intelligent animals and the more we perfect our mechanization so much the more nearly do we approach the impersonal life of bees or ants.

And if I might attempt to state in one paragraph the work which I have chiefly tried to do in my life it is this: to make a cell of good living in the chaos of our world. Lettering, type-designing, engraving, stone-carving, drawing — these things are all very well, they are means to the service of God and of our fellows and therefore to the earning of a living, and I have earned my living by them. But what I hope above all things is that I have done something towards reintegrating bed and board, the small farm and the workshop, the home and the school, earth and heaven.

The thing about Christianity, the thing about the Cross, about Calvary, is that it is true to man. Man, not that creature, that biped known to Science — measured as to his dimensions, his comparative dimensions, for there are no others; dissected as to his physiology; analysed as to his psyche — but man, the person known to himself and to God, the creature who knows and wills and loves, master of his acts (however much he be hindered by and subject to heredity and circumstances), therefore responsible. That is the creature who desires happiness and by the very nature of things, by his own nature, cannot find it except in God. That is why death is the gate of life.

— From Eric Gill, *Autobiography*
(New York: The Devin Adair Co)

The idea of "the cell of good living" is expressed by Ignatio Silone, by Arthur Koestler, by Aldous Huxley. Not by the movement of masses swayed by any demagogue will things be changed. But the yeast will leaven the dough, the salt will add savor, the candle will shine out, and as Juliana of Norwich wrote, "All will be well, and all will be well, and all manner of thing will be well."

(When Susie fell and bumped her head today, T. gathered her up and, rocking her, murmured, "Everything's going to be all right, my

89

darling. Everything's going to be all right." And I know she was making an act of hope, because outside a blizzard is raging, and already the snow is a foot thick on these country roads. However, it is the month of the Holy Family. They must take care of us. God will temper the wind to the shorn lamb. So we reassure ourselves, but O how uneasy I am nonetheless!)

And now I read this quotation from a review of the work of Dr. Martin Buber by Ann Freemantle in the *Commonweal*. According to Buber, constructive socialism "becomes possible only through the formation of small voluntary groups of men who not merely share the means of production, or the forces of labor, but who, as human beings, enter into a direct relationship with one another and live a life of genuine fraternity. Such a socialism would have to resist any mechanization of living. The association of such groups would have to resist the dictates of an organized center, accumulation of power, and a political 'superstructure.' The focus of such groups, or cells, is not a political but a religious motivation."

January 30
St. Martin

THE WEATHER has been bitter, fourteen below zero one morning — never above ten above zero. Which is very cold, even for New York. Every now and then we have a winter when it is colder in Alabama than in Alaska, just to turn things upside down.

All through the snow the redbirds and bluebirds go in flocks. There are foxes and black bears in the woods and deer that come to the doorstep. David is not a hunter, and besides, we have not the right kind of a gun.

For meat we have a side of bacon which will last us the winter. We have just finished some sausage friends gave us. Once a month we have chicken. Once every few weeks we buy liver.

But in general our meals are pancakes and coffee and applesauce for breakfast, beans and raw cabbage for lunch, bread and cheese and stewed tomatoes for supper. Once a week eggs, sometimes pies, suet puddings. It is fun to seek out recipes — to use what is at hand. The potato crop around here has not been good — they are green, scabrous, some soft and spongy. So they are no good for mashing or baking, only boiling with salt and margarine on them. But everything tastes delicious, and best of all is the smell of fresh-baked bread in the house.

January 31
St. John Bosco

FOURTEEN BELOW zero again. Up at five-thirty to build fires, and Susie has been staying obediently under the covers, what with a few slaps. So we stayed in bed until 7:00. The living room warmed up, but it took till afternoon to heat the kitchen, which is a north room, even with washing, baking of bread, rolls, and apple pies.

We were afraid to wipe up the floor for fear of leaving a coating of ice, because in the four corners of the room things like canned milk, the water bucket, the clothes in the sink were still frozen at ten o'clock. But we did it anyway with a well wrung-out mop.

How the day goes! Outside it is unbelievably beautiful, with the snow-covered fields and hillsides, the green pines and the red roads showing through the snow. But one does not take much time to contemplate this beauty. If you go out, it is for wood, to empty ashes on the icy path, to take down clothes and to hang others, and it is breathtakingly cold, and the clothes freeze as you hang them up.

Men always — I am sure from my experience in the past — wonder what women do with their time. My son-in-law is too polite to say so, but I am sure he thinks, "Two women to two children and one house!" But the work never ends.

I thought of Margaret Bosco, the mother of St. John Bosco, today, and how she helped him in his gigantic work of caring for boys, and how she prayed while peeling potatoes and mending, etc., but with little children tugging at your apron strings, it is hard to pray. I manage to get in the psalms of Matins every day (next week I'll try Laud), and Vespers in the evening. I vary the hours in order to get more familiar with all the psalms. This new English translation from the new Latin translation, arranged as the breviary is, brought out by Father Frey, is wonderful. Every day something new shines forth.

I had read somewhere that Moses, one of my favorite characters in history, was denied entrance to the Promised Land because he turned bitter against his followers, failing in love and trust. I had thought that only a legend until I read in today's, Saturday's, Matins, "Then they angered him at the waters of Meribah, and it went ill with Moses on their account, for they embittered his spirit, and he spoke rashly with his lips"; Ps. 106:32-33. (The old translation is "They provoked him also at the waters of contradiction; and Moses was afflicted for their sakes: because they exasperated his spirit. And he distinguished with his lips.")

This is a lesson in holy optimism, an argument for faith in and love for those who depend upon us. How often I fail in these ways, in plain, ordinary kindness and love and hope. Father Faber's spiritual conferences on kindness are an eye-opener. They are out of print now but can be obtained in any religious library.

This last month has been the month of the Holy Family; now this coming month, I'm going to think of Margaret Bosco, who has not been canonized yet but was undoubtedly a saint. Her life was much like ours, and she certainly did not have any electric washing machine, or gasoline ones, as they do hereabouts.

On a recent trip to the West Coast, I was much struck by the price of land. Some friends of ours in Portland recently bought a place for sixteen thousand dollars, and the house on it could not be lived in, so they had to rent another house a mile away. They have five or six children and are quite isolated, though they do have electricity. But there was going to be a shortage of electricity, the papers warned, urging people not to have lights on their Christmas trees. One friend with a deep-freeze locker reported a tremendous spoilage of food because of failure of electricity for several days. Another said that recently when her mother had the dinner all preparing for company in the electric range, the power went off for four hours, so dinner was ready by eleven at night.

This is not just sour grapes. In all the suburbs of New York City during a recent ice storm, the power was off for days, and heating power as well as cooking facilities were done away with. And, of course, no one had kerosene or wood stoves handy!

But to return to prices, Leslie, our neighbor down the road, says, "Where do people get so much money [to buy] such expensive farms?" In this case, the girl had received insurance after her brother's death in the war, and it was on the strength of that insurance that they bought their farm. The husband works in a factory to keep it going.

Down here in West Virginia, or up in Pennsylvania, or in Vermont, I have seen farms for twelve hundred, fifteen hundred, two thousand — beautiful farms — bottomlands, wooded hillsides, springs and wells, houses [with] seven and eight rooms, from fifty to a hundred years old, low ceilinged, high ceilinged, log houses, clapboard houses, tin-roofed houses, with pigpens, chicken coops, woodsheds, and barns; but humble houses too, with a pump on the back porch and no plumbing, only the tubs hanging on a nail. Five hundred dollars' down payment will buy one of these houses, but it would be far better to have cash, and not have to pay four percent interest to the bank. Cash is hard to come by; people exchange help in these country parts.

Down here in West Virginia, cows sell at this time of the year for $100 or $125. Up in New York state, for $260. Food for humans is standardized, of course, and also the commercial feed for animals. The prices have gone up about 300 percent in the last few years.

"And where is cash to come from?" young married people in the cities say. Around here, farmers cut pulpwood, nine dollars a cord collected at your farm, and eleven a cord if you deliver it. There is work in the sand mines or for girls in a stocking factory, and in the summer in the tomato cannery.

But if the men are away all day in winter, who is going to cut wood for the wife? One needs a power saw, a car for transportation, etc. But people hereabouts do without these things, even if they have to walk miles to work, and they prepare all summer for the coming winter, etc.

Anyway, there is quite as much security here as in the city: once you get here, you see that. Really more. Employment in this machine age is tied up with preparedness, armaments, war, and recovery from war. Most of us cannot forget the depression of 1929-1939. Then one depended on the State, on the relief — and the investigator said as she surveyed the coffeepot on the stove and looked for signs of expenditures or dissipations, "What right have you got to have another baby when you cannot support the one you have?"

Land, and a home and liberty — the liberty of Christ that St. Paul often talked of. These are what a man craves, and a woman too. But they do mean hard work, real drudgery. How dead tired one gets at night, and how wonderful sleep is. "Just resisting the cold consumes your energy," Tamar says, after standing on her feet most of the day, cooking and washing.

There is the question of school, of course. Down here it would be necessary to go to a public school. "But that certainly keeps the parents awake to their responsibilities," T. said today. "Besides, in Easton, Helen said the children were always being urged by the sisters to bring money. With a big family there just is no money."

February

FOR A long time there are no visitors; then suddenly the day is full of them. Everyone is wondering when T. is going to have her baby. The mailman asks; neighbors send over presents. This morning Bud Yost came in with a bundle of baby clothes outgrown by some of his nieces and nephews. His mother is so young a looking woman that I had taken her for her husband's daughter at the apple-paring last fall. They are local people, and the farms now priced at twelve hundred dollars are worth, to them, eight hundred; and this one, which we are renting, priced at twenty-five hundred dollars, worth twelve hundred. They themselves [were] renters all their lives, until suddenly the father, coming into a little legacy, was able to make a down payment on a place selling for fifteen hundred. He works; his wife cans at home and sells her produce; the children, a son and two daughters, all help too. The son who visited us this morning has been cutting pulpwood.

One cannot help thinking that the men have an easier time of it. It is wonderful to work out on such a day as this, with the snow falling lightly all around, chopping wood, dragging in fodder, working with the animals. Women are held pretty constantly to the house. Tomorrow I shall take to reading and pacing the porch, one of my favorite occupations. I've been reading the psalms for Matins and Vespers, and by taking a stroll midmorning or afternoon I can get in the Little Hours. Susie is so crazy to get out, and suffers so with cold when she does.

I was reading in *David Copperfield* how Betsy Trotwood paced the floor for two hours while she unraveled problems, and at eighty could still do a five-mile stretch! She reminds me of my mother-in-law, who at eighty plays croquet, walks, swims, listens to Churchill on the radio, and in general is a vigorous old Englishwoman.

In the afternoon Joe came in — he is moving, and the problem of packing [and] finding a place for himself, wife, and four small children is a hard one. He brought jam from his wife. Then in the late afternoon, Alma and Leslie — who are on the next farm — came, Leslie to fetch home a goat he was buying from Joe, and Alma to take a lesson in hooked-rug making and knitting. Her baby will be due next August. She is a wonderful little housekeeper and cooks and cans and bakes. Their house is of logs, very uneven, low-ceilinged, irregular, only three of the seven rooms inhabitable. But they are managing. She canned twenty roosters last week. Last month they slaughtered, and the other day Leslie brought us some of her scrapple. She boiled the head and feet, picked the bones and ground them up, mixed them with home-ground cornmeal, and cooked them like mush. The scrapple comes out of the pan in a firm cake to be sliced down and fried.

Little by little I learn more about the neighborhood. No Negro families, for instance. All of Dutch or Irish descent. No unions. Stocking factory, Victor plant, sand mines all unorganized. This week there is an election to decide whether the workers in the Victor plant want a union. The local paper in an editorial urges against it. How can a union organizer get in one of these tight little communities? It certainly demands courage. And in spite of Republican propaganda to the contrary, it is not just "business is business," and the desire to increase the dues-paying members of a great union like the C.I.O. Auto Workers, of which this will be an affiliate. Power, perhaps, and the desire of the worker to feel his strength, his importance, his responsibility as a man, and not just a wage slave — this desire motivates men.

Yesterday we went to Dr. Tobias — T. has been going weekly to him. His office is in a store just off the square. There were a dozen there before us. All poor people, all shabbily dressed, all workers of farm background.

There was one young mother with five children. When T. has her two trying to tear up magazines and spit on the windows, she is not at all embarrassed, because all the mothers bring their children everywhere. They have to.

Dr. Tobias is an all-around family doctor, a tired, youngish man, full of common sense. He dispenses calcium pills to the expectant mothers, cough medicine to the children, etc. No prescriptions or going to the drugstore. His charge for delivering the baby is thirty-five dollars. The hospital, "The Pines," [charges] four dollars a day for the mother, one dollar for the baby.

Friday, February 6
Feast of St. Dorothy

ST. DOROTHY is the patroness of gardeners, and when I think of a garden, I think of a garden enclosed, as the Blessed Mother is described to be. A wall is a lovely thing — with fruit trees and hollyhocks and tall things growing against it. A garden not too small to have a grape arbor at one end, where there can be tables and chairs and benches for outdoor meals. Such a garden is for women and children, so that there can be no straying of little feet.

St. Dorothy, pray we may one day have such a garden, that we may settle long enough in one place to put roots in, if not our own, since we are pilgrims, at least a tree's, a vine's.

One of the vows the Benedictines take is *stability*. And there is such wandering today, from job to job, from home to home. Most people want a settled place, but economic circumstances make it hard.

Our life is made up of meals. We have been making beautiful

cakes, pies, and cookies, much to the delight of David and the children, to vary our monotonous diet.

Susie has a good appetite and ploughs her way sturdily through a breakfast of wheat cereal, applesauce, and a full eight ounces of milk. But Becky eats like a bird. A bit of whole-wheat bread, a piece of apple, a handful of wheat when the chickens are fed, a piece of raw carrot, a bit of raw oats. She has a great liking for these things. T., when she was a baby, refused a bottle after she was weaned at ten months, drank only a few swallows of milk, and made each meal a torment. Then, when she had to be away from home at the hospital for a week with abcessed ears, she almost starved, since she would not take a bottle, and no one had the patience to feed her. I can remember bringing her home from the hospital looking gaunt and starved, weeping over her all the way. Then she was so ravenous I had to get up in the middle of the night to make cereal for her. She had bronchitis that winter, and I worried over her constantly. I remember one doctor telling me, "Throw away your thermometer. Babies are hard to kill." He was a clinic doctor and saw many sicker than mine.

O, the generations of mothers! Of women and babies! I have pictures of my mother's mother and grandmother on the one hand, and myself and daughter and granddaughter [on the other]. Six generations of us.

My mother used to nurse her baby sister as a little girl, and so had a taste of motherhood long before she had five of her own. That little sister died last year, and my mother four years ago. Charity Washburn, Anna Satterlee, Grace Day, Dorothy, Tamar, Rebecca — six generations living during wars, revolutions, earthquakes, hurricanes, and more war.

My mother said as she was dying, "I have lived enough." But up to a week or so before her death, her appetite for life had not diminished. She loved life passionately, intensely, wanted to live, and felt that life was full, was thrilling even at seventy-five.

Her last child was born when she was forty-five, and of course I thought of her as old then. She was not well after that for a year or so, and every morning I used to get up with my brother at four-thirty — change him, feed him, and put him into a warm carriage beside the fireplace in the library to take another nap while I studied Virgil before getting breakfast. I was in my last year of the Robert Waller High School in Chicago, and I loved Latin so much that I read the *Ecloques* besides the *Aenead*.

Our teacher, Dr. Matheson, so inspired us with enthusiasm that he offered to teach Greek to any who wished to remain an additional period after school. A number of us did, and got through Xenophon and the New Testament. There are not many such teachers today.

I should not have studied half so well if I had not had that baby to get up with in the morning.

We were very poor then. My father's newspaper had failed, and he was without a job for some time. It was not long after that he got another post as racing editor of a New York paper, and our difficulties were over — we had recovered as we had many times before. Our status was that of most professional people in the cities. We owned nothing, only personal effects — we had nothing in the bank. We lived from week to week. We were poor, but we lived as though rich. Our standards were American standards. On my father's side there were farmers and doctors in the South — Tennessee. The farmers were landowners, but the moneyless doctor was the respected one.

My mother's people, on the other hand, were whalers or mill workers. Her father had been a chairmaker, so his discharge from the army stated, after the Civil War. But he had been a war prisoner, had tuberculosis, and died young, leaving a widow with five children, so my mother at fourteen went to work in the local shirt factory.

Workers and scholars. How mixed up we are in the United States. And what misconceptions the rest of the world has of us. There is so much pose of prosperity in our big cities that when one sees a farm mother with homemade clothes on herself and her brood of children in a city bus station, she has the appearance of destitution. And yet she and her husband may own their acres, their home, their means of production.

In the slums, in the most crowded, noisome tenements, young girls emerge for work as for the evening's pleasure, dressed like movie stars.

Taking people all in all, it is hard to tell who are the oppressed, who are the proletariat, the dispossessed, the propertyless. Until suddenly (if there is peace, no threat of war, no increase of armaments) there is a depression, [and] wheels stop turning, chimneys stop smoking, and fourteen million people are out of work.

And that fear hits the countryside too. The stocking factory has closed down. The sand mines are idle. The Victor plant is pulling out. No cash income. How will we live? It is lonely in the country. There is relief in the city. There everyone's disaster is no one's disaster. Misery loves company. And so the farms are deserted.

Well, how do you live without cash anyway?

February 11

I BEGAN to write this on the Feast of our Lady of Lourdes when I went to my bookshelves to find something about our Blessed Mother to read. I picked up two books, opened them for a bit and closed them both with horror, and sat down with my missal instead. I'm not going to mention the names of the two books nor their authors. I'd prefer to talk of the splendid hagiography of Father Thurston and Donald Attwater (the revised Butler), Gheon, Ida Coudenhove, Margaret Monroe, and other modern writers.

In the first of the two books aforementioned, the saint-writer declares that the Blessed Mother, with lighted torches, was seen setting fire to a dance hall where couples were carousing, and burning it to the ground with four hundred people therein! The second book had a little chapter about eating: "The saints went to their meals sighing. St. Alphonsus, when sitting down, would think only of the sufferings of the souls in purgatory, and with tears would beseech Our Lady to accept the mortifications he imposed upon himself during meals. Blessed de Montford sometimes shed tears and sobbed bitterly when sitting at table to eat. If such have been the feelings of the saints, what shall we say of those of Mary? . . . St. Jerome (in a letter to Heliodorus) said that this wonderful child only took, toward evening, the food which an angel was wont to bring her."

100

No wonder no one wants to be a saint. But we are called to be saints — we are the sons of God!

Thank God for the missal! I turned for refreshment to the Mass for the day.

"The flowers have appeared in our land, the time of pruning is come." (That is literally true. In the country they have been pruning the fruit trees and grapevines the early part of this month.) "Arise, my love, my beautiful one, and come; my dove in the clefts of the rock, in the hollow places of the wall. Show me thy face, let thy voice sound in my ears, for thy voice is sweet, and thy face comely."

Filled with joy at this so different address to the Mother of Christ, I went on reading that chapter in the Canticle of Canticles — "Behold, my beloved speaketh to me: Arise, make haste, my love, my dove, my beautiful one, and come. For winter is now past, the rain is over and gone. The fig tree hath put forth her green figs; the vines are in flower with their sweet smell. Arise, my love, my beautiful one, and come. . . . Catch us the little foxes, that destroy the vines."

The little foxes — it is about the little foxes I wish to write — the little foxes that destroy the beautiful vines that prevent the grapes from coming to fruition. In other words, the little misconceptions of feastings and fastings that keep us from rejoicing in true devotion during this season of Lent.

In the Mass of this very day there were two prayers begging for "health both of soul and of body" and "that physical and moral health which we desire." I want to write about feasting and fasting and the joys and beauties of both, because, although this is a feast day on which I begin this writing, it is also Ash Wednesday.

How much there was about food in the Old Testament. Adam raised food for himself and Eve, and did it with pleasure. After the fall of Adam, ploughing and seeding and harvesting, earning one's daily bread either as a husbandman like Cain or shepherd like Abel, was a difficult and painful affair. Sacrifices of food were offered to the Lord, whether of beasts or of bread and wine — food because it represented our life — what we live by. We offered our lives to the Lord. We also lust after food as Esau did when he sold his birthright for a mess of pottage. The Israelites complained of their food in the desert and yearned after the fleshpots of Egypt, even with the bondage and slavery it entailed, even though the Lord fed them bread from heaven and water from the Rock, food that had every delight and taste.

Who can forget the widow's cruse of oil which was never diminished; Ruth gleaning in the corn; Daniel and his three companions living on "oats, pea beans, and barley corn"; and the meal that was served Daniel in the lion's den by the prophet Habakkuk? St. Bonaventure said that after the long fast of our Lord in the desert, when the angels came to minister to Him, they went first to the Blessed Mother to see what she had on her stove, and got the soup she had prepared and transported it to our Lord, who relished it the more because His Mother had prepared it. Of course.

How many times fasting is enjoined in the Old Testament. Whenever there was war, as penalty for their sins, the Jews were told to fast, and to fast joyfully, not with long faces. Over and over again the chosen people were urged to do penance, to fast, even their cattle, not only as a sign of sorrow for sins, an offering to God of their life, but also to have the means to show their love for their brother who was afflicted.

How shall we have the means to help our brother who is in need? We can do without those unnecessary things which become habits — cigarettes, liquor, coffee, tea, candy, sodas, soft drinks, and those foods at meals which only titillate the palate. We all have these habits, the youngest and the oldest. And we have to die to ourselves in order to live; we have to put off the old man and put on Christ. That it is so hard, that it arouses so much opposition, serves to show what an accumulation there is in all of us of unnecessary desires.

Instead of quoting Father Lacouture or Father Hugo, I'd like to quote Father Zosima, that very much alive character in Dostoyevsky's *Brothers Karamazov*:

The world says, You have desires, and so satisfy them, for you have the same rights as the most rich and powerful. Don't be afraid of satisfying them and even multiply your desires. . . . I knew one "champion of freedom" who told me himself that, when he was deprived of tobacco in prison, he was so wretched at the privation that he almost went and betrayed his cause for the sake of getting tobacco again! And such a man says, "I am fighting for the cause of humanity."

How can such a one fight, what is he fit for? He is capable perhaps of some action quickly over, but he cannot hold out long. And it is no wonder that the people instead of gaining freedom have sunk to slavery and instead of serving the cause of brotherly love and the union of humanity have fallen on the contrary, into dissension and isolation.

The monastic way is very different. Obedience, fasting and prayer are laughed at, yet only through them lies the way to real, true freedom.

I have always meant to go through the New Testament to see how many times food is mentioned, how many times Christ dined, supped, picnicked with His disciples. He healed St. Peter's mother-in-law, and she rose to serve them. He brought the little girl back to life and said, "Give her to eat." He broiled fish on the seashore for His apostles. Could it possibly be that Mary was less solicitous for the happiness and comfort and refreshment of others?

It is a part of woman's life to be preoccupied with food. She nurses her child; she has nourished him for nine long months in her womb; it is her grief if her breasts fail her; she weeps if her child refuses to eat. Her work as food provider is her pleasure and her pain, pain because of the monotony and because right now the cost of food has gone up 100 percent.

There are many ways to write about the problem of food. The heretical attitude of mind which feels shame of the body, disgust at its functions, distaste at supplying its necessities, fear of its joys, has resulted in a most exaggerated attention to food. First we neglect it because we think of eating as a gross pleasure. Then we lose interest in preparing food for the family. Then we turn to store and factory foods with all their talk of vitamins and calories.

From the standpoint of health, there are two good books which stimulate many thoughts on food. Dr. Price's *Nutrition and Physical Degeneration,* and Alexis Carel's *Man the Unknown.* We eat to have strength in order to serve God. If there are pleasures of taste to oil the heavy labor of production, we should take them gratefully from the good God. I'm sure the Blessed Mother did not neglect her family duties. I am sure St. Joseph provided a good piece of wood which Mary kept scrubbed and perhaps waxed, and she who "with her bosom's milk didst feed her own Creator, Lord most high," must have seen to it that suitable meals were served on that board to Him who was "like unto us in all things save only sin."

I have been getting an idea as to what was eaten in those days by what is eaten now by people in the same region. Reviewing a book for the *Commonweal, In the Footsteps of Moses,* led me to T. E. Lawrence, and then to Doughty's *Arabia Deserta.* At the same time, I was reading Bazin's *Life of Fr. Charles de Foucauld.* And, of course, *The Desert Fathers.*

Wheat, butter, and honey, dates, wine, and oil, mutton, calves, fish, and quail — these are all mentioned in the Bible. Aside from feasts there was a monotony of diet that we should get back to for the sake of simplifying our lives, for the sake of being more truly poor with Him, for the sake of fasting, and for the sake of health. A handful of ground wheat with honey and milk on it makes a most delightful collation. A slice of whole-wheat bread makes a fast day breakfast. You can buy a sack of wheat, a hundred pounds. You can live this way in city or country. This is Lent, and Lent is a wonderful time to begin again.

Back in May 1741, Pope Benedict XIV said, "If this observance of Lent comes to be relaxed it is to the detriment of God's glory, to the dishonor of the Catholic religion, and to the peril of souls; nor can it be doubted that such negligence will become a source of misfortune to nations, of disaster in public affairs, and of adversity to individuals."

As in the days of the Old Testament, that prophecy of Pope Benedict XIV has come true with us.

February 16

STILL NO baby! When a mother nurses her children and conceives while nursing, there is no way of telling the date of the new arrival. It was usually thought that a nursing mother did not conceive, but we know several who do, most regularly, so they do not know whether the next is due January, February, or March. Nor can the doctors tell! When my child was born, I could be pretty accurate as to the date, but the doctor informed me I was two months' pregnant when I knew I was five. Another young woman I knew in the twenties kept going to the doctor for seven months, being treated for anemia, but by that time it was obvious she was pregnant. Some women show their pregnancy most obviously, others so little that one often reads of young women giving birth to babies when no one expected it. One of the strangest cases I ever heard of was of a young woman working in Margaret Sanger's birth-control headquarters (Planned Parenthood, they call it now) who confessed one day, to the girl at the desk next to her, that she was going to have a baby that very day! There was a great hullabaloo in the office.

Today is a great day even though no baby has arrived. A farm has been bought. Three hundred dollars' down payment has been made to Mr. Unger at Stotler's Crossroads. The total price is twelve hundred dollars for seventy acres of land that has not been farmed for twelve years, although people rented there and lived there up to last summer.

There are seven rooms, and an attic for storage. There is a good tin roof, good wood walls, badly papered, good hardwood floor; the doors and windows are bad. The porch is falling down. The chimney is slightly askew; there is a flood in the cellar under the living room. Water is to be had from a spring five hundred feet away. There is a well by the barn, long unused. There is a well by an abandoned schoolhouse next door, cemented over. The schoolhouse is also torn down. All the water must be fetched. All the wood must be chopped.

Right now, though the new farm is only half a mile across the creek, we must go ten miles around, up hill and down dale, because the creek is high. People go around on horseback hereabouts; we are always passing them, we, who have no horse, in a borrowed car. They carry saddlebags. Sometimes they ride sidesaddle, and look very ruminative, meditative, as they ride along.

Last Saturday there was a high wind roaring around the house. There was pouring rain that night and the night before, melting all the snow. Then when the wind died, there was everywhere the sound of rushing waters.

Sunday at 6:30 we were able to get to Mass. (And by leaving before the last gospel, we were able to get home in time for D. to go to the second Mass at 9:00.) The pastor is ill in the hospital, so every Sunday a different priest arrives. He talked last Sunday of the "Tribunal" of penance — a court where everyone was forgiven. What a strange court, indeed, when over and over, repeating our offenses again and again, we are forgiven; where everyone is forgiven! How different from *The Trial* of Kafka, where men are tried, found guilty, and sentenced.

Today and yesterday it was like spring outdoors. I got up and made the fires as usual at seven, but by ten the children were on the porch without their coats. T. and D. took a two-mile walk Sunday. She washes heavy clothes, today trousers and woolen underwear and shirts, yesterday blankets, besides the ordinary baby wash. She bakes, she knits, she crochets, she weaves, she pores over seed catalogues, she makes lists, her face is placid, happy, calm; but her feet drag, she shuffles along, and she feels heavy. She says it is a long wait.

We look at her and say, Is it today? How do you feel? It is St. Ignatius' Day, it is St. John Bosco, it is St. Martin — all good names. It will be a girl, T. says hopelessly, and D. shouts, "Don't you dare come home with a girl! We bought a farm. We need a boy to farm it."

March

THE BABY has arrived! A boy was born, and now T. says she will never worry again as to what her next will be, now that there is a son! One week a payment was made on a farm; the next week a son was born. Mother and father and grandmother all are content!

The baby was born on February 20 and christened on March 7, which happens to fall this year on Laetare Sunday. It is also the feast of St. Thomas Aquinas. Laetare Sunday, "rejoicing" Sunday, a fine day for a baptism. Alma and Leslie were godparents, and Father Ignatius performed the baptism whereby Eric was made a son of God and an heir of heaven. All the day before, Tamar and I were busy cooking for the baptismal feast. The farm at Newburgh had sent a fine ham, and we boiled that all afternoon. She made lemon meringue pies and a fine cake, and we put candles on it in the shape of a little fish, the symbol of a Christian. I had to finish making the baptismal robe, which was made of a straight piece of white linen which I had bought stamped as though for a table runner, in a Woolworth store. The stampings wash out nicely, and I had embroidered it around the edges with little red crosses and on one side a large red cross, and on the other a blue shell and below it flowing water and another little fish. It was very attractive, and the priest smiled as he used it, when he said, "Take this white garment, which

107

mayest thou bear without stain before the judgment seat of Our Lord Jesus Christ, that thou mayest have life everlasting." We had also a beautiful decorated candle, which the priest handed to the godfather for the infant, saying, "Receive this burning light and keep thy baptism so as to be without blame; keep the commandments of God that when the Lord shall come to the nuptials, thou mayest meet Him together with all the saints of heaven and mayest have eternal life, and live forever and ever."

The ceremony of baptism is certainly impressive, with the priest beginning, "What dost thou ask of the Church of God?" and the sponsor answering for the child, "Faith."

It made me think of my days of struggle coming into the Church, how I did not know whether or not I had faith or believed, or just wanted to believe. Things that I questioned I just put out of my mind then, and reconciled myself with the thought, "After all, why should I expect to understand everything? That would be heaven indeed." I knew that if I waited to understand, if I waited to get rid of all my doubts, I would never be ready. So I went in all haste one December day right after Christmas and was baptized a Catholic. I did not think of it at the time — I understood so little that when I went to be baptized I asked for faith. But I knew that prayer, "Lord, I believe, help Thou mine unbelief," and that comforted me. Father Roy used to teach us to pray, "Lord, I love you because I want to love you." And recently I read in Garrigou-Lagrange the quotation "Thou wouldst not seek Him if Thou hadst not already found Him." That is Pascal. So much has to be accepted by faith, and faith is so much an act of the will. And though we are informed by our senses — we hear with our ears, we read with our eyes, we understand with the interior senses — still, when it comes down to it, we cannot look for sensible consolations from our faith (except very seldom). People often talk about not going to church because they do not "feel" like going. They only pray when they "feel" like it, and when they force themselves they seem hypocritical to themselves. I used to get down on my knees with such hesitation, thinking self-consciously, "What kind of a gesture is this I am making? What am I doing this for anyway? Am I trying to induce an emotion of religion?" It is true that I was performing an act of religion, and by going through the gestures I would be more likely to "feel" reverent, adoring.

It is strange how self-conscious we Americans are about exterior acts of courtesy, how haltingly we perform them. Yet certainly if we act with courtesy and respect toward people, we will feel it more.

Speaking of comfort in religion, I like to think how our Lord loved women and how tender He was of them. Now that I have become a mother-in-law, I like to think of St. Peter's mother-in-law and how our Lord healed her (and also how she got up and served them). Women do love to be active; it is natural to them. They are most happy in doing that for which they are made, when they are cooking and serving others. They are the nourishers, starting with the babies at the breast, and from then on their work is to nourish and strengthen and console.

So Tamar and I had a very good time that Lenten Saturday, cooking for the mid-Lenten feast. We invited the Clarks, our neighbors, but they had to go to Baltimore that day. . . . Since it snowed and they did not go, and yet did not come, we decided that it was because they were Brethren, who [do] not believe in infant baptism, that they did not wish to come and celebrate with us. We are glad, however, that they believe, and know what they believe, and go to church to worship every Sunday. They are an earnest crowd. A notice in the local paper of a revival carried on a few weeks ago reports: "Each night we count the chapters read in the Bible from one night to the next. The highest count was five hundred and eighteen chapters. One person read 96 chapters. The revival is a renewed interest in the word of God."

Leon Bloy wrote, "Like the Eucharist, the Words of the Sacred Book feed the soul and even the mind, without its being necessary to understand them."

He also wrote, "The only profitable way to read the psalms or the book of Job, for instance, is to put yourself in the place of the speaker, since he who speaks is always, necessarily, the Christ, whose members we are."

It is early in the morning (I must grab the chance to write while I may), and the pails of water are heating on the stove. Since we have not washed since Saturday, there is a great wash for today. Becky

109

and Susie are both eating peanuts and singing happily. Becky sounds like a Chinese singer, having a peculiar plaintive wail that delights her heart. Yesterday when the sponsors and the priest were reciting the Apostles' Creed together, both children joined them with a mumbling of their own. Not that the priest or the sponsors mumbled as some I have heard do. They spoke clearly and distinctly. Many a priest does swallow his words in the most peculiar fashion, thinking that he is fulfilling his obligation of praying aloud as long as some sounds come out. But the effect is horrible, scarcely human. No wonder the Protestants at the time of the Reformation talked of "hocus-pocus," which is a corruption of the sacred words, "Hoc est corpus meum."

Meditations for woman, these notes should be called, jumping as I do from the profane to the sacred over and over. But then, living in the country, with little children, with growing things, one has the sacramental view of life. All things are His, and all are holy.

I used to wish I could get away from my habit of constant, undisciplined reading, but in the family one certainly is cured of it. If you stop to read a paper, pick up a book, the children are into the tubs or the sewing machine drawers. And as for praying with a book — there has been none of that this Lent for me. Everything is interrupted, even prayers, since by nightfall one is too tired to pray with understanding. So I try to practice the presence of God after the manner of Blessed Lawrence, and pray without ceasing, as St. Paul advised. He might even have had women in mind. But he himself was active enough, weaving goats' hair into tents and sailcloth to earn a living, and preaching nights and Sundays. So I am trying to learn to recall my soul like the straying creature it is as it wanders off over and over again during the day, and lift my heart to the Blessed Mother and His saints, since my occupations are the lowly and humble ones, as [were] theirs.

THE BABY will be three weeks old tomorrow night, and both baby and mother are fine. Tamar walked the three-quarters of a mile over to the new-old house, over the swinging bridge, over the rushing creek, and came back across the meadow following the brook, which made the walk longer. She wanted to give Dave directions about putting up shelves; to measure the stairwell to see if the double bed and bookcases could go upstairs, because it is one of those old-fashioned houses with tiny, narrow enclosed stairs, both from the kitchen and living room. How they are going to get their double bed up, they do not know. Dave wanted to put all his books upstairs in the large room which used to be the smoke room over the kitchen, but that looks impossible too.

Tamar has been active since she came home, baking a cake one day (though she sits at a high stool by her kitchen cabinet while she does so), packing boxes of clothes for Europe on still another, and now out for walks! I'm glad she is so strong. She is better after this baby than after the two others, she says. Marge said the same thing last year. As a matter of fact, Marge had five days in the hospital only, and when she came home, she found me and Peter sick in bed with flu and took care of both of us too as to meals.

St. Teresa of Ávila has a great deal to say of women's ailments. "The first thing we have to do," she writes firmly in *The Way of Perfection,* "and that at once, is to rid ourselves of love for this body of ours — and some of us pamper our natures so much that this will cause us no little labor, while others are so concerned about their health that the trouble these things give us (this is especially so of poor nuns, but it applies to others as well), is amazing. Some of us, however, seem to think that we embraced the religious life for no other reason than to keep ourselves alive, and each nun does all she can to that end. In this house, as a matter of fact, there is very little chance for us to act on such a principle, but I should be sorry if we even wanted to. Resolve, sisters, that it is to die for Christ, and not to practice self-indulgence for Christ, that you have come here. The Devil tells us that self-indulgence is necessary if we are to carry out and keep the Rule of our Order, and so many of us, forsooth, try to keep our Rule by looking after our health, that we die without having kept it for as long as a month — perhaps even for a day."

Newman writes that the greatest tragedy is that so few of us have even begun to live when we die. Not even to make a beginning!

St. Teresa goes on, "No one need be afraid of our committing excesses here, by any chance — for as soon as we do any penances, our confessors begin to fear that we shall kill ourselves with them."

Every time I am making what I consider a thorough confession — that is, telling tendencies that I wish I could overcome, like eating between meals, indulging in the nibbling that women do around a kitchen, and mention it in confession as a venial sin not only in regard to myself but my neighbor who is starving all over the world — the confessor makes no attempt to understand, but speaks of scruples. One confessor said, "I order you to eat between meals!"

These are tendencies to gluttony, and gluttony is one of the seven deadly sins. So little is expected of us laypeople, that as Father Joseph, our dear Benedictine friend, once said, "The moral theology we are taught is to get us into heaven with scorched behinds."

What kind of an unwilling, ungenerous love of God is this? We do little enough, and when we try to do a little more, we are lectured on Jansenism! I don't even know what it is. I only know that I am self-indulgent.

St. Teresa is sharp enough with nuns who want to go in for their own kind of penance:

> It is really amusing to see how some people torture themselves; sometimes they get a desire to do penances, as one might say, without rhyme or reason; they go on doing them for a couple of days; and then the devil puts it into their heads that they have been doing themselves harm, and so he makes them afraid of penances, after which they dare not even do those that the Order requires — they have tried them once! They do not keep the smallest points in the Rule, such as silence, which is quite incapable of harming us. Hardly have we begun to imagine that our heads are aching, then we stay away from choir, though that would not kill us either. One day we are absent because we had a headache some time ago, another day because our head has just

been aching again, and on the next three days in case it should ache once more. Then we want to invent penances of our own, with the result that we do neither the one thing nor the other. Sometimes there is very little the matter with us, yet we think that it should dispense us from all our obligations and that if we ask to be excused from them we are doing all we need.

But why, you will say, does the Prioress excuse us? Perhaps she would not if she knew what [was] going on inside us. But she sees one of you wailing about a mere nothingness as if your heart were breaking, and you go and ask her to excuse you from keeping the whole of your Rule. . . . Sometimes the poor Prioress sees that your request is excessive, but what can she do? She feels a scruple if she thinks she has been lacking in charity, and she would rather the fault were yours than hers; she thinks too it would be unjust for her to judge you harshly. . . .

Think how many poor people there are who are ill and have no one to complain to, for poverty and self-indulgence make bad company. Think too how many married women have serious complaints and sore trials and yet dare not complain to their husbands about them for fear of annoying them. Sinner that I am! Surely we have not come here to indulge ourselves more than they! How free you are from the great trials of the world! Learn to suffer a little for the love of God without telling everyone about it. When a woman has made an unhappy marriage, she does not talk about it or complain of it, lest it should come to her husband's knowledge; she has to endure a great deal of misery, and yet has no one to whom she may relieve her mind. Cannot we then keep secret between God and ourselves some of the ailments He sends us because of our sins? The more so since talking about them does nothing whatever to alleviate them. . . . Believe me, my daughters, once we begin to subdue these miserable bodies of ours, they give us much less trouble. Unless we resolve to put up with death and ill health once and for all, we shall never accomplish anything. And believe me, slight as it may seem in comparison with other things, this resolution is much more important than we may think; for if we continually make it, day by day, we shall gain dominion over the body. . . . No one will regret having gone through trials in order to gain tranquility and self-mastery.

St. Teresa points out that she is talking of ailments to which women particularly are subject, and knowing that some nuns would say, "What will people think if you write thus and so?" she adds that she is writing for them, that the matter is important, and that all convents are the same.

And all women are the same, I might add, and such advice goes for us all. And I add too that I am writing this for women, so I do not mind being considered indelicate if these notes bring solace or comfort or help to some women.

I remember an old Irish woman who had raised eleven children saying that she had suffered at one time or another, and sometimes all at once, varicose veins, piles, and fallen womb, and with the passage of years all these ailments had disappeared. Mostly from being able to take more rest, keep off her feet, as the children got older.

I do know that the fetish for order, for making one's house look like something from *Better Homes and Gardens* is partly responsible for the ills of the world, for ill health, jagged nerves, nagged husbands, broken homes, etc.

One has to learn to look on outward disorder with a humble serenity, not minding what the neighbors will say.

March 11

DAVID AND TAMAR are getting enough eggs now to sell some, and since eggs are good for forty-eight cents a dozen at the crossroad's store a mile away, that means that four dozen eggs will buy a few staples. Coffee is fifty-four cents a pound now, bread sixteen cents a loaf, oleo forty-five a pound. We make our own bread, however, from good whole-wheat flour, and I am very proud of mine, made according to an English recipe with only one rising; so short in time and easy to make. You just knead your ingredients together — flour, salt, lard, sugar, yeast, and water — and make [the dough] stiff enough so that you can pat it into loaves with well-floured hands, put it in the pans, let rise for half an hour, and then bake for an hour. It can be done of an evening, or before breakfast. It certainly is good to eat with a bit of onion — a poor man's feast.

Spring is coming, though it is still only twenty above zero when we get up in the morning. The frogs are croaking, and have been this week past, in the runs along the road, and green things are pushing up on the hillsides, and the barley and wheat fields are green. The sun is warm in the middle of the day, but oh dear, how sharp the wind is, so that the children come wailing in off the porch after too short a respite for us who are working in the house. Right now they are in again. I write at the kitchen table, and Becky is going around singing, "The baby is all baptized," putting it to various tunes. They have brought their cart in from the porch and are riding each other around in it with great noise. Their favorite toy[s] right now [are] all the canned goods in the house, which they play with like blocks — soups, tomato paste, deviled meat, and small cans of baby food, which my sister sent for the babies, to help out in an emergency. What with moving, Tamar did not do much preserving last fall.

Becky is always asking for a washboard so she can help with the washing. She has a little mop and a little carpet sweeper — which are a great delight to her — to help clean the floor. Already, though she is not three, she helps with the dishes after every meal. How I hope she continues this love of work.

St. Benedict, after St. Joseph, is my patron, and his motto was "Work and Pray." A Benedictine monk, Father Rembert Sorg, writes,

> We are of the opinion with Cassian, St. Benedict, and St. Thomas that the true, positive ascetical exercise of the body to mortify concupiscence of the flesh is honest manual labor. It is apostolic, wholesome, and as far as positive violence to be inflicted on the body is concerned, sufficient. But it has to be noted with reference to the sufficiency that the true ascetic, like St. Paul, has the readiness to undergo any hardship of body rather than be separated from the charity of Christ. The spirit of this, however, does not so much involve a case of seeking these things out as of taking whatever comes in a full love of Christ.

115

The bill came from the doctor today, and with all our visiting at his office and his delivery of the baby, it came to thirty-seven dollars. The hospital bill was forty-nine: four dollars a day for the mother in a three-bed ward, and a dollar a day for the baby. Tamar stayed for seven days. The remainder of the cost was for medicine, delivery room, and circumcision. All reasonable enough and to fit the purse of people hereabouts. For her other two babies, Tamar paid a flat rate of fifty dollars at the Easton Hospital, and that is the rate at most of the hospitals in New York, provided you take any doctor or intern on duty. If there is anything extraordinary about the birth, specialists are always called in. It is only the poor and the rich that have such care; the middle class, mainly because they insist upon it, pay far higher. Quite a few young women whom I know have had to pay two hundred dollars to the doctor just because they were ashamed to say their husbands were getting so little salary. The doctor judged by their pretensions to prosperity rather than the actual wage of the father.

Ray Michael just came by and wanted someone to come and help cut pulpwood. He has some kind of power tool, and he holds one end (he needed a man for the other), and they walk through the woods, the trees going down before them like grass before the mower. Pulpwood must not be less than four inches in diameter, and it grows very fast, practically replacing itself, they all say around here. I suppose it goes to the paper mills and the Dupont people. Ten dollars a cord if they come and get it and thirteen if they haul it in. Normally by hand a man can cut a cord a day, according to the size of the tree, of course. Larger trees, less work.

There are always casual jobs showing up like that. The wage here would be sixty cents an hour. And a day's work would suffice to get in a supply of staples, and a week's work would pay the taxes. But the farmers in the springtime have so many things they want to do that the only time such labor is done is when they are driven to it. With the young boys it's another matter.

One can get by if one's wants are modest. One can withdraw from the factory, refuse to make munitions, airplanes, atom bombs. In sections like this, rent is ten a month, sometimes even five dollars, and there are empty houses. But city people are afraid, afraid of the country, afraid of the dark, afraid to be alone, afraid of the silence. They confess to it. And I remember myself, once, as a little girl, wandering out along the beach down at Fort Hamilton, sitting at the edge of a swamp and listening to the cicadas on a hot summer day, and suddenly being overcome by fear. Even as a little child of six I often awakened in the dark and felt the blackness and terror of nonbeing. I do not know whether I knew anything of death, but these were two terrors I experienced as a child, a terror of silence and loneliness and a sense of Presence, awful and mysterious.

March 22

SPRING IS HERE. The frogs are clamorous, the birds awaken us at six or before, the crocus is in bloom; one can actually see things grow from hour to hour. Lilies of all kinds bursting up out of the ground, buds coming out on the pear tree and apple trees and hedges.

Today it rains, a sudden downpour. The roads are ridges of mud running with water. There is the monotonous pattering of rain on the tin roof (all the roofs are tin hereabouts) and on the grass outside. But it is good to be out in it too, going to and from the barn, the chicken house, the sheds. There is much activity, for we have moved, just in time before the spring rains began and the creek rose again. We moved [on] St. Patrick's Day, bright and sunny, and by the next night were installed in the new-old house, as we call it. When I shopped for cold meat and beer at the tavern, down on the highway, the woman there said, "We've been married seventeen years and moved nineteen times, and thank God we've got our own place now."

The Yosts down the road moved from one farm to another, share-cropping, always tenants and working desperately hard until finally a little legacy enabled [Mr. Yost] to buy his own place for fifteen hundred dollars. There is a five-room house, many outbuildings, and fifty acres, and "I wouldn't take five thousand for it if I was offered," he said proudly.

Mrs. Yost said she certainly was tired of fixing up other people's houses. Eve Yost, one of her daughters, had gone out to work at [the age of] twelve for two dollars a week, and she really worked, scrubbing clothes on a washboard, cooking, baking bread, cleaning. She was home from Washington, where she works at the comparatively easy job of waitress now, married to a filling-station attendant and sending money home to her mother to raise her twelve-year-old son, her only child. They drive up every month or so in a fine big car, making the hundred miles in two hours flat.

Moving — what a job it is! In the book of Job, hell is described as a place where "no order is," and our disorder, certainly with its attendant restlessness, is a vision, a sample of hell.

Never to be at home, never to be settled, never to have one's own belongings at hand!

Eric Gill said, "Property is proper to man," and certainly one's tools, implements, clothing, utensils — no matter how one tries to simplify one's life — are important.

One time David was helping move a friend of ours from farm to town, from a two-room cabin to a five-room house. There were six children in the family, and there were boxes upon boxes of clothes, rags mostly, that another helper, a kindly friend, wanted to throw out.

It impressed me very much to see the understanding care my son-in-law took of all these possessions. "To the poor," he said, "everything has its value." What looked like rags and junk were part of the everyday living of that poor home.

Well, we had plenty of what to others would look like junk and rags. But Tamar can make hooked rugs or braided rugs. And any number of old wool skirts her sisters-in-law have sent her have been made into little jumper dresses for the two little girls. We like to look at the ads in the Sunday papers to see the prices of the dresses that T. so handily turns out on her machine. Eight dollars for a tiny skirt; five dollars for a little blouse.

My mother used to make all our clothes when we were children, but her great lament was that they did not look *bought*. "Homemade" was her sad comment, after hours over the machine.

What strange standards we Americans have! We judge so much

by the cost — we must keep up with the Joneses. I see it in myself and in my desire not to appear different. I look longingly at the new styles in coats and dresses.

There is some excuse for it now, for the styles may in a way be termed Christian styles, with their decent long skirts, full and graceful. As a grandmother especially, I need long skirts with children clambering all over me, climbing in my lap, hiking my dress over my knees. I have concocted one long housedress by adding a foot length of goods around the bottom, and Becky insists on calling this a "nightgown"!

2 P.M.

THE RAIN CONTINUES. Tamar is busy making Easter candies with fondant (made a few days ago), chopped candied lemon peel and orange peel, and black walnuts. The whole to be dipped in bitter chocolate and made to resemble an egg. She also experimented with hot cross buns this morning, though it is only Tuesday. To be more liturgical, she neglected to put the cross on them until Friday. We were surprised that Alma had never heard of them in the South. I suppose the custom is a New England one.

Yesterday was a busy and glowing day. The sun shone, [and] Ray came over to help rake up dead grass, broken glass, high weeds, wallpaper, tin cans, [and] stones from around the house. All day Becky helped him, raking valiantly. She sat on her high stool after meals, washing "disses," she helped get the milk, [and] she all but witnessed the delivery of three baby goats, one of which was born dead. The two little survivors were brought in behind the kitchen stove, and that evening she helped feed one, pushing its head down into a coffee can, where it learned immediately to lap up the milk. Tamar used to feed them with a bottle and nipple, but with the last few kids, she found they learned immediately to suck the milk up out of a pail.

The kitchen is a busy place, filled with babies, baby goats, kittens, three adults. Around suppertime it is bedlam. It reminds me of

119

the riotous picture presented in that Christmas carol — of milk-maids milking, lads a-leaping, drummers drumming, pipers piping, etc.

> "On the first day of Christmas
> My true love gave to me
> A partridge in a pear tree" (is the way the song begins).

March 28

"NOW IS the time . . . that we must say good-bye . . ."

Every day during Holy Week we had Mass at St. Vincent's Church in Berkeley Springs, and I drove down. Afterwards I stopped for a cup of coffee before the twelve-mile drive home. There was a jukebox, of course, in the coffee shop (one cannot get away from them), and every morning that same slow, sad, sentimental and haunting song blared forth.

"Now is the time . . . that we must say good-bye," sung with incredible slowness, almost with a wail.

It irritated me and yet moved me, because I had to leave the following Sunday. After all, I am still at work, I am still in harness, and I had to return to New York, to the house of hospitality, to the farm at Newburgh, where the retreats are beginning again for the spring and summer.

Tamar has had her baby; the moving is done; spring is here. Much as I would love to stay, I have no excuse to stay. It has been two-and-a-half months that I have been away, and though I have been able to keep up with letters and some little bit of writing, my mind and heart have been absorbed in the work at hand, "the family."

So now tomorrow I start off again "on pilgrimage," for we have here no abiding city. Much as we may want to strike our roots in, we are doomed to disappointment and unhappiness unless we preserve our detachment. It is the paradox of the Christian life, to hate father and mother, sister and brother and children on the one hand, if they stand between us and God, and on the other to follow the teaching of St. Paul: "If any man have not care of his own, and especially those of his house, he hath denied the faith and is worse than an infidel"; not to be solicitous for the things of the world, and yet to do everything with love, for the love of God. Moreover, much as I appreciate St. Peter's mother-in-law and how "she rose and ministered to them," and much as I love St. Paul's talk of grandmothers, I know that mother-in-law and grandmother should not be too much in evidence or trying to live the lives of the younger people. If we are there to serve, it is one thing. But usually we are not nearly so much needed as we think we are. There are such things as guardian angels, and our dear Lord watches over all.

April

WHENEVER I groan within myself and think how hard it is to keep writing about love in these times of tension and strife, which may at any moment become for us all a time of terror, I think to myself, "What else is the world interested in?" What else do we all want, each one of us, except to love and be loved, in our families, in our work, in all our relationships? God is Love. Love casts out fear. Even the most ardent revolutionist, seeking to change the world, to overturn the tables of the money changers, is trying to make a world where it is easier for people to love, to stand in that relationship to each other. We want with all our hearts to love, to be loved. And not just in the family but to look upon all as our mothers, sisters, brothers, children. It is when we love the most intensely and most humanly that we can recognize how tepid is our love for others. The keenness and intensity of love brings with it suffering, of course, but joy too, because it is a foretaste of heaven. I often think in relation to my love for little Becky, Susie, and Eric: "That is the way I must love every child and want to serve them, cherish them, and protect them." Even that relationship which is set off from other loves by that slight change in phraseology (instead of "loving," one is "in love") — the very change in terminology, denoting a living in love, a dwelling in love at all times, being bathed in love, so that every wak-

123

ing thought, word, deed, and suffering is permeated by that love — yes, that relationship above all should give us not only a taste of the love of God for us but the kind of love we should have for all.

When you love people, you see all the good in them, all the Christ in them. God sees Christ, His Son, in us and loves us. And so we should see Christ in others, *and nothing else,* and love them. There can never be enough of it. There can never be enough thinking about it. St. John of the Cross said that where there was no love, put love and you would take out love. The principle certainly works. I've seen my friend, Sister Peter Claver, with that warm friendliness of hers which is partly natural (she is half-Jew and half-Irish) but which is intensified and made enduring by grace, come into a place which is cold with tension and conflict, and warm the house with her love.

And this is not easy. Everyone will try to kill that love in you, even your nearest and dearest; at least they will try to prune it. "Don't you know this, that, and the other thing about this person? He or she did this. If you don't want to hear it, you must hear. It is for your good to hear it. It is my duty to tell you, and it is your duty to take recognition of it. You must stop loving, modify your loving, show your disapproval. You cannot possibly love — if you pretend you do, you are a hypocrite, and the truth is not in you. You are contributing to the delinquency of that person by your sentimental blindness. It is such people as you who add to the sum total of confusion and wickedness and soft appeasement and compromise and the policy of expediency in this world. You are to blame for communism, for industrial capitalism, and finally for hell on earth."

The antagonism often rises to a crescendo of vituperation, an intensification of opposition on all sides. You are quite borne down by it. And the only Christian answer is *love,* to the very end, to the laying down of your life.

To see only the good, the Christ, in others! Perhaps if we thought of how Karl Marx was called "Papa Marx" by all the children on the street, if we knew and remembered how he told fairy stories to his children, how he suffered hunger and poverty and pain, how he sat by the body of his dead child and had no money for coffin or funeral, perhaps such thoughts as these would make us love him and his followers. *Dear God, for the memory of that dead child, or that faithful wife, grant his stormy spirit "a place of refreshment, light, and peace."*

And there was Lenin. He hungered and thirsted, and at times he had no fixed abode. Madame Krupskaya, his widow, said that he loved to go into the peace of the pine woods and hunt mushrooms like old Mrs. Dew down at Easton did, and we with her one October. He lived one time in the slums of Paris, and he lived on horse meat when he had meat, and he started schools for the poor and the workers. "He went about doing good." Is this blasphemy? How many people are dying and going to God their Father and saying sadly, "We have not so much as heard that there is a Holy Spirit." And how will they hear if none preaches to them? And what kind of shepherds have many of them had? Ezekiel said in his day, "Woe to the shepherds that feed themselves and not their sheep!"

And if there have been preachers, has there been love? If people will not listen, one can still love, one can still find Christ in them to love, and love is stronger than death. Dear God, may Lenin too find a place of refreshment, light, and peace. Or don't we believe in retro-active prayers? There is no time with God.

It is an easy thing to talk about love, but it is something to be proven, to be suffered, to be learned. That's why we have our retreat house at Newburgh. Last week after my return from Berkeley Springs, I went up on a foggy day, taking a train at Grand Central because the bus which leaves at 6:30 and passes our door at Newburgh was on strike. The train was slow, and the ferry slower. A fog which kept us floundering in the middle of the river for half an hour was so heavy that it was hard to breathe. It was a great relief from oppression to reach the high ground, where the retreat house stands, six miles inland, and to get to bed early after the oppression of the city.

It is always a terrible thing to come back to Mott Street. To come back in a driving rain, to men crouched on the stairs, huddled in doorways, without overcoats because they sold them perhaps the week before when it was warm, to satisfy hunger or thirst — who knows? Those without love would say, "It serves them right, drinking up their clothes." God help us if we got just what we deserved!

It is a terrible thing to see the ugliness and poverty of the cities, to see what man has made of man. I needed those few days at Newburgh to brace myself for work. Father Anthony, a young Benedictine from Newton, New Jersey, was with us that week, giving a retreat on the sacraments, and the conferences I was in time for continued what I had been pondering of the love of God for man and man for man. "From Genesis to Revelation," he said, in one conference, "it is the story of God's love for man. All the story of God's dealing with man is a love story. Some say the Old Testament tells of God's justice and the New of his love. But there is not a page but emphasizes God's folly in ever forgiving and drawing man back to him." I remembered the book of Hosea, the prophet and holy man who was commanded by God to love and marry a harlot, who had children by him, and who left him again and again, having children also by her lovers. And how Hosea again and again took her back. How he must have been scorned by his generation, he a holy man, so weak and uxorious, so soft-minded that again and again, "he allured her" to him, on one occasion even buying her back from her lover, even providing her, while she was with her lover, with corn and wine and oil. And God even commanded it so that down through the ages there would be this example of God's love for a faithless people, of the folly of love, a foretaste of the folly of the Cross. If we could only learn to be such fools! God give us the strength to persist in trying to learn such folly.

We had three conferences a day, of an hour each, and a fifteen-minute period of prayer after each conference. There was silence for the week, and manual labor, in the house and out. There was rosary after lunch and a holy-hour midnight on Thursday. Every morning the day began with Prime, the first prayers of the Church for the day (after Matins and Lauds), and then there was a sung Mass, the first Mass in the Kyriale for the festive season, and it was pure beauty that strengthened the heart to learn to love.

There was just a handful of us there, since we have not begun to send out our retreat notices for the year. We are urging our friends to study the following dates and figure out their vacations, and try to plan to spend some time with us this summer and fall.

May 1 there will be a study weekend on WORK.

Memorial Day weekend there will be a retreat for men conducted by Father Francis Meenan, Holy Ghost Father from Norwalk.

June 13-19 — First study week.

July 4th weekend — A basic retreat for women.

July 18 — Father Veales, [a] Josephite from Washington, D.C., will give a basic retreat for men.

August 14 there will be another study week.

Labor Day weekend — Father Purcell, an Augustinian, will give a retreat for families, and there will be several girls to care for the children, who will have their own little retreat at the same time.

There will be extra weekends and also through the fall, to be announced later.

We cannot overemphasize the importance of these retreats and beg our readers to try to plan to come to some of them. While it is true that love sweetens all of life and makes light of pain and suffering and brings us to the happiness we all desire, one must learn to love, and there is no place better than a retreat house to learn such lessons. We must withdraw for a time to renew our strength for the great struggle of the apostolate. Without the use of our spiritual weapons of love, which include prayer and penance and work and poverty and suffering, our future is harsh and ugly to contemplate. Great struggles lie before us in this era of war and revolution through which we are passing, and which we in America have not begun to suffer as yet. We must prepare, so we do beg you to come and help us. "A brother helped by a brother is a strong city."

The retreat house, of course, is not just for our readers who can afford to take train or bus and get to us for this time not only of rigor but of delight. ("All the way to heaven is heaven, since He said, 'I am the Way.'") But it is also for the poor, the lame, the halt, and the blind. We always have a few from our House of Hospitality, and come the summer, we are also going out on the highways and byways and persuade our brothers in. There is many a sick one just out of Bellevue or off the breadline who needs "refreshment, light, and peace," here and now. The retreat house is for us all, but most especially for those who can go no place else for lack of funds or because difference in race, color, and creed has kept them from this sweet rest of a retreat. God will raise up amongst us all those He wishes to work for Him, and He will give us all the strength we need for the work we all will have to do.

The farm of ninety-six acres, attached to the retreat house, is going to provide meat and vegetables also for our breadline at Mott Street. It was a wonderful sight to see John Filliger out there on the horizon at the end of a long field, ploughing with his team, and the hound dog trailing along behind. A number of the fields are ploughed now, and the greenhouse is filled with cabbages and to-mato plants, not to speak of spring salads. Hans and Charlie and Louis Owen and a new arrival by [the] name of Murphy are busily at work these spring days, and before he left Father Anthony blessed the house and the fields. Our chapel has been greatly enlarged, thanks to Hans Tunneson, and the conference room floor painted, and we are ready for our friends and fellow workers.

Peter will be taken up to the farm again next week, where for some hours every day he can sit under the crab apple tree out in front of the adobe-like house which the men and the priest share. Nothing is blooming yet, no buds show green, and the wind is still harsh. But the spring sun is warming, and after the desperately hard winter on Mott Street, the warmth is a touch of God's love on us all.

Now there is much time being spent in arguments against Universal Training [and] Conscription, and the fog of threatened war hangs so heavy over us all. We beg the prayers of all our readers that we may hold our stand with strong love, with warm love, because without it we know that all arguments will be unavailing.

April 15

I HAVE just read a review of the Kinsey report, which appeared in the spring number of *Politics,* that very interesting quarterly which Dwight McDonald puts out on Astor Place. (I understand they have open nights Thursdays and intend to go up there sometime.) It was the completest review I've seen yet. I've not read Father Kennedy's, nor any other Catholic review, but intend to look some of them up. Anyway, here are some of the things I was thinking about the book.

In the first place, I remembered how I came across Havelock Ellis's *Sexual Pathology* at the age of seventeen, in the home of a professor at the University of Illinois, where I was working my way through —

cleaning, cooking, caring for children — for my room and board. It was an ugly shock to me. I had been as knowing as most children, speculating about the things of sex at an early age indeed. (I can remember talking about it when I was six.) One might also say that an ugly tide rose in me, a poisonous tide, a blackness of evil, at reading there so many things that certainly do not need to be known by other than doctor or priest, by those who are schooled to bear it and trained to help in relation to it. Dr. Von Hildebrand writes about the poisonous fascination of sex, its deadly allure in the abstract. I felt it then in its most hideous form, and there was no beauty in it, no love, but it was like the uncoiling of a dank and ugly serpent in my breast. These may be extreme ways of expressing myself, but I am sure that at times there has been this consciousness of evil in us all. Evil as a negation, as an absence of good, as a blackness, a glimpse of hell "where everlasting horror dwelleth, and no order is."

In physical depression, after illness, or after physical excess, there are feelings of guilt in us all, I am sure, and even those who deny there is a conscience feel this. I wonder why that very testimony of guilt in us all is not a witness against such books as Kinsey's. But of course, these days they are trying to make people overcome their sense of guilt, to deaden consciences. When we are little children, our consciences tell us what is right or wrong, and we know full well when we are choosing evil. The trouble with the Kinsey report is that it makes people cease to regard themselves as the least of all, as the guiltiest of all, as the saints say we should, and instead we say, "I'm as good as he is," or "He is as bad as I am, in fact much worse." And we compare ourselves with others instead of with God, horizontally instead of vertically. Christ said, "Be ye therefore perfect, as your heavenly Father is."

St. Paul said, "Let these things be not so much as mentioned among you." And he also said, "Whatsoever things are good and true and beautiful and chaste, and of good repute, think on these things," and the lesson for Easter season is, "If ye be risen with Christ, seek the things which are above." People say, "But it helps you in guiding and guarding your own children to know these things. You cannot be like ostriches, with your heads in the sand. You've got to know these things, regardless of how much they make you suffer (or what they do to you in the way of shock)."

I thought of a paragraph in a book review in *Time* magazine which spoke of two women who kept an inn at Dunkirk and who, in the thickest of the war, went . . . calmly, tranquilly, and serenely about their work, making an atmosphere of peace in the midst of war and horror, bringing courage to thousands by their very example. They went right on about their work in their routine, living as they had always lived, keeping to their work, and by thus maintaining strength and calm, helped build up a resistance movement that continued all through the war. They probably never knew what they inspired in the way of work.

I thought too of a story I read of the expulsion of the Jesuits from Spain, how they lived on a boat and were rejected at one port after another, and were years at sea, and still kept to their life of prayer, penance, and study, running as it were a house of studies in the middle of the Mediterranean. "We have here no abiding city." They were like desert fathers, except that they lived in the middle of the sea in their monastery, which floated about between heaven and earth, seemingly rejected for a time by both.

And I remembered an old friend, wife of a member of the I.W.W., who traveled about the country, and in every little room she stopped, she made a home with a couple of scarves, pictures, a deft arrangement of furniture and her suitcase of belongings. To live here and now the life of the spirit, to live as though this dear flesh were not the burden of pleasure and pain that it is — this is a great gift and to be cultivated in our time. "All the way to heaven is heaven," said St. Catherine of Siena, "because He said, 'I am the Way.'" We have too many samples of hell, and the Kinsey report is one of them.

Yes, we know what is in man. Cy Echele recognized that man is but dust, as well as little less than the angels, when he wrote this note this spring:

This evening Margaret and I set up Gregory's first bed. It is quite an event for a little boy to graduate from the basket and crib stage to his own bed. What declares his coming dignity more effectively than having a special place like this allotted for his retiring in the evening, and for those precious lying-awake hours in the morning, when the gift of reflection surely begins to come to man? An important occasion calls for a blessing, and we went to the Ritual to find something appropriate.

In the end I composed a new prayer, adapted from the old, and based on the style of the collects, which are so beautiful and majestic. I simply read the prayer and sprinkled the bed with holy water, asking God if He might bestow a blessing through me, a layman and head of the family.

The words were composed new because we wanted a particular application on this occasion. The bed was bought with my labor; the mattress and pillow, the two sheets and pillowcase were made by Gregory's grandmother, who has provided so much for our physical sustenance during our eight years of married life.

Here is the prayer:

O Lord, God Almighty, Creator of heaven and earth and of all things, who has willed that by rest and sleep our bodies are restored to freshness and a measure of integrity after periods of activity and labor: Bless this bed which we Thy servants, Cyril and Margaret, have disposed for the use of our dear son, Gregory. May it be the means to him of Thy great blessing of health, soul, and body. Guard him also, we beseech Thee, against all defilements which the evil one may in his stealth attempt to impose upon him during the hours of peace and passivity of body. Through this creature, a bed, may he come to Thee, our only true and lasting God, to enjoy the blessed fruit of a life spent in Thy love and service. Through Jesus Christ, Thy Son, our Lord, who liveth and reigneth with Thee in the unity of the Holy Spirit, God, world without end. Amen.

Every night at Compline we say the ancient hymn,

Procul recedant somnia,
Et noctium phantasmata;
Hostemque nostrum comprime
Ne polluantur corpora.

Our beds may be altars at which we kneel to pray, and on which we receive the sacrament of matrimony, giving and receiving in a communion which is a foretaste of the beatific vision, and which *can be* consummated with recollection and dignity and joy. Or they may be something else again, to the sardonic and the cynical and sensual, who in all their talk and writing of sexual play smack more of the goat or rooster than the lamb. After all, we are not animals, we are men, and as Eric Gill said, man must ever be more or less than the animals; he can never be on their plane.

Among the sets of books my father bought for the household and which included Dickens, Hugo, Stevenson, and Scott, there was also de Maupassant, which was kept locked away from us children. Of course, we read him, and I found nothing glamorous or attractive in his stories, which were frankly fleshly. They contained to me all the ugliness, the sadness, and the degradation of the flesh, which I saw aging and corrupting and dying all about me. Children at times are very conscious of death, of the penalty of original sin. And I think it was in de Maupassant that I read his lament that bodily functions the most repulsive as well as the most sublime were bound closely to the same organs, so that often there was an element of the grotesque in what should be the greatest and most dignified act of man, when he was co-creator with God. It is this consciousness that has led to what people term the Jansenism of the Irish and Anglo-Saxon prudishness in regard to sex. We know our children are being presented with other points of view, and it is time indeed that there should be more talk on the subject of sex and marriage on the part of Catholics.

God knows women have enough of the ugly and the lowly to do in the work of this world. In their sufferings they see clearly the result of the Fall. They are closer both to heaven and to hell than men are in a very literal, material, earthy sense.

I'm certainly not going to read the Kinsey report. But it needs to be considered and thought about. What people ought to read is Eric Gill's *Autobiography, The Life of Thomas More* — and here are good books on the shelf in front of me right now: *The Meaning of Love* by Solovyov; *The Mind and Heart of Love* by Father D'Arcy.

Here is a letter I received this week from a young mother:

I haven't read the Kinsey report either, but I have read several reviews, including the one you mentioned in *Politics*.

I do not wonder that it is a best-seller, that people turn to books of this kind and to Freudian psychologists for help. There is no part of Catholic doctrine so neglected as the teachings of the Church on sex and marriage. Not even those on social justice are so unknown and unpracticed.

There is good and plenty taught on the negative side — what is forbidden — but when it comes to holding up the vision of a holy marriage with sex as an integral part, to any positive and integrated teaching on this vital subject, there is a conspiracy of silence, an attitude of embarrassment and evasion.

Being a product of the Catholic middle class, Irish-American, I know that tinge of Jansenism well. Sex is shut off from the rest of life, tolerated in marriage as a necessary evil for the procreation of children. Instruction is given reluctantly and with embarrassment, and delayed until adolescence, when the problem becomes impossible to ignore or suppress. That our parents and teachers did not intend to produce such an effect I am certain. It arose from a panicky concern to protect us, whom they loved, from the sins of the flesh. Also, they knew that sex life fell with the Fall. But it can be renewed by the graces of the Redemption received in the Sacrament of Matrimony, and this is what they forgot to tell us or make real to us.

All things must be restored to Christ; our bodies were redeemed too. Children should be learning healthy and holy attitudes unconsciously as well as consciously from infancy so that they can fuse the natural and supernatural in every part of life. The beautiful prayers of the Nuptial Mass could be studied with profit long before it is time to think of being engaged.

I agree with you, there is very little of the evils of sex that anyone needs to know, but kept in ignorance of the good made by God, we turn to the evil made by man. Coition is grotesque, yes, but then the union of spirit and matter which makes man is a grotesquerie. That a man should put food into a hole in his face is grotesque: that is why gluttony is so repulsive, whether it expresses itself in taking too much food or "wolfing it down," in fussiness, Epicureanism, or excessive preoccupation with eating. But who thinks of the grotesque side of eating when he is taking his food as befits a Christian and a man, properly, in company, with the object of nourishing himself, that he may be a better servant to God? And knowing that this eating is a kind of sacrament, a natural figure of the Agape, of Christ's feeding our souls with Himself in the Eucharist. Our Lord gives us Himself in bread and wine. He knows we are flesh and blood as well as spirit, and we need a visible sign. Yet we eat quite naturally and simply, aware of these things, although we are not always thinking of them at the moment of eating.

In the same way, one does not perceive that sexual union is grotesque when engaged in making love (a beautiful and homely phrase, the *making* of love). I think that the communion of husband and wife could be thought of as a visible sign of the Sacrament of Matrimony, and in the Nuptial Blessing the priest prays, "O God, Thou hast sanctified marriage by a mystery so excellent that in the marriage union Thou didst foreshadow the union of Christ and the Church."

The marriage union has always seemed to me to be an earthly shadow of the Blessed Trinity. As the love of the Father and Son is the Holy Spirit, the union of man and woman produces a child; the family is a little trinity of love.

Some choose evil because they have not seen the good, and I could write a little Kinsey report myself of sin and damage and unhappiness in the lives of people I know who never learned to bring grace into the realm of sex. Those who suppress sex wrongfully, who hate the flesh, either become neurotic prudes or fall into the opposite extreme of excess. Those unwilling or unable to accept the attitudes of the conventional and puritanical bourgeoisie are easily betrayed by that "poisonous fascination" of which Dr. Von Hildebrand writes. They begin the descent to the Dark Angel, through the mysticism of Evil, only half knowing what they are doing. The novels of Aldous Huxley, who savagely strips away the fascination, are the best antidote I know to this kind of poison, and I shall always be grateful that I read them in early youth. But he, in his turn, is a Manichee with no compassion for this dear flesh.

For a more Christian view of life, the best books I have run across are *Life Together* by Wingfield Hope (which I frequently re-read for the vision — for its true idealism and refreshing common sense); *In Defense of Purity* by Dietrich Von Hildebrand; *Love in the Western World* by Denis de Rougemont; the Encyclical on Christian marriage by Pope Pius XI. And the Nuptial Mass in the Missal.

There are such treasures of wisdom and beauty within the Church — buried treasure. Remember how Peter used to go around saying that on the subject of sex the Catholic Church is foolproof? He was quoting some doctor in the middle west — Minneapolis or Chicago. There is so much that is good and beautiful to mediate. Do you know *At the Wedding March* by Hopkins? It was written, I think, for his brother's wedding. Lettered and framed, it makes a good gift to give a bride and groom.

AT THE WEDDING MARCH

God with honour hang your head.
Groom, and grace you, bride, your bed
With lissome scions, sweet scions,
Out of hallowed bodies bred.

Each be other's comfort kind:
Deep, deeper than divined.
Divine charity, dear charity,
Fast you ever, fast bind.

Then let the march tread our ears:
I to Him turn with tears
Who to wedlock, His wonder wedlock,
Deals triumph and immortal years.

And of course, the chapter from the *Imitation* beginning, "Nothing is sweeter than love, nothing stronger, etc."

I did like Cy Echele's blessing for the bed so much, and I read it at an appropriate time, as we have just bought their first beds for Elizabeth and Michael. They are to be delivered tomorrow, and we shall set them up, sprinkle them with holy water, and

135

read the prayer composed by Cyril. So many thanks for sending it on and much love to you.

In Christ
Mary

April 18

"WOMEN'S JOB is to love," Sister Peter Claver used to say to me when I was overflowing with indignation over the injustices and suffering I saw around me. She was always reminding me that the greatest weapon we had to overcome evil and hatred was to love all men for the Christ that was in them.

The more I thought on this subject of the love of God and the love of man, the more I thought of the nuptial love spoken of so often in the Bible. There are other relationships used as an expression of the kind of love which must govern our conduct. On this earth we must often be thinking in terms of the love a child has for its parent. When the heart is dull and work oppresses, we think in terms of the duty of servant to master, the created to the Creator.

Strangely enough, even though this love is so often spoken of not only in the Bible but by the saints in their writings, there have been many objections because of it, made to the retreat we have at our Newburgh farm (when we can get the retreat masters who give this retreat), a retreat which has also been given in Pittsburgh by Father Hugo and by Father Lacouture in Canada.

A great controversy has arisen about this retreat which is not settled yet, mainly because of the implications of the teaching that we are sons of God and must so behave. The controversy is over nature and the supernatural and man's death and resurrection to a new life, putting off the old and putting on the new man.

The teaching has been that love which is of the Lover for the Beloved can only be between equals, and so to achieve this we must die to the natural and live supernatural lives, doing everything for the love of God.

Not being a theologian or a philosopher, I have written little on the subject and wish to talk and write less.

But while we are on the subject of the Catholic teaching in regard to love and sex, I should like to quote from a book by Father John J. Hugo called *A Sign of Contradiction*.

He is dealing with one objection made by a Censor in the Society of Jesus to this aspect of Father Lacouture's teaching.

The quotation is extensive, but because it deals so beautifully with the love of God and man, I wish to quote it in full, and I am sure that Father Hugo will not mind, and that our readers will be glad to have this clear expression of the teachings of the saints.

Excerpt from *A Sign of Contradiction*

The comparison between sexual union and the Beatific Vision, the Censor says, is to be viewed "with horror." And why, pray, with horror? Is it that there is something evil in sexual union? If there is anything evil in it, then indeed we would have to view "with horror" any comparison between it and God. But is it evil? To say so would be to fall into that very Manicheanism (teaching that material nature is evil) of which Father Lacouture himself has been falsely accused. Here, however, we see how wide a circuit Father Lacouture cuts around Manicheanism: far from regarding nature as essentially depraved, he is ready to find even in sexual union itself — most deeply wounded of all our faculties by the Fall, if St. Thomas is correct — the very image of the Creator and of that most glorious attribute of the Creator, His love. In *Le Seminaire* Father Lacouture was condemned for teaching the very Manicheanism that he is here condemned for so clearly avoiding. Just where may the poor man turn? "John came neither eating nor drinking, and they say, 'He has a devil!' The Son of Man came eating and drinking, and they say, 'Behold, a glutton and a wine-drinker!'" (Matt. 11:18-19).

But if sex and sexual union are to be considered creatures of God, as indeed they are, then there is no reason why they may not be compared, by way of analogy, with Him Who made them.

137

For the Creator leaves His image, more or less perfectly, in all His creatures. And this tracing of analogies holds an honored place in Catholic theology: outside of divine revelation itself, it is the only *positive* means we have for studying and contemplating God. By means of it theologians seek to fill in the gaps left by revelation in our knowledge of God. And in this particular case, the analogy between sexual union and the union of love between God and the soul is at once affirmed by reason and pointed out by divine revelation itself.

The trouble is that the Censor himself is not free from a certain Manichean tendency! Like so many others, when he thinks of sexual union, he's thinking only of the physical union of sex; and he speaks of this as though it were in some sense evil. Now sexual union of course is at once physical and psychic (or spiritual). When the physical union of sex is divorced from the spiritual element of genuine love, as in prostitution, then sexual union is just that: prostitution. But when the union of sex is spiritual as well as physical, as God intended it to be, then it is a noble thing, the consummation and fulfillment of the highest human love, that between man and wife, which is blessed by the Church in the Sacrament of Matrimony. All love is perfected in union; in its fullest sense, it *is* union; so that sexual union, being the climax and consummation of the highest human love, is the very noblest of God's creatures; there is nothing in all creation which provides a more apt or truer analogy for the contemplation of God. Is it to be wondered at that almost all of Father Lacouture's comparisons are taken from sexual union? I think not; you will find the same thing, if you care to look, in all the mystical writers of the Church. Let us glance at some examples.

God Himself indicated this analogy; its source is the Holy Scripture. Should we, for example, view "with horror" such passages as the following from the Canticle of Canticles, which not only point out the comparison but describe it with some intimacy of detail?

> Show me, O thou whom my soul lovest, where thou feedest,
> where thou liest in the midday. . . . Thy cheeks are beautiful

as the turtledove's, thy neck as jewels. . . . Behold, thou art
fair, my beloved, and comely. Our bed is flourishing. . . . His
left hand is under my head, and his right hand shall embrace
me. In my bed by night I sought him whom my soul loveth.
(Canticle I, 6, 9, 15; II, 6; III, 1)

This Canticle, ever a treasure to Catholic mystics, is so perfectly
a love poem that rationalistic Bible critics maintain plausibly that it
is *only* a love poem and not the inspired word of God at all.

Does the Censor subscribe to this interpretation? Or will he
accept the orthodox view that the Sacred Writer is here writing
of divine love by allegory and analogy?

Jesus, when He appeared, described Himself as "the Bridegroom." A bridegroom is a man having a bride: who is the bride
of Jesus? Obviously, He was speaking in a spiritual or mystical
sense: He was fulfilling the prophecy of the Canticle. So, Catholic nuns speak of themselves as brides of Christ. But not nuns
alone — every Christian soul is the bride of Jesus. Hence every
Christian soul can find in the sexual union of bride and groom
the best analogy and most perfect illustration of the relationship existing between himself and God.

Saint Paul (we hope the Censor is not too oppressed with
"horror") does not fail in turn to point out this analogy: "Husbands, love your wives, just as Christ also loved the Church"
(Eph. 5:25). Again, he says, "For I have betrothed you to one
spouse, that I might present you a chaste virgin to Christ"
(II Cor. 11:2).

Without knowledge of this imagery, the Catholic mystics
could not be understood at all. One unacquainted with it might
be shocked, for example, at the poems of St. John of the Cross:

O night that guided me,
O night more lovely than the dawn,
O night that joined Beloved with Lover,
Lover transformed in the Beloved.

Upon my flowery breast,
Kept wholly for himself alone,

139

There he stayed sleeping, and I caressed him,
And the fanning of the cedars made a breeze.

I remained lost in oblivion;
My face I reclined on the Beloved.
All ceased and I abandoned myself,
Leaving my cares forgotten among the lilies.

Such imagery is very bold — what the Freudians could make of it! Should it, however, be viewed "with horror"? Presumably one who undertakes the office of censor is acquainted with such works as these. How then can he condemn a brother religious and priest for using language and illustrations that are wholly in accord with the age-old teaching tradition of the Church? True, St. John of the Cross, whom we have quoted, is a mystic. Nevertheless, the relationship he speaks of is that of every Christian to God. Accordingly, not to mystics alone but to every Christian, and that in the very ceremony of baptism, the Church addresses these words:

> Observe the commandments of God, that when Our Lord shall come to His nuptials, thou mayest meet Him together with all the saints in the heavenly court, and live forever and ever.

The only thing peculiar to the mystics is their vivid realization of the nature of the soul's relationship with God, and their actual possession, following great fidelity to grace, of a very perfect degree of union with Him. It is one of the excellences of Father Lacouture's teaching that he brings forcibly to the minds of ordinary Christians the essential nature of the soul's union with God, as illustrated by the analogy of Bridegroom and Bride. Otherwise, for the most part, we will have to go to the mystics to hear these divine nuptials celebrated and described — so reluctant are most Christians, including numbers of their teachers, even to hear of the King's invitation to the wedding feast of His Son. St. Bernard (to go on with our citations) describes this union:

> For although the *Spouse*, as a pure creature, is less than her Creator, and hence also loves less, yet if she loves with her

140

whole being, her love is perfect and wanting in nothing. It is love of this kind that constitutes the *spiritual marriage* of the soul with the Word.

Mark that the Saint speaks of the spiritual marriage *of the soul* — not of the mystic — with the Word. He goes on:

Happy the spouse to whom it has been given to experience *an embrace* of such surpassing delight! This spiritual embrace is nothing else but a chaste and holy love, a love most sweet and ravishing, a love perfectly serene and perfectly pure, a love that is mutual, intimate, and strong, a love that joins two not in one flesh but in one spirit, according to the Apostle's testimony: *"He that is joined to the Lord is one spirit."*

Nor is the description of this love in terms of an embrace a mere accident:

This is in truth the alliance of a holy and spiritual marriage. But it is saying too little to call it an alliance: it is rather an embrace.

Not forgetting that the Bridegroom in this case is divine as well as human, and must therefore be treated with reverence as well as with love, St. Bernard nevertheless says:

The Word is indeed one Who deserves to be honored, Who deserves to be admired and wondered at; but He is better pleased to be loved. For He is the Bridegroom, and *the soul* is His Bride. And between a bridegroom and his bride, what relation would you look for other than the bond of mutual love?

The Church, moreover, gives her approval to this language. Here, for example, are the words she addresses to the newly wedded bride in the Nuptial Blessing, clearly indicating the symbolical and spiritual character of the marriage union:

O God, Who has made marriage sacred by a significance so sublime that in the nuptial union Thou wast pleased to forecast the mystical union of Christ and the Church. . . . Deus

qui tam excellenti mysterio conjugalem copulam conse-
crasti, ut Christi et Ecclesiae sacramentum praesignares in
foedere nuptiarum. . . .

Priests, especially, will observe that the word used in this
blessing to designate nuptial union, *copula,* is employed in theology to describe not only sexual union in general but coitus in
particular. Such a choice of words, fully justifying St. Bernard's
reference to the marriage embrace, cannot be regarded as an accident; had the Church experienced the Censor's horror, she
would have carefully avoided this term.

Other spiritual masters use the same language. St. Francis de
Sales, for example, describing the attractiveness of the Bridegroom to the Bride, writes,

> The sacred spouse wished for the holy kiss of union: Oh,
> said she, *let Him kiss me with the kiss of His mouth* (Cant. I, 1).
> But is there affinity enough, O well-beloved spouse of the
> well-beloved, between thee and thy loving one to bring to the
> union which thou desirest? Yes, says she: give me it; this kiss
> of union, O Thou dear love of my heart: *for thy breasts are
> better than wine, smelling sweet of the best ointment.*

The same saint makes quite explicitly the very comparison to
which the Censor most strongly objects — that between sexual
union and the Beatific Vision:

> In fine, the heavenly King, having brought the soul He loves
> to the end of this life, assists her also in her blessed depar-
> ture, *by which he draws her to the marriage bed of eternal glory.*

Again, this is no exaggeration: the Church sanctions the
thought by her own usage. It is with a similar thought that she
speeds her children into eternity. Over the grave of the Christian
departing from this world she prays:

> Teach us to watch and pray, that when Thy summons comes,
> we may go forth to meet the Bridegroom and enter with
> Him into life everlasting.

These various prayers of the Church that we have been quoting have a real doctrinal value; according to the axiom *lex orandi est lex credendi* (the norm of prayer is the norm of belief), they give us the official teaching of the Church.

Since Newman describes a gentleman as one who does not willingly give pain, it can be only the great importance of the subject that justifies so complete a departure from the gentlemanly ideal as is involved in setting down the above passages from the saints and prayers of the Church, which undoubtedly have caused convulsions of horror in the Censor and any others who share his views. For the matter is important; it is not simply a question of propriety in the choice of literary metaphors. We touch here, in truth, the very heart of Christianity, the essential relationship that it establishes between God and the soul, a relationship that marks it off from merely natural religion and a merely rational code of upright conduct. That relationship is one of love: the end of Christianity, the final goal to which everything else in the Church is ordered, is to unite the souls of the faithful to God in the love of eternal friendship. Therefore, the essential supernatural relationship between God and man is one of personal, intimate, eternal love. Natural religion, on the other hand, observes its correct norm of conduct coldly and exactly according to reason. Without doubt, there is also a natural love of God, enjoined upon man as a rational creature, but it differs *toto coelo* from supernatural love, sharing in the coldness, the abstractness, and the remoteness of the reason which is its principle. Christianity transforms this relation, makes it genuine affection, intimate, personal, tender — in a word, changes it into a true friendship, a most sublime love. Thus (not to speak here of membership in the Church and participation in the sacraments, which is presupposed in a Christian), the *practical* difference between Christian and pagan, that is, the difference in actual conduct, is that the Christian is motivated and inspired by love. After all, a Christian is human, and must, like a pagan, observe the ordinary conditions of human life; however much he may fast, he will also eat, drink, sleep, work, take his recreation. The kingdom of God is within. The Christian King Alfred, in a song that

Chesterton put on his lips, thus describes the difference between pagan and Christian to his heathen conquerors:

> Our monks go robed in rain and snow,
>   But the heart of flame therein,
> But you go clothed in feasts and flames
>   When all is ice within.

Now in order to bring home to our minds this essential relationship of love between God and the soul, the Scripture employs two analogies: it represents God as Father and Christians as His children; it also represents God as Bridegroom and the soul as Bride. These are the two ways, given to us by God Himself, for studying His love, for learning its exigencies, for discovering the manner in which it is to be expressed. Each of these analogies is useful, yet each by itself is insufficient; hence God has provided the two together. The relationship of child to parent reminds us that our love of God is one of dependence as well as of tenderness, and must therefore be accompanied by filial fear and reverence. The analogy of Bridegroom with Bride teaches us, as no other method could, that the love of God is one almost of equality (we having been elevated to the supernatural plane by grace), of deep and intimate and lasting affection, as between spouses.

Of these analogies, the most perfect is that between Bride and Groom: better even than the other it shows us the real nature of love: union between those who are beloved of each other. It also shows us the perfection of the union that should exist between God and the soul, since the union between husband and wife is the most perfect known to human love and friendship. Accordingly, St. Bernard, in distinguishing his four degrees of love, illustrates the third by filial love, but the fourth and highest degree he compares to nuptial love:

> O truly a great thing is love. But it has degrees of greatness.
> In the very highest of these degrees stands the love of the
> Bride. The children also love, but they have an eye to the inheritance, the thought of losing which makes them suspi-

cious of everything and causes them to regard with more fear than affection Him from whom they hope to receive it.

Showing again the superiority of this highest degree, which can be adequately described only in terms of nuptial love, he says,

> For the soul that is such desires nothing for herself with a private affection, neither happiness nor glory nor anything else whatever, but loses herself completely in God, and has but one most eager desire, namely, that the King should bring her into His bedchamber, that she might belong to Him alone and enjoy his sweet caresses.

Clearly, to forget this essential relationship is to remove the heart from Christianity and reduce it, in practice, to the observance of the precepts of natural religion. It is to eliminate from Christianity Christ Himself, His teaching, His way of life, the End that He has fixed for our strivings. The special command that He laid upon us is that we should love God with our whole heart, that is, exclusively, as a faithful bride loves the bridegroom; and the highest gift and power that He gave us — charity — is that which binds us to God by Love. Accordingly, to throw discredit on the analogy, by which, better than all other means, it is possible to teach the meaning of supernatural love, is, in actual fact and effect, to eliminate that essential relationship of love from the practice of our religion, reducing it to a formal observance of rationally imposed duties, a reduction that the other analogy, with its accent on fear, is powerless to prevent.

As we have progressed in discussing this point, the reader must have been experiencing a mounting excitement; for we have come upon one of the most closely guarded secrets in the Grand Strategy of the High Command in Hell. It is really a magnificent plan, devised with such genius as might be expected from angelic intelligences resolved to divert Christians generally and Christian teachers in particular from attaining, or even pursuing, the essential purpose of Christianity. The devils, close students of human psychology that they are, accomplish this end by taking advantage of the false delicacy, on the one hand, and the prurience, on the other, with which sexual union nowadays is usually regarded: both attitudes, although quite different in themselves, are equally useful in causing sexual union to be regarded as something shameful and therefore unworthy, as the Censor has expressed it, of comparison with the Beatific Vision. And in this manner the analogy revealed to us by the Holy Spirit Himself for disclosing the secrets of divine love is thrown away in fear, contempt, and even "horror," as though it were monstrous to suggest the thought.

Let those who share the Censor's views look to their employ.

And if the Censor, or others like him, whether moved by sham-delicacy or prurience, regard this comparison "with horror" or similar sentiments, let them know that others, free from such distortions of spiritual insight, think very differently on this subject. There was, for example, the Catholic layman, married, who, hearing this comparison brought out clearly on one of our retreats, exclaimed to the priest directing it, "For the first time in my life I understand the true beauty and sublimity of Christian marriage, the reason why our Lord made it a sacrament, the spiritual significance of the wedding union, and its place in the overall plan of Providence."

May

"WITH WHAT praises to extol thee we know not, for He whom the heavens could not contain rested in thy bosom."

Mother of fair love, it is hard to write about you, who have given us God. I can only write very personally in thanksgiving for bringing me to the Faith through motherhood, for sending me sweet reminders even through Communist friends (a gift of a rosary on one occasion and a little statue on another).

"The feast of our life is often sad," the Hungarian Bishop Prohaszka writes. "There is much heavy food which science and politics provide, but our wine is missing, which should refresh the soul and fill it with pure noble joy of life. Oh, our Mother, intercede with thy Son in our behalf. Show Him our need. Tell Him with trust, 'They have no wine.' He will provide for us.

"Sweet wine, fiery wine, the Lord Jesus gives to our bridal soul; He warms and heats our hearts. Oh, sweet is the wine of the first fiery love, of the first elating zeal!"

White goats leaping in the violets,
Goats with their wattles,
Ducks with their waddles,
Black crows feasting on brown ploughed earth,
Walking in line by the green wheat field.

This is a poem written for my grandchild Rebecca, who was made a child of God May 6. So I always remember this day as well as her birthday. Some days we think of ourselves as mourning and weeping in this valley of tears. Other days we feel like shouting, "All ye works of the Lord, bless ye the Lord! Praise Him, adore Him, above all forever!"

Spring in the country, with its countless duties of ploughing, planting, and the care of new creatures! One of the greatest joys in life is bathing a new baby who stretches and yawns and opens its mouth like a little bird for provender. "Give us this day our daily bread!"

Thank God for everything. Thank God that in other countries peasants are ploughing and planting and tending new things — all of them samples of heaven, all of them portents of that new heaven and earth wherein justice dwelleth.

Leaving out of account Divine Providence, there is chaos and destruction ahead, and injustices breeding new wars. But we cannot leave out of account Divine Providence, so we can live in hope and faith and charity, and rejoice and continue to pray and do penance to avert another war.

We must rejoice this month of May and let our glance of joy rest on beauty around us. It would be thankless to do otherwise.

If there are such keen joys and beauty in such times as these, how heaven will shine forth. I like to think of Father Faber's writings on life and death. He quotes at the conclusion of one of these sermons, "'My beloved to me and I to Him, who feedeth among the lilies till the day break and the shadows retire.'" And then he repeats with joy, "Till the day break, and the shadows retire. Till the day break and the shadows retire. Till the day break and the shadows retire!" If these joys are shadows, what can such bliss be?

It is May Day again, and we will begin our sixteenth year. *The*

Catholic Worker has finished fifteen years in the lay apostolate. People look at our masthead and say, "Yes, but it says Vol. XV, No. 3. What does that mean?" It just means that we have skipped an issue now and again, and it means that we come out eleven times a year, not twelve, but according to some regulation of the post office department, you have to number a journal in that way.

Last year I tried, taking the whole issue of the paper to do it in, to write a general article on what we were trying to do, summing up what our program meant. But a thing like that is most unsatisfactory. One is always leaving out the most vital things. Peter Maurin's program of action was for round-table discussions for the clarification of thought; houses of hospitality for the practice of the works of mercy, for the study of Catholic Action; farming communes or agronomic universities where the unemployed could learn to raise food, build shelters, make clothes, and where unemployed college graduates could do the same, where the worker could become a scholar and the scholar a worker.

And who are those with whom we have cooperated through the years, and whom we admire and love in the lay apostolate, in spite of differences?

There is first of all the N.C.W.C. labor action groups, with whom we first came in contact back in 1933 and who were pioneers in the field. Peter used to go to all their meetings, not only to hear but to be heard.

There was the *Commonweal* group of scholars, who were by their writings and thought studying the "theory of revolution." George Shuster, now president of Hunter College and then an editor of *Commonweal,* sent Peter Maurin to me and so started off the Catholic Worker movement.

There were the Friendship House groups, first in Canada and then in the United States, who worked so steadily in the interracial field, among the poor, performing works of mercy and having centers of meetings and study, days of recollection and retreats.

There is the Association of Catholic Trade Unionists, with their papers throughout the country, and the papers they have influenced, and the priests who have entered the field of trade unionism and gone on picket lines, into the factories, into the homes of workers, and into strike headquarters. There is *Work* in Chicago, edited by Ed Marciniak, one of the founders of the Chicago House of Hospitality, which is no more, and there are the ACTU publications, *The Wage Earner* in Detroit and *Labor Leader* in New York.

There is the Grail at Loveland, Ohio, and there is the Center for Christ the King [at] Herman, Pennsylvania, schools of the apostolate for women and for men, centers of study not connected by any close ties.

There are such publications as *Today* in Chicago and *Integrity* in New York, animated by much the same spirit, and to whom we owe much, as they owe much to us. There is official Catholic Action, not recognized yet in many a diocese, but making a beginning here and there about the country and stimulating and arousing the laity. Fides publications at South Bend, which recently published Cardinal Suhard's *Growth or Decline? Concord*, the student publication gotten out by the Young Christian Students, *The Catholic Lawyer*, published also from Notre Dame — all these are evidences of specialized Catholic Action, of the apostolate of like to like.

There are the retreat movements, and we refer especially to our own because it is a basic retreat open for both colored and white, Catholic and non-Catholic, men and women, young and old, for the poorest of the poor from the Bowery as well as for the young seminarian or student.

There are the Cana conferences for the family, started in St. Louis by Father Dowling and spreading throughout the country.

And we are part of it all, part of this whole movement throughout the country, but of course we have our own particular talent, our own particular contribution to make to the sum total of the apostolate. And we think of it as so important that we are apt to fight and wrangle among ourselves on account of it, and we are all sensitive to the accusation that we are accenting, emphasizing one aspect of the truth at the expense of another. A heresy overemphasizes one aspect of the truth.

But our unity, if it is not unity of thought in regard to temporal matters, is a unity at the altar rail. We are all members of the Mystical Body of Christ, and so we are closer to each other, by the tie of grace, than any blood brothers are. All these books about discrimination are thinking in terms of human brotherhood, of our responsibility one for another. We are our brother's keeper, and all men are our brothers whether they be Catholic or not. But of course the tie that binds Catholics is closer, the tie of grace. We partake of the same food, Christ. We put off the old man and put on Christ. The same blood flows through our veins, Christ's. We are the same flesh, Christ's. But all men are members or potential members, as St. Augustine says, and there is no time with God, so who are we to know the degree of separation between us and the Communist, the unbaptized, the God-hater, who may tomorrow, like St. Paul, love Christ.

This past month or so we have all been reading such books as *The Worker Priest in Germany,* translated by Rosemary Sheed; *France Alive* by Claire Bishop; *Growth or Decline?* by Emmanuel Cardinal Suhard; *Souls at Stake* by Rev. Francis Ripley and F. S. Mitchel, with a foreword by Archbishop Bitter.

Chesterton used to start off writing in answer to things he had been reading, or because he was stimulated by what he was reading, and I am sure that all of us on *The Catholic Worker* this month are doing just that. One of the books I have been reading by a non-Catholic, Richard Gregg, about the work of Gandhi along economic lines, led me to think of just how the Catholic Worker movement is distinguished from all these other movements, just what it is we emphasize, just what position we take which is not taken by them. Not that we wish to be different. God forbid. We wish that they all felt as we do, that we had that basic unity which would make us agree on *Pacifism* and *Distributism*.

We feel that the two go together. We feel that the great cause of wars [is] maldistribution, not only of goods but of population. Peter used to talk about a *philosophy of work and a philosophy of poverty*. Both are needed in order to change things as they are, to do away with the causes of war. The bravery to face voluntary poverty is needed if we wish to marry, to live, to produce children, to work for life instead of for death, to reject war.

A philosophy of work is essential if we would be whole men, holy men, healthy men, joyous men. A certain amount of goods is necessary for a man to lead a good life, and we have to make that kind of society where it is easier for men to be good. These are all things Peter Maurin wrote about. (He is not writing anymore; we are just reprinting what has appeared by him in *The Catholic Worker* over and over again for many years. The fact that people think Peter is still writing is an evidence of the freshness of all his ideas. They strike people as new. They see all things new, as St. John said.)

A philosophy of work and a philosophy of poverty are necessary if we would share with all men what we have, if we would each try to be the least, if we would wash the feet of our brothers. It is necessary if we would so choose to love our brother, live for him, and die for him, rather than kill him in war. We would need to reject the work in steel mills, mines, [and] factories which contributed to war. We would be willing to go on general strike, and we intend to keep talking about general strikes in order to familiarize each other, ourselves, [and] our fellow workers with the phrase, so that they will begin to ponder and try to understand what a different way of working, different jobs, a different attitude to work would mean in the lives of all. (There is plenty of other work besides factory work. Not all workers are factory workers. There are the service jobs, the jobs that have to do with food, clothing, and shelter. There are the village jobs. Not all would have to be farmers. We are not shouting for all to rush to the land. There is the village economy. A destruction of cities may force us to consider it in the future.)

The Catholic Worker movement is distinguished from other movements in its attitude to our *industrial civilization,* to *the machine,* and to *war.*

To make a study of the machine, it would be good for our readers to send to India and get this book of Richard Gregg's called *The Economics of Khaddar* (hand-spun and handwoven cloth). It is published by Jivanji Dahyabhai Desai, Navajivan Press, Kalupur Ahmedabad, India. "The symbol of the unity given to all Christians by Christ himself was food, bread and wine; so the symbol of unity of all India given by Gandhi was means to food — the spinning wheel."

Gandhi was concerned with the poor and with unemployment. So was Peter Maurin. He started his movement in 1933, when unemployment reached the peak of 11,000,000. It was war which put all these men back to work, and it is recovering from war which is keeping them at work, though unemployment is again setting in. Peter did not believe in the use of force any more than Gandhi did to settle disputes between men or nations. He was inspired by the Sermon on the Mount, as was Gandhi, and there was no talk in that of war. It was turning the other cheek, giving up your cloak, walking the second mile. It was feeding and clothing your enemy. It was dying for him on the Cross. It was the liberty of Christ that St. Paul talked of. Christ constrained no one. He lived in an occupied country all his years, and he made no move to join a movement to throw off the yoke. He thought not in terms of the temporal kingdom of the Jews.

The problem of the machine is the problem of unemployment. Or rather, the problem of *power*. "The right use of power is the important thing; the machine is only an incident." A spinning wheel is a machine; so is a typewriter, a churn, a loom, a plow. These machines use the available mechanical energy of men, women, and children, young and old. The old man (anyone over forty-five in our industrial era) can use any of these machines. Mechanical energy is derived from food eaten by the person. Not from gasoline and water-power or electricity or coal. Men have to eat, employed or unemployed. The efficient thing to do is to use the available energy, human energy, to combat unemployment. Then we would not have to fight about oil and such like raw materials.

There have been many tributes paid to Gandhi for his nonviolent resistance, his pacifism in a world at war. But little to the "economic validity of his program." That is what this book is about. And I would wholeheartedly recommend it to all missionaries who have been sending us their desperate appeals these last years. We must continue to help them of course, but the works of mercy are not enough. Men need work as well as bread to be co-creator with God, as He meant them to be, in taking raw materials and ennobling them.

Richard Gregg synopsized his book as follows (paragraphing mine):

In addition to being a consideration of the economic validity of Mr. Gandhi's programme, and of one aspect of the Indian renaissance, it may be regarded as a discussion of a special instance of the economic validity of all handicraft work versus power-machine industry;

or as a discussion of a special method of unemployment prevention and relief;

or as a new attack on the problem of poverty;

or as an indigenous Indian form of cooperation;

or as illustrating one phase of the relations between Orient and Occident;

or between Western capitalism and some other forms of industrial organization;

or as a fragmentary and tentative investigation of part of the problem of the limitation or balance of use of power and machinery in order to secure a fine and enduring civilization;

or as a partial discussion of the beginning of a development of a sounder organization of human life.

If India will develop her three great resources, (1) the inherited manual sensitiveness and skill of her people; (2) the wasted time of the millions of unemployed; (3) a larger portion of the radiant energy of the sun,

and if she will distribute the resulting wealth equably among all her people, by the wide use of the spinning wheel and the hand loom, she can win to her economic goal.

"You have to take a position on our contemporary civilization, to judge, condemn, or correct it," Cardinal Suhard says. "You must draw up an objective evaluation of our urban civilization today with its gigantic concentrations and its continual growth, inhuman production, unjust distribution, exhausting form of entertainment . . . make a gigantic synthesis of the world to come. . . . Do not be timid. . . . Cooperate with all those believers and unbelievers who are wholeheartedly searching for the truth. You alone will be completely humanist. Be the leaven and the bread will rise. *But it must be bread, not factitious matter.*"

That is why we rebel against all talk of sanctifying one's surroundings. It is not bread in the first place. It is not worth working with. We must think of these things, even if we can take only first steps out of the morass. We may be caught in the toils of the machine, but we do not have to think of it for our children. We do not just think in terms of changing the ownership of the machine, though some machines will remain and undoubtedly will have to be controlled municipally or regionally.

Peter Maurin's vision of the city of God included Pacifism and Distributism. And that is what distinguishes us from much of the lay apostolate today. It is the talent Christ has given us, and we cannot bury it. The April issue of *The Catholic Worker* has devoted its space to pacifism, and that was the issue distributed on May Day through the streets of New York. These May Day notes are again a recapitulation.

May 7

ALL OUR talks about peace and the weapons of the spirit are meaningless unless we try in every way to embrace *voluntary poverty* and not work in any position, any job that contributes to war, not to take any job whose pay comes from the fear of war, of the atom bomb. We must give up our place in this world, sacrifice children, family, wife, mother, and embrace poverty, and then we will be laying down life itself.

And we will be considered *fools for Christ*. Our folly will be esteemed madness, and we will be lucky if we escape finally the psychopathic ward. We know — we have seen this judgment in ourselves and in others. The well-dressed man comes into the office, and he is given respect. The ragged, ill-clad, homeless one is the hobo, the bum. *"Get in line there. Coffee line forms at six-thirty. Nothing to eat until four. No clothes today."*

Peter Maurin, visiting our Buffalo house one time, showed his face inside the door and was so greeted. "Come back at five and have soup with the rest of the stiffs." And then the comment, "One of those New York bums came in this afternoon, said he was from the New York house."

One of the friends of the work, in laughing at the incident that evening, said, "Where did you go, Peter?" "I went to see *Grapes of Wrath*." Peter was always meek, obedient to all. His speech with everyone when he was not indoctrinating was always Yea, yea, nay, nay. Another story told of him was that when he went to see a professor's wife at Columbia, the wife thought he was the plumber and ushered him into the cellar. He followed her confusedly, wondering why she was entertaining in the cellar. If he knew or thought of such things as rumpus rooms or basement bars, he might have thought he was being ushered into one of them.

Another tale told is of his going to speak at a Midwest college where the door brother was known for his great charity. At the very sight of Peter, the brother ushered him down into the kitchen and sat him down before a good meal, which Peter gratefully ate. As the time for the lecture drew near, the harassed fathers were telephoning and hunting all over the college, finally finding him in the cook's domain, having a discussion there.

Another case I know of, of my own knowledge, is a time he went up to Rye, or New Rochelle, or some Westchester town to make a morning address to a women's club. He always went where he was asked. An hour or so later, we received frantic calls. "Where is Peter?" People always called him Peter. Sometimes they were even more familiar and called him "Pete." Since I had put him on the train myself, I told them that he had left on the train designated, that he must be in the station.

"There is only an old tramp sitting on one of the benches, asleep," was the reply. We knew it was Peter, and it turned out to be so.

We have seen many an occasion when he was silenced at a meeting by a cautious chairman before he had even gotten underway. More courteous chairmen allowed him so many minutes to "make his point" and without listening sat him down or called him to order. I have seen Father La Farge and Bishop Boyle come to his rescue and explain who he was, what he was trying to say.

Bishop Boyle likes to speak of the time he had an all-day discussion with Peter after one of these encounters in the lecture hall. "I had to get up and tell them what he was trying to say," the bishop beamed. And it was not just the case of an accent, for Peter, even after forty years in this country, has an accent. If the accent goes with the well-groomed appearance, people make an attempt to understand it. Coming from a ragged old apostle, people make no attempt to listen.

"People will not listen," Peter used to say sadly. Or else, more directly, he would rebuke, "You are listening with one ear, making your answers before you have heard what I have said. You do not want to learn, you want to teach, you want to tell me." He knew he was a man with a message.

And now Peter is more than ever in absolute poverty. He has achieved the ultimate in poverty. This last chapter is necessary for a complete picture of Peter as he is today. It is hard to make our readers understand it. They read or half-read the articles that we run month after month, and no matter how many times we explain that they are reprinted from much earlier issues and that Peter has not written for four years, they write enthusiastically and tell us how they profited by his last essays. "His mind is as keen as ever," they say enthusiastically.

But something has happened to his mind. We must say it again because it is of tremendous significance. It reveals more than anything else his utter selflessness, his giving of himself. He has given everything, even his mind. He has nothing left; he is in utter and absolute poverty. The only thing he really enjoyed, exulted in, was his ability to think. When he said sadly, "I cannot think," it was because that had been taken from him, literally. His mind would no longer work. He sits on the porch, a huge old hulk. His shoulders were always broad and bowed. He looks gnome-like, as though he came from under the earth. He shambles about one-sidedly, as though he had had a stroke. His head hangs wearily, as though he could not hold it up. His mouth, often twisted as though with pain, hangs open in an effort to understand what is going on around him. Most of the time he is in a lethargy; he does not try to listen or to understand. Doctors say that it is a hardening of the arteries of the brain. Some talk of cardiac asthma to explain his racking cough. He has a rupture which gives him pain. Sometimes he has headaches. We only know when we ask him, and he says yes or no.

"I have never asked anything for myself," he said once, and he made every conscious effort to give all he had, to give the best he had, all of himself, to the cause of his brother. The only thing he had left in his utter poverty which made Skid Row his home and the horse market his eating place and the old clothes room his haberdasher was his brilliant mind. Father McSorley considered him a genius. Father Parsons said that he was the best-read man he ever met. Now he remembers nothing. "I cannot remember." "I cannot think."

One time we acted charades before him at the retreat house at Easton. Irene Naughton arranged three scenes in which the men acted out . . . three essays, "When the Irish Were Irish a Thousand Years Ago," "When a Greek Met a Greek," [and] "When a Jew Met a Jew." The contrast was that of the teachings of the fathers of Israel and the Fathers of the Church with the present. The men dressed in sheets and angora goats' hair to give them a venerable appearance and did a delightful job of it. Afterwards we asked Peter what were the essays which the charades exemplified. He did not know. We read aloud his essays to him, and he did recognize them as he had written them, but as they were acted and spoken in the charade, he "could not remember."

John Cort, of the Association of Catholic Trade Unionists and one of the editors of the *Commonweal,* who spent a few years with us on Mott Street, said once that he thought the most significant message we had for the world today was poverty.

All the world admires and talks of the poor man of Assisi. Christ is honored even by the unbeliever, the hater of churches, as the poor man who washed the feet of His disciples and had no place to lay His head. Poverty is praised and sung of in song and story. But its reality is little known.

It is a garden enclosed, a secret beauty. It is to be learned by faith, not by reason or by sense. It is not just *simplicity,* which can be a very expensive proposition indeed.

Peter's poverty might have been thought to be that of an old peasant who was used to nothing better. "After all, he never had anything — he was one of twenty-three children. They lived like animals;

their manure pile was their greatest possession." I have heard just such remarks as these.

And of course there is truth in the fact that he was not used to soft garments nor the homes of comfort. He was always in good trim to practice the life of poverty.

One of Newman's Lenten sermons talks of our endeavors to multiply comforts and get rid of daily inconveniences and distresses of life.

"Cold and hunger and hard lodging, humble offices and mean appearance are considered serious evils," he writes. "All things harsh and austere are carefully put aside. We shrink from the rude lap of earth and embrace of the elements, and we build ourselves houses in which the flesh may enjoy its lust and the eye its pride."

Cold and hunger and hard lodging and all things that affront the senses were well known to Peter. But what of the interior senses, the memory and the understanding and the will? These last years we have seen all these mortified in him. Much of his memory and his understanding are gone, and his will is fixed on God. When we wake him in the morning, all we have to say is "Mass, Peter," and he is struggling and puffing and panting to get out of bed. At night it is the same for Compline and rosary unless we forbid him to get up and make him lie still.

There is a dear priest who used to talk to us about being *victims*. I could write a book about him, so great was his love of God and of souls, but this is about Peter. He too became a victim. What he loved most, after his spiritual work, was to do active work for souls — build houses, work his electric saw, make things for the chapel, travel about to talk of the things of God. He was known for his activity. Then, at the age of fifty-seven, paralysis and loss of memory set in. Incontinent and bedridden, he has spent the last two years away from all those he loved, far from the activities he craved. I asked him if he had offered himself as a victim, and he said wryly, "One doesn't realize what one is saying often. We offer God so much, and maybe we think we mean it. And then God takes us at our word!"

Peter gave himself, he offered himself to a life of poverty, and he has been able to prove his poverty. It is not just something he was used to or was attracted to in a superficial way. His poverty, his self-abnegation was complete.

And now he is dying (if not already dead) to the things of the world. "His life is hid with Christ in God." He is not even appreciated for the saint he is. (And understand that I use this term as one uses it for one not passed upon formally by the Church. A rector of a seminary once said to his students, "I want you all to be saints, but not canonized ones. It costs too much.")

Father Faber describes what Peter's actual death may be like in one of his spiritual conferences on death entitled "Precious in the Sight of the Lord":

> Let us speak of one more death, and then close our list. Let it be the death of saintly indifference. This is a death so obscurely veiled in its own simplicity that we can hardly discern its beauty. We must take it upon faith. It is the death of those who for long have been reposing in sublimest solitude of soul in the will of God. All complications have disappeared from their inward life. There is a bare unity about it, which to our unseeing eyes is barren as well as bare. All devotions are molten in one. All wishes have disappeared, so that men look cold, and hard, and senseless. There is no glow about them when they die. They die in colorless light. They make no demonstration when they go. There is no pathos in their end, but a look — it is only a look — of stoical hardness. They generally speak but little, and then it is not edifying, but rather on commonplace subjects, such as the details of the sick room or news about relatives; and they speak of these things as if they were neither interested in them nor trying to take an interest. Their death, from the very excess of its spirituality, looks almost animal. They lie down to die like beasts, such is the appearance of it, independently as if they needed none of us to help them, and uncomplainingly, as if fatalism put them above complaining. They often die alone when none are by, when the nurses are gone away for a while. They seem almost as if they watched [for] the opportunity to die alone. As they have lived like eagles, they mostly die high up, without witnesses, and in the night. This death is too beautiful for us to see its beauty. It

rather scares us by something about it which seems inhuman. More of human will would make it more lovely to us; for what is there to be seen when the will of the saint has been absorbed long since in the will of God? Like the overflow of some desert wells, the waters of life sink into the sand, without a tinkling sound to soothe the ear, without a marge of green to rest the eye.

Precious in the sight of the Lord is the death of His saints.

May 10

NATURALLY SPEAKING, people are filled with repulsion at the idea of holiness. We have so many sad examples of Pecksniffs in our midst. But now we are filled with encouragement these days to find that it is not only the Catholic Worker lay movement but writers like Ignazio Silone, Aldous Huxley, and Arthur Koestler who are also crying aloud for a synthesis — the saint-revolutionist who would impel others to holiness by his example. And recognizing the difficulty of the aim, Silone has drawn pictures of touching fellowship with the lowly, the revolutionist living in voluntary poverty, in hunger and cold, in the stable, and depending on "personalist action" to move the world. *Bread and Wine* [and] *The Seed Beneath the Snow* are filled with this message.

According to St. Thomas, "The perfection of divine love is a matter of precept for all without exception, so that even the perfection of heaven is not excepted from this precept, since it is the end to which one must tend."

We are either on the road to heaven or hell. "All the way to heaven is heaven, for He said, 'I am the Way,'" St. Catherine of Siena tells us. And likewise all the way to hell is hell. We have some pretty good visions of hell around us these days and these last years. Dante wrote his great vision of hell. St. Teresa of Ávila has a picture of hell in her autobiography. The latest vision of hell is Aldous Huxley's in *Time Must Have a Stop*. One night last winter I went to Tannhauser and realized then that Venusburg was another vision of hell, to which, in the old Christian legend, Tannhauser is condemned at the end, to repeat his senseless and cloying pleasures for all eternity. Bernanos wrote that hell was "not to love anymore." After the last war, everyone was talking about the lost generation. After this war, thank God, they are talking more about saints. A few years ago there was a book review in the *New York Times* about Greek and Christian tragedy and *Moby Dick* as an allegorical novel. In that review it is pointed out that unlike Greek tragedy, where one's fate is written, where it is only up to the hero to play the heroic part, the Christian has a *choice*, and each and every lowly Christian is forced to make that choice. W. H. Auden was the author of the review in the *Times*, and he writes,

There is the possibility of each becoming exceptional and good; this ultimate possibility for hero and chorus alike is stated in Father Mapple's sermon, and it is to become a saint, i.e., the individual through his own free will surrenders his will to the will of God. In this surrender he does not become the ventriloquist's doll, for the God who acts through him can only do so by his consent; there always remain two wills, and the saint therefore never ceases to be tempted to obey his own desires.

The saint does not ask to become one, he is called to become one and assents to the call. The outward sign that Ahab is so called is the suffering which is suddenly intruded into his life. He is called to give up hunting whales — "the normal, cannibalistic life of this world."

Archbishop Robichaud, in his book *Holiness for All* (New Man Press), emphasizes the fact that the choice is not between good and evil for Christians — that it is not in this way that one proves his love. The very fact of baptism, of becoming the son of God, presupposes development as a son of God. C. S. Lewis, the author of *Screwtape Letters*, points out that the child in the mother's womb perhaps would refuse to be born if given the choice, but it does not have that choice. It has to be born. The egg has to develop into the chicken with wings. Otherwise it becomes a rotten egg. It is not between good and evil, we repeat, that the choice lies, but between good and better. In other words, we must give up over and over again even the good things of this world to choose God. Mortal sin is a turning from God and a turning to created things — created things that are good.

It is so tremendous an idea that it is hard for people to see its implications. Our whole literature, our culture, is built on ethics, the choice between good and evil. The drama of the ages is on this theme. We are still living in the Old Testament, with commandments as to the natural law. We have not begun to live as good Jews, let alone as good Christians. We do not tithe ourselves; there is no year of jubilee; we do not keep the Sabbath; we have lost the concept of hospitality. It is dog eat dog. We are all hunting whales. We devour each other in love and in hate; we are cannibals.

In all secular literature it has been so difficult to portray the good man, the saint, that a Don Quixote is a fool; the Prince Myshkin is an epileptic in order to arouse the sympathy of the reader, appalled by unrelieved goodness. There are, of course, the lives of the saints, but they are too often written as though they were not in this world. We have seldom been given the saints as they really were, as they affected the lives of their times. We get them generally, only in their own writings. But instead of that strong meat we are too generally given the pap of hagiographical writing.

Too little has been stressed the idea that *all* are called. Too little attention has been placed on the idea of mass conversions. We have sinned against the virtue of hope. There have been in these days mass conversions to Nazism, fascism, and communism. Where are our saints to call the masses to God? Personalists first, we must put the question to ourselves. Communitarians, we will find Christ in our brothers.

May 12

HERE ARE some quotations from my winter's reading:

Travels in Arabia Deserta by Doughty makes good background reading for one's study of the Bible. "Cheerful is the bare Arabic livelihood in the common air, which has sufficiency in a few things snatched incuriously as on a journey; so it is a life little full of superfluous cares; their ignorance is not brutish, their poverty is not baseness."

In another part he writes, "There is a winter proverb of the poor in Europe, 'Fire is half bread.'" I thought of this many times when we were cold during January and February.

❧

"Attend to reading," St. Paul said to Timothy. St. Jerome writes to Eustochium, "Let sleep creep over you holding a book, and let the sacred page receive your drooping face." St. Augustine said, "Do you know how we should read Holy Scripture? As when a person reads letters that have come from his native country, to see what news we have of heaven." Rodriguez says that reading is sister and companion to meditation. St. Jerome wrote, "Where is this fire [of the love of God]? Doubtless in the holy Scriptures, by the reading whereof the soul is set on fire with God and purified from all vices." St. John 6:63: "The words that I have given you are spirit and life."

❧

Thoughts on holy silence: St. Gregory kept silence during Lent.

Holy Abbot Agatho for three years carried a pebble in his mouth to gain the virtue of silence.

Abbot Deicoola always had a smile on his face, and when asked why he was so happy, he said, "Be what may be and come what may come, no one can take God from me."

Newman's picture of a Christian character: free from excitement or effort, full of repose, still, equable. "Act then as persons who are in a dwelling not their own. . . . What matters it what we eat, what we drink, wherewith we are clothed, what is thought of us, what becomes of us, etc."

On the other hand, there is the sacramental attitude toward life:

"Whatever you do, whether you eat or drink, do all in the name of the Lord Jesus."

Isaiah 32:17-18: "The work of the righteous shall be peace, and the effect of righteousness, quietness and assurance forever. And my people shall dwell in a peaceable habitation and in sure dwellings and quiet resting places."

To think nothing of ourselves and always to judge well and highly of others is great wisdom and high perfection. — *The Imitation of Christ*

Prayer is what breath is to the body. Prayer is the hand of the body, waits on it, feeds it, washes it, tends it — as the hands do everything, so prayer. "If Stephen had not prayed," writes St. Augustine, "the Church would never have had St. Paul."

Buddha says that community life is like sword grass in one's hand.

St. Apollo formed a community of 500 monks near Hermapolis, who received daily Communion and listened to a daily homily. "In these he often insisted on the evils of melancholy and sadness, saying that cheerfulness of heart is necessary amidst our tears of penance as being the fruit of charity, and requisite to maintain the spirit of fervor. He himself was known to strangers by the joy of his countenance."

"The grace of the Holy Ghost, like a good mother, has put aloes on the breasts of the world that that might become bitter to me which before was sweet, and sweetest honey on the things of virtue and religion in order to make that tasty and sweet to me which before seemed bitter and disagreeable." — Rodriguez

"It was a rule among the Jews that all their children should learn some handicraft in the course of their studies, were it but to avoid idleness and exercise the body, as well as the mind, in some sensible pursuit." — Butler

Charles de Foucauld wrote, "Manual labor is necessarily put into the second place, to make room for studies, at present, because you and I are in the period of infancy; we are not yet old enough to work with St. Joseph; we are still with Jesus, the little child at the Virgin's knee, learning to read. But later on, humble, vile, despised manual labor will again take its great place, and then Holy Communion, the lives of the saints, prayer, the humble work of our hands, humiliation and suffering!"

June

EVERY DAY the planting goes on. Tomato plants, cabbage, celery, asparagus, rhubarb, peppers, carrots, beets, beans — so much that I cannot think of it all. Today, a hot June day, it has been onions. Jane has begged onions from the wholesalers, and John Filliger and Tom and George and Jim have been out since lunch putting them in. They were soft ones which they were unable to sell. We have not been able to buy onion sets; the time for them is past, the onion growers around Florida, New York, tell us.

The cow is giving twenty-four quarts of milk a day, and we can use every bit of it, with eighteen sitting down to table, quite aside from retreats. People come to retreats and stay awhile. People pass by on the road and come in to stay weeks. Several leave and several arrive.

Last week it was Father Francis Meenan's retreat that brought the crowds, a retreat for men, and they all said it was the best yet. I went to New York to take care of the office so that all at Mott Street could come to the farm over the Memorial Day weekend. No one on our block seemed to be going away for the holiday. It was as noisy, as crowded as ever. On Sunday morning there was one of those tragedies which attracted a still greater crowd. A woman

167

down the street who had lost her husband a few months ago was washing her windows on a Sunday morning, fell three stories to the ground, and was killed instantly. I passed her on my way home from Mass. With the crowd and the ambulance out in front, I thought it was someone being brought to the hospital, a routine we had become used to. It was a terrible shock as I passed down the middle of the street to see the figure of a woman lying in the gutter, amongst all kinds of litter, half-covered with a piece of brown paper from a neighboring butcher shop. It always seems [to take] an interminable length of time for police, ambulance, doctor to arrive. The priest arrived first.

It was quiet enough around the office. A few visitors came in, bringing boxes of clothes. Marge was housebound, what with the children having measles, German measles, and chicken pox right after each other. Women were sick in the house, and some who were not sick were disorderly.

During the last two months, Johanna and Tommy have been praying for a [new] station wagon to take children and their mothers to the farm. They had gone up in [one] to Newburgh last year, but this year the old wagon has fallen apart. So they had started to pray. Lo and behold, a friend of the farm turned over his 1932 Chevrolet to me, and after seventy-five dollars' worth of work on it, I was able to drive Bridget, Anne, and Dave back to New York in it with no mishaps. We came over the new Storm King highway, picked sweet clover on the way, [and] enjoyed the view of the river if we did not enjoy the sound we made between the echoing mountains. We sounded either like a Mack truck or an aeroplane, but I trust after we get the muffler fixed (there are a few large holes mended with tin cans), we will have a little more holy silence. I was afraid the children would feel that St. Joseph had let them down. I myself was much pleased with the car. But the children were delighted and insisted on calling it their station wagon. I had no sooner arrived boastingly in my new conveyance when Tom Sullivan informed me that another friend had given a 1924 Columbia which was in much better shape all around — upholstery, engine, tires, general appearance, etc. To think of it — a car for the farm and a car to pick up stuff around New York! Both small cars that do not use too much gas. The men in the office talk of exchanging the two for a truck, but I am dead against it. These will get us there.

When I returned to the farm last Tuesday, I brought Johanna with me to recover from her measles, German measles, and chicken pox. Since she arrived she has fallen on her nose, barked her shins, had a skirmish with the dog, made friends with the bull, and helped milk the cow. Now we learn from New York that Tommy has mumps, so she just won't go home until this awful siege is past. The only thing left is whooping cough.

As I write, suppertime approaches. Helen has gone down the road to collect some promised rhubarb, Florence is mending here on the porch where I write, Peter is reading, and Charlie is tearing around inside, concocting one of his wonderful desserts. He has been serving us tender milkweed tops which taste like asparagus, and we have also had lamb's-quarter, dock weed, and dandelion greens aplenty.

Hans Tunnesen is busy working on a new floor in the unused barn, which will be a dormitory for mothers and children. (The barnyard will be made into the bull pen for the youngsters that Tim O'Brien wrote about some years ago.) We got the lumber for two hundred and seventy-five dollars, and we haven't a cent to pay for it. Brescia, the lumber man in Montgomery, is trusting us, and we told him we would have to pay in dribs and drabs, just as we could beg it. So those of you who are interested in family retreats are invited to chip in. There are six retreats scheduled for the summer months, and there will be weekends in the fall. We have already had three retreats this spring. Of course it will be during the summer months that the families will wish to come, so we could not wait for the lumber. St. Joseph was so prompt in sending the cars, we are sure he will take care of the barn floor and staircase and chimney for us.

June 20

SOME TIME ago, Douglas Hyde, one of the editors of the *London Daily Worker,* became a Catholic. In an article in the *Catholic Herald* of England, he wrote,

169

In 1943, I libeled, in the course of my work on *The Daily Worker,* a Catholic paper, *The Weekly Review,* and a number of its contributors. In preparation for an anticipated court case, which in fact was never heard, I read through the paper's files for the preceding year and studied each issue as it appeared.

I had accused it of providing a platform for Fascists at a moment when Fascist bombs were raining down on Britain. I came in time to realize that not only had I libeled it in law but also in fact.

For years my cultural interests had been in the Middle Ages. My favorite music was also pre-Purcell; in architecture my interest was in Norman and Gothic; in literature my favorites were Chaucer and Langland. We had a family joke which we made each year when holidays were discussed: "Let's go on a trip to the thirteenth century."

And these were the interests of the people behind the *Weekly Review.* I came to look forward to the days when it appeared on my desk. A natural development was that I became increasingly interested in the writings of Chesterton and Belloc. . . .

A good Communist must never permit himself to think outside his Communism. I had done so, and the consequences were bound to be fatal to my Communism.

That, as it were, is the mechanics of my introduction to Catholicism.

Not long ago at a mass meeting of the workers in a Finnish factory, when the question was asked which they would prefer, Communism or capitalism, they shouted, "Neither."

It is never too late to begin. It is never too late to turn over a new leaf. In spite of the atom bomb, the jet plane, the conflict with Russia, ten just men may still save the city.

Maybe if we keep on writing and talking, there will be other conversions like Mr. Hyde's. It was reading an article that got Father Damien his helper Brother Joseph, at Molokai. It was reading that converted St. Augustine. So we will keep on writing.

And talking, too. They always said in England that the Distributists did nothing but talk. But one needs to talk to convey ideas. St. Paul talked so much and so long that in the crowded room one young lad, sitting on the windowsill, fell out of the window and was killed like a woman down the street from us, last week. Only she was not listening to the word of God but washing windows on a Sunday morning. And it was sad that there was no St. Paul to bring her to life. Her life finished there. But we are still alive, though we live in a city of ten million, and one can scarcely call it life, and the papers every day carry news of new weapons of death.

However, we are still here. We are still marrying and having children, and having to feed them and house them and clothe them. We don't want them to grow up and say, "This city is such hell that perhaps war will be preferable. This working in a laundry, a brass factory, the kitchen of a restaurant, is hell on earth. At least war will teach me new trades, which the public school system has failed to do. This coming home at night to a four-room or a two-room tenement flat and a wife and three children with whooping cough (there are usually not more than three children in the city) is also hell." And what can be done about it? We are taught to suffer, to embrace the cross. On the other hand, St. Catherine said, "All the way to heaven is heaven, because He said, 'I am the Way.'" And He was a carpenter and wandered the roadsides of Palestine and lived in the fields and plucked the grain to eat on a Sunday as He wandered with His disciples.

~

This morning as I went to Mass my eyes stung from the fumes of the cars on Canal Street. I crossed a vacant lot, a parking lot filled with cinders and broken glass, and longed for an ailanthus tree to break the prison-gray walls and ground all around. Last night all of us from Mott Street were at a meeting at Friendship House to hear Leslie Green, Distributist, and the talk was good and stimulating so that in spite of the noise, the fumes, [and] the apathy which the city brings, I was impelled this morning to write. My son-in-law, David, has also been deluging me with pamphlets. He has one of the best libraries in the country on the subject, and deals with the books and pamphlets which discuss Distributism.

We could list perhaps fifty among our friends, and if we went through the files of our readers we could find many more who have gone to the land. These toeholds on the land have meant, however, that the young, married couples had a little stake to start with. They had, or could borrow, a bit of money to make a down payment on a farm. Their families could give them a start if it was only a few hundred dollars. (There was an ad in the *New York Times* yesterday of a farm for sale for twelve hundred dollars, three hundred down and twenty-five dollars a month.) Even with the bit of money, however, faith, vision, [and] some knowledge of farming or a craft are needed. People need to prepare themselves. Parents need to prepare their children.

On the one hand, there are already some toeholds on the land; there are those farmers already there who have the right philosophy; there is still time, since we have not as yet a socialist government or nationalization of the land. We have some government control, but not much yet. Not compared to what there may be soon.

On the other hand, there are such stories as that in the last issue of *Commonweal* about the de Giorgio strike in the long central valley of California, of fifty-eight thousand acres owned by one family, of two thousand employees, of horrible living conditions, poor wages, forced idleness, "times of repose" between crops, when machines are cared for but not men, women, and children. *The Grapes of Wrath* pattern is here, is becoming an accepted pattern. Assembly-line production in the factory and mass production on the land are part of a social order accepted by the great mass of our Catholics, priests and people [alike]. Even when they admit it is bad, they say, "What can we do?" And the result is palliatives, taking care of the wrecks of the social order, rather than changing it so that there would not be quite so many broken homes, orphaned children, delinquents, industrial accidents, so much destitution in general.

Palliatives, when what we need is a revolution, beginning now. Each one of us can help start it. It is no use talking about how bored we are with the word. Let us not be escapists but admit that it is upon us. We are going to have it imposed upon us, or we are going to make our own.

If we don't do something about it, the world may well say, "Why bring children into the world, the world being what it is?" We bring them into it and start giving them a vision of an integrated life so that they too can start fighting.

This fighting for a cause is part of the zest of life. Father Damasus said once at one of our retreats that people seemed to have lost that zest for life, that appreciation of the value of life, the gift of life. It is a fundamental thing. Helene Isvolsky, in a lecture on Dostoyevsky at the Catholic Worker House last month, said that he was marked by that love for life. He had almost been shot once. He had been lined up with other prisoners and all but lost his life. From then on he had such a love for life that it glowed forth in all his writings. It is what marks the writings of Thomas Wolfe, whose writing was a Niagara.

～

But how can one have a zest for life under such conditions as those we live in at 115 Mott Street? How can that laundry worker down the street, working in his steamy hell of a basement all day, wake each morning to a zest for life?

In the city, very often one lives in one's writing. Writing is not an overflow of life, a result of living intensely. To live in Newburgh, on the farm, to be arranging retreats, to be making bread and butter, taking care of and feeding children there, washing and carding wool, gathering herbs and salads and flowers — all these things are so good and beautiful that one does not want to take time to write except that one has to share them, and not just the knowledge of them, but how to start to achieve them.

The whole retreat movement is to teach people to "meditate in their hearts," to start to think of these things, to make a beginning, to go out and start to love God in all the little things of every day, to so make one's life and one's children's life a sample of heaven, a beginning of heaven.

The retreats are to build up a desire, a knowledge of what to desire. "Make me desire to walk in the way of Thy commandments." Daniel was a man of "desires." Our Lord is called "the desire of the everlasting hills."

Yes, we must write of these things, of the love of God and the love of His creatures, man and beast, and plant and stone.

"You make it sound too nice," my daughter once said to me, when I was writing of life on the land, and voluntary and involuntary poverty, which means in specific instances . . . doing without water, heat, washing machines, cars, electricity, and many other things, even for a time the company of our fellows, in order to make a start.

And others have made the same accusation who are making a start on the land. And I know well what they mean. One must keep on trying to do it oneself, and one must keep on trying to help others to get these ideas respected.

At Grailville, Ohio, there is not only the big school of the Grail Apostolate, where there is electricity, modern plumbing, [and] a certain amount of machinery that makes the work go easier and gives time for studies; but there is also a sample farm, twelve acres, with no electricity, no modern plumbing, no hot water, where the washing is done outside over tubs and an open fire, and yet there, too, the life is most beautiful and a foretaste of heaven. There one can see how all things show forth the glory of God, and how "All the way to heaven is heaven."

Artists and writers, as I have often said, go in for voluntary poverty in order to "live their own lives and do the work they want to do." I know many a Hollywood writer who thought he was going out there to earn enough to leave to buy a little farm and settle down and do some really good writing. But the fleshpots of Egypt held him. And I knew many a Communist who had his little place in the country, private ownership too, and not just a rented place, a vacation place.

Property is proper to man. Man is born to work by the sweat of his brow, and he needs the tools, the land to work with.

The principles of Distributism have been more or less implicit in much that we have written in *The Catholic Worker* for a long time. We have advised our readers to begin with four books, Chesterton's *What's Wrong with the World?* [and] *The Outline of Sanity,* and Belloc's *The Servile State* and *The Restoration of Property.*

These are the books which Douglas Hyde must have read, which gave him the third point of view, neither industrial capitalist nor Communist.

In a brief pamphlet by S. Sagar, made up of a collection of articles which ran in *The Weekly Review,* Distributism is described as follows:

> To live, man needs land (on which to have shelter, to cultivate food, to have a shop for his tools) and capital, which may be those tools, or seeds, or materials.

> Further, he must have some arrangement about the control of these two things. Some arrangement there must obviously be, and to make such an arrangement is one of the reasons why man forms communities. [Men being what they are, every society must make laws to govern the control of land and capital.]

> [The principle from which the law can start is] that *all* its subjects should exercise control of land and capital by means of direct family ownership of these things. This, of course, is the principle from which, until yesterday, our own law started. It was the theory of capitalism under which *all* were free to own, none compelled by law to labor. [Popular magazines like *Time* and the *Sat-*

175

urday Evening Post are filled with illustrations of these principles, which all men admit are good, but unfortunately the stories told are not true. It is the reason why great trusts like . . . Standard Oil and General Motors have public relations men, why there is a propaganda machine for big business, to convert the public to the belief that capitalism really is based on good principles, Distributist principles, really is working out for the benefit of all, so that men have homes and farms and tools and pride in the job.] Unfortunately, in practice, under capitalism the many had not opportunity of obtaining land and capital in any useful amount and were compelled by physical necessity to labor for the fortunate few who possessed these things. But the theory was all right. Distributists want to save the theory by bringing the practice in conformity with it. . . .

Distributists want to distribute control as widely as possible by means of a direct family ownership of land and capital. This, of course, means cooperation among these personal owners and involves modifications, complexities, and compromises which will be taken up later.

The aim of Distributism is family ownership of land, workshops, stores, transport, trades, professions, and so on.

Family ownership in the means of production so widely distributed as to be the mark of the economic life of the community — this is the Distributist's desire. It is also the world's desire. . . . The vast majority of men who argue against Distributism do so not on the grounds that it is undesirable but on the grounds that it is impossible. We say that it must be attempted, and we must continue to emphasize the results of not attempting it.

❧

The Catholic Worker farm at Newburgh has ninety-six acres. We are raising hay, corn, vegetables, pigs, chickens, a cow. Every few days the dog, King, has brought in woodchucks, and some of them weigh eight pounds. He must have caught fifty this year. Down at the docks on the Hudson River the Negroes fish without a license for fish and eels. It is woodchuck season, and you can eat the wood-chucks now. You skin them as you do rabbits, and roasted with sage dressing they make a good meal, and they are cleaner than chicken or hog. Right now Carmela and Florence are sitting out under the crab apple tree, stringing beans. There are peas and broccoli and Swiss chard besides lettuce for salads. It is getting easier to feed the forty or so retreatants who come every few weeks to the farm, and the twenty who are here all summer.

I tell these things to make the mouth water. In the fall we are go-ing to put in a field of wheat, and next summer, God willing, we will have our own flour for the good whole-wheat loaves that come out of the oven every day.

For the average worker it is more and more difficult to get food. Butter, oleo, and fat are sky high. Meat costs a fortune. Food prices have gone up 133 percent and milk 85 percent. We saw these figures in a magazine recently to advertise milk as a food. How to live, how to feed a family! Most of all, how to find shelter!

We are not expecting utopia here on this earth. But God meant things to be much easier than we have made them. A man has a natural right to food, clothing, and shelter. A certain amount of goods is neces-sary to lead a good life. A family needs work as well as bread. Property is proper to man. We must keep repeating these things. Eternal life begins now. "All the way to heaven is heaven, because He said, 'I am the Way.'" The cross is there, of course, but "in the cross is joy of spirit." And love makes all things easy. If we are putting off the old man and putting on Christ, then we are walking in love, and love is what we all want. But it is hard to love, from the human standpoint and from the divine stand-point, in a two-room apartment. We are eminently practical, realistic.

~

Irene has charge of the clothes distribution at Mott Street (besides having charge of the women's house and writing for the paper and seeing visitors), and the other day a mother of eleven children, nine of them living, came in to get clothes. They are all living at the municipal lodging house on Third Street. The other afternoon when the rain had stopped, Irene and I walked down Mott Street to Bleecker where Mott Street ends, then over to the Bowery and up one block to Third Street, and there, just to the east of the Bowery, is the big building that used to be the Bowery Y.M.C.A. and which is now a municipal shelter.

I was familiar with the place because it used to have a "clean-up system" before the days of D.D.T. (which you can use like a talcum powder), and there once in a while I used to bring my old friend Mr. Breen. He was a very dignified old man, with a beautiful beard, and he walked with a cane. He looked like Chief Justice Hughes. He had worked as Sunday editor of the *Washington Post,* and he had worked for the *New York World,* written reviews for the *Commonweal,* poetry for us, and had assisted us, during his last years, in answering our large correspondence. His wife and children had died, he had fallen into bad times, and during the Depression we became his family. For a time he had slept in the world's largest bedroom, on a dock down at South Ferry, where the municipality put up about twelve hundred men every night. He used to tell us a story of one old man who evidently thought he was in a cathedral, so vast was the long, dim dock at night, and in his nightshirt, with his long sticks of legs making him look like a strange bird, he used to "make the stations" down the inner aisle between the double-decker beds, pausing at every seventh bed to pray.

Mr. Breen had many such stories of the poor. We had to take him, as I said before, to the Bowery Y for a clean-up every now and then. One could bathe at leisure, have one's clothes cleaned and pressed, and have a shave and a haircut — all for seventy-five cents. We used to go in state in a taxi cab. It was very hard to get Mr. Breen to go, and he would only go with me. As we went up to the desk and the very courteous young man behind it, Mr. Breen would look at him haughtily and say in lordly fashion, "I have come to be deloused." Then he would turn to me with a sweeping bow, thank me for my escort, and I would leave him there for the night.

Now this building is part of the municipal lodging house. On either side of the entrance hall there are beautiful rural scenes painted on the walls, a road through the woods, a country field, and around the tiled halls, children from one year old and up are playing, slipping in and out between the hordes of young and old, black and white, drunk and sober men who are also served, who also are "clients" getting their lodging for the night and several meals a day. The men were registering at the desk as we came in. They all could write their names on the ledger; they were all literate. After they registered, they were all taken upstairs to the dormitories to bed. It was five-thirty. No one was taken in after nine.

Downstairs, meals were still being served. They had soup or stew, as we could see from the windows outside, two slices of bread, and huge mugs of cocoa.

I don't know how many thousands of men are served every day, are lodged every day. What was occupying our minds was the fact that forty-five families were lodged there too, with six, eight, nine children. The mothers sat around, the fathers came in to report the result of their day's search for rooms. (And who wants families of four children even, let alone nine?) The children restlessly ran from end to end of the hall, and we tried to talk.

"Isn't there a playroom?" Yes, but the colored, the Puerto Rican, the Italian, and the "American" children fought. It was nerve-racking. There were separate bedrooms for different members of the family; it was not overcrowded. There is a doctor for the women and children. The city was doing what it could. Up at 26th Street, another branch of the municipal lodging house, there were other families and more men. What they were trying to do was bring all the men down to Third Street and get the women and children away from the Bowery and up to 26th Street, where there was a playground, a dead-end street, the river, and more light and air.

❧

Yesterday two Irish Christian Brothers came to call and told us of Harlem, where their order had a school in what was the largest parish in the world. There were thirty thousand people in it, it was esti-

179

mated. Families fleeing the hunger of Puerto Rico were living three families to an apartment. It was the most congested, most neglected section of the city. With all these thousands, the church on Sunday was only half full. It is not a leakage from the Church; it is a landslide.

We have been working on these problems at the Catholic Worker for the past fifteen years, and we can say with all sincerity that things have never been so bad as they are now, even in the worst of [the] Depression. Now men may have work, but they lack homes. There may be odd jobs, poorly paid jobs, something coming in the way of work, but the housing situation gets worse and worse. Everywhere it is the same. In every city and town the story is the same. There are no apartments; there are no houses.

Mr. O'Daniel, father of the eleven we were visiting, had had a job as janitor. In order to make their profits and avoid the penalties of rent gouging, the owners of the building he was in had transformed a twelve-apartment house into a twenty-four apartment house of two-and-a-half rooms each. The board of health got after the owner for having a large family of children in the basement, and he had let them go. No one wants to employ families; none want to rent to families.

And of course we can understand the homeowners' point of view. Once we saw a cartoon in the *Saturday Evening Post* of a mother rebuking her child. "Don't deface the wall, William. We *own* this house." In other words, what you own is taken care of. Property means responsibility. Property is proper to man.

But what a need there is to arouse the conscience! To call attention to the poor! "Are there any more poor?" This fatuous question has been asked me so often by well-meaning listeners at meetings that one must answer it. "What about the bricklayer and his huge wages? Never have wages been so high." And what do high wages mean when there is no just price? Anyway, with all the talk of high wages, most of the people around here that I know are working for thirty and thirty-five dollars a week. Also, the great white-collar class of young men and young women are getting along by living at home, profiting by the industry and thrift and better housing opportunity of their parents.

People sooner or later will have to admit that things are rapidly getting worse, not better. People said during the war that Hitler had the theory that the bigger the lie, the easier it was to get people to believe it. It seems to me we have quite a number of these big lies.

There is the lie of high wages.
There is the lie of widespread ownership.
There is the plentiful production lie.
There is the everyone-consuming-more lie.

S. Sagar says that the great danger of today is not a revolt of the proletariat but the lethargy of the proletariat. He also says that the "preliminary to any steps taken towards Distribution was the creation of the *will* to take them."

Here is one quotation from Pope Pius XII which ought to be considered a mandate along these lines:

We confirm what only recently we had occasion to expound. For Catholics, the only path to be followed in solving the social problem is clearly outlined in the doctrine of the Church. The blessing of God will descend on your work if you do not swerve in the slightest degree from this path. You have no need to think up specious solutions or to work with facile and empty formulas for results that prove only a delusion. What you can and ought to strive for is a more just distribution of wealth. This is and this remains a central point in Catholic social doctrine.

Joseph T. Nolan writes in *Orate Fratres,*

Too long has idle talk made out Distributism as something medieval and myopic, as if four modern Popes were somehow talking nonsense when they said: The law should favor widespread ownership (Leo XII); wages should enable a man to purchase land (Leo XIII and Pius XI); the family is most perfect when rooted in its own holding (Pius XII); and the tiller of the soil still represents the natural order of things willed by God (Pius XII). . . .

181

But in general there is so little facing of the problem of the land, or of machinery, which the Franciscan Belliot called one of the gravest and most disquieting elements in the social problem. How many Catholics, especially liturgists, share the anxiety of the present Pope at the agglomeration of huge populations in the cities "and the diminution of modern man by the domination of the machine"? Neither the nihilists nor the optimists who still dream of abundant production can fill our present need; a lot closer are the realists who are willing to rebuild an organic Christian society from the ground up, from the soil, who might escape the very real prospects of unemployment, hunger, and despair.

There are numerous steps that can be taken, outlined in *The Restoration of Property* by Hilaire Belloc. But how to create in men a *desire* to take them, a hope that they will be able to take them?

Things have gotten so desperate, Mr. Sagar says, goods have gotten so scarce, the effort to find housing has become so heartbreaking, that now at last today, after these many years, Distributism is going to be discussed.

The alternatives are not capitalism or socialism. We must take into consideration the nature of man and his needs, not just cash [for] commodities, food, and clothing, but a home, a bit of land, and the tools with which to work, part ownership in workshops and stores and factories.

Distributism does not mean that everyone must be a farmer. The Distributist thinks in terms of the village economy, and as for the size of the CITY (the city of God) which Cardinal Suhard talks of our building, that is a matter of situation. It may be five hundred, it may be five thousand, it may be fifty thousand population. The main thing to do is to *distribute* the cities before the atom bomb does it. We are not suggesting that it be done by force but by education. If that seems too slow a method, probably depression, war, hunger, and homelessness will play their part. We only know it is not human to live in a city of ten million. It is not only not human, it is not possible. "Cities are the occasion of sin," Father Vincent McNabb said, and of course any theologian will say that we should flee the occasions of sin. Pope Pius XII pointed out that it was difficult for modern youth to live in the cities without heroic virtue. (And it was never intended that the good life should demand *heroic* virtue.)

Distributism does not mean that we throw out the machine. The machine, Peter Maurin used to say, should be the extension of the hand of man. If we could do away with the assembly line, the slavery of the machine, and the useless and harmful and destructive machines, we would be doing well.

In the psalms it says, "Lord, make me *desire* to walk in the way of Thy commandments." Daniel was called a man of desires, and because he was a man of desires, the Lord heard him.

Cardinal Suhard of Paris and Father de Lubac, S.J., both cry out against the refusal of some traditionalists to be co-creators with God and use the tools which science has put in man's hands. But Father de Lubac also writes (in *The Dublin Review*), "Does not the discovery of new values involve the depreciation of other, perhaps more fundamental ones? And does it not breed, even while the discovery is still modest and tentative, a kind of intoxication, so that the passionate interest it arouses tends to make men oblivious of everything else, even of essentials? And so ambiguous situations pile up, leading inevitably to crises whose outcome no one can safely prophesy."

But the essentials are food, clothing, and shelter. The essential is ownership, which brings with it responsibility, and what is more essential than the earth from which we all spring, and from which comes our food, our clothes, our furniture, our homes?

It is as a woman, a mother, speaking for the family and the home, that I protest the work of "priest-sociologists," who in their desire to help the worker are going along with him in his errors and are accepting the easy way of capitalist industrialism, which leads to collectivism and the totalitarian state.

The warning is there, [in] Isaiah 26:5-6:

He shall bring down them that dwell on high; the high city he shall lay low. He shall bring it down even unto the ground; he shall pull it down even to the dust. The foot shall tread it down; the feet of the poor, the steps of the needy.

[So] "strengthen ye the feeble hands, and confirm the weak knees. Say to the fainthearted, 'Take courage and fear not. Behold, your God will bring the bread of recompense. God Himself will come and save you.'"

July-August

JUNE AND JULY I have spent on the farm at Newburgh, where the retreats have been going on apace. There was a study week in June with Father Victor White and Father Pierre Conway, Dominicans, and then retreats with Father Taggart, Vincentian, [and] Father Fiorentino [and] Monsignor Betowski, both from the New York diocese; and Father Veale, Josephite. One of the retreats was a family retreat, though we had not expected it to be, but the long weekend of the Fourth of July was a temptation, and there were four families, one with five, two with two, and one with one child.

Hans had just finished laying the floor of the barn in time, puting up the stairs and screening it in. Michael Kovalak helped as he always does in a crisis, and Bob Campbell showed up in time to make the screens for the windows and the doors. The great difficulty of the weekend lay in the fact that a nest of swallows [was] shut in by the screen door, and it had to be left open so that the mother swallow could fly in and out with food. By the end of the weekend, both mother and father bird were teaching the young to fly. Now the screen door can be closed again.

Although the only family retreat was planned for Labor Day weekend, and we are receiving reservations for that all the time, still another family of six has asked to come for the mid-August retreat,

185

and now there is a mix-up as to whether we can have it on August 15th or whether it must be changed to the 22nd.

This has been a month of much housekeeping, extra responsibilities sent to us for care, extra people arriving we did not expect, including two extra retreats not scheduled. Among the guests were Clara Faviano, Edith Pietraniello, Anne Ricupero, and Frances Palmiotti, with their own children and some others besides, making fourteen in all. They were Celia Ricupero, Chickie Sclafani, Jimmy Deodato, Anthony Deodato, Cosmo Ricupero, Anthony and Mary Ann Pietraniello, Nicholas and Morris Palmiotti, and Frank Faviano, all from Mott Street. . . . They liked the Newburgh farm so much that they thought it would be wonderful if some of the neighbors would chip [in] together and buy an old inn which is for sale down the road. We wish they would. We could practice mutual hospitality, each taking the other's overflow, not to speak of enjoying the wonderful Italian cooking. The girls made spaghetti while they were on their Friday-to-Monday visit, and I was an appreciative guest, since in addition to taking over the new barn dormitory, they used the canning kitchen and cooked their own meals. They arrived the same weekend as Monsignor Betowski and his retreat group, but Monsignor Betowski is well used to the Catholic Worker and its friends, and joined them one evening after conference for coffee and conversation.

"Your column will not be a pilgrimage this month," one of the men on the farm says, "since you have not been off the place for two months almost." I had begun to feel not only that life was like a "night spent in an uncomfortable inn," as St. Teresa has it (and the weather has been so very hot that the group of us who sleep up under the roof have felt that our inn is indeed not what it should be in the way of comfort), but I also had begun to feel like an innkeeper. And then suddenly, on a moment's notice, I went to West Virginia for a five-day visit to my daughter and her family.

Walter Vischer and I drove down in the Chevrolet, '32, and we started off at dawn on a rainy, humid morning. Going through Montgomery and Port Jervis and over through the mining section, running south of towns such as Tamaquay and Pottsville, we hit the superhighway and traveled along it at a smooth clip of thirty-five miles an hour (the car would not make more) until we reached Fort Littleton, where we emerged, thirty miles or so from Tamar and Dave's. We had no lights on the car and went through four tunnels with fear and trembling. The first two seemed barely lit, and we stayed in back of another car. We were off the highway by three o'clock, and in another hour or so, traveling due south, we reached the Rock Gap district south of Berkeley Springs, where Tamar and Dave have their seventy-acre farm. Our only troubles had been two flat tires. Tamar was out berrying, and during the few days I was there, we picked blackberries and dewberries and ate berry short-cake and made jam. The orchard had some early apples, and the babies, Rebecca and Susannah, brought in pails of them, which we made into apple jelly, which with goat's milk cheese goes most delightfully on whole-wheat bread. When we were not doing up jams and jellies, we were down in the brook, which is deep enough to swim in, and shallow enough, with a good sand bank, for the children to play on, so it was a vacation indeed. I do not know of a happier way to spend an afternoon than sitting in a shallow brook with babies paddling happily around. There were little crawfish on the bottom, little minnows darting between your fingers as you try to catch them, boat flies on the surface, and beautiful blue dragonflies flying just above the water. There were neither mosquitoes nor flies nor gnats. The sun-warmed waters of the brook made up for all the "pail baths" we had been taking through the heat. We washed the children's clothes before we went back to the house, and we picked Indian pipes and pennyroyal as we went back through the field.

Within a radius of a mile, there are four or five farms for rent either for five or ten dollars a month. The houses can be lived in, and if one owned them (the price range is from two to three thousand), repairs could be done little by little. The ground is good bottom-land. There are streams for fishing, and there is hunting. There are pines and black walnut and locust on the gentle hills, and there is pulpwood to be cut for selling and plenty of wood for the fires in winter. Taxes are low, and there are no gas or electric bills. But, and here is the rub, the nearest town, of 1,500 inhabitants, is twelve miles away with its church and schools and hospital. The larger towns of Martinsburgh and Winchester are each about thirty miles away. But it's surprising how much company one has, how neighborly people are. And the joy for the children in such surroundings! But there is a price to pay for all this beauty, and that price a willingness to accept the poverty of the people on the land. Old houses, oil lamps, wood heat, water to be carried in pails, the tattletale gray of clothes so washed, and the quiet, the solitude of life with neither radio, newspaper, nor telephone, . . . where the daily mail becomes the event of the day.

People are more afraid of such a life than they are of the atom bomb! And so Peter talked of agronomic universities, farming communes, so that people could go in groups, and in groups hold each other up. Man is not made to live alone; he is a social being. So where there is a crowd, they flock together. Peter used to say, "They are not communitarian; they are gregarious."

Let us hope that Maryfarm at Newburgh will give a taste for the simplicity of life on the land and the courage to face it, and that other Maryfarms throughout the country will be performing the same function. A place to make retreats, to learn to meditate, to think in the heart, "to be quiet and see that I am God," a place to learn to work, and a place to go from, as apostles, and make a life for the family.

August 8

AN ACCOUNT of a day in my life, the first day of a retreat, spent in silence and prayer. I am not the author of these retreat notes, since I was taking down what I heard. Yet the priest who gave the retreat would not claim them either. He would give credit to St. Paul, to St. Thomas Aquinas, to St. John Chrysostom, St. John of the Cross, St. Francis de Sales — to any and all of the saints quoted. Or he would give credit to Father Lacouture, S.J., or Father Pacifique Roy, S.S.J., or Father John J. Hugo, secular. They all give the same retreat, having made it with the first-named priest.

The cost of our retreats (there are four or five through the summer) is what one can pay. If one is just able to pay fare, one pays nothing. Maybe a poor visitor pays two dollars, maybe five, and then someone comes along and pays a hundred, so as to include his poorer brothers. These retreat priests believe in sowing what they have — food, shelter, spiritual wealth. The Lord has to take care of things. If we get down to bread and water, well, then all the better [the] retreat. As it is, we had very good meals three times a day — so good, so enjoyable, that it was a pleasure to fast on Friday to thank our Lord.

My notes are incomplete! I am just taking bits of them here and there and using them. I had made the retreat many times before and had made copious notes.

For inexactitude in quoting, for putting the emphasis here or there (where I needed it, probably), please excuse me. I realize that it is hard to print such fragments as this without doing a grave injustice to those priests who give the conferences. But I do want just to give a taste of my retreat, as though to say to others, "Come and see that the Lord is sweet." Learn of Him and find rest for your souls.

Or as Isaiah wrote and St. John paraphrased, "All ye that have thirst of desire, come to the waters, and all ye that have no silver of your own will and desires, make haste; buy from Me and eat; come and buy from Me, wine and milk [that is, spiritual sweetness and peace] without the silver of your own will, and without giving me any labor in exchange for it, as ye give for your desires. Wherefore do you give the silver of your will for that which is not bread — that is of the Divine Spirit — and set the labor of your desires upon that which cannot satisfy you? Come, harkening to Me, and ye shall eat the good ye desire, and your soul shall delight itself in fatness."

For years, in houses of hospitality around the country, speaking and writing and working, we have been trying to change the social order. Now these last years I realize that I must go further, go deeper, and work to make those means available for people to change themselves, so that they can change the social order. In order to have a Christian social order, we must first have Christians. Father Lallemant talks about how dangerous active work is without a long preparation of prayer. Aldous Huxley quotes him at length in *Gray Eminence*.

The desert fathers had these same ideas. When times became so bad (when there was universal conscription, for instance), they retreated by the tens of thousands to the desert wastes to pray, to work, and God knows what the world would have been without them. St. Ephrem came out when there was need and started a hospice during a pestilence and retired again to pray.

First Conference

Christ is with us, though our eyes are blinded, just as He was with the disciples at Emmaus. To keep the attitude of listening! The retreat will be as successful as our silence. Silence of the whole being, all our senses, all our powers. Keep only the power of loving. Control our eyes. The eyes let in much noise, just as do the ears. We need solitude, silence of mind. The mind definitely makes a noise. Stay in the company of God. By not looking at others, as well as by not speaking to others, we keep in solitude. Renew resolutions of silence every day.

[Just before coming on this retreat, I was reading Newman's historical essays on St. Basil and St. Gregory, their friendship, their differences. St. Gregory made resolutions of silence very often, for all of Lent, for instance. Newman admired this great discipline, "at his age," too.]

Our prayer should be, "Speak Lord, for thy servant heareth." We should ask God to teach us the secrets of His love. Insist on this love with importunity. No other love is happy unless it finds its roots in this. Loving God seems to be loving nothing? But there is a definite way. We must learn the rules. There is infinite happiness waiting. Also, it will free us from the slavery of other loves. God is nothing else but love. "Where love is, there God is." All other loves pale in comparison. Our nature is not built for so strong a love, so we must change our nature. "Enlarge thou my heart, that thou mayest enter in." How can you tell if a person loves you? By their thoughts, words, and deeds. Our love is made up of our actions. There is a conformity, a union of desires, tastes, deeds. Many people want to and do make sacrifices,

190

but there is not much change in the temperature of their love for God. On this retreat we study ourselves first. Our Adam life. Everyone has that. But there is our Christ-life too. We are children of God. Grace is participation in the life of God. Human life is natural to us. Supernatural life is added unto us. We have new powers.

Second Conference

Good actions may be human or divine. There is confusion in regard to these. The only actions which lead to God are divine actions. Supernatural action has God for its end. The natural has ourselves. Action has value according to whom the action is directed. The act of eating, for instance. For our own pleasure, or to build our bodies to strengthen them to serve God (I Cor. 8). There is such great waste in our lives in just good actions. The whole burden of the retreat is to do all actions for the love of God. Divine love is as different from human love as human is from animal.

Our greatest danger is not our sins but our indifference. We must be in love with God. It is not so much to change what we are doing, but our intention, our motive. It is not sufficient that we refrain from insulting a person; we must love. This retreat is to increase our love for God. When we say that we love God with our whole heart, it means whole. We must love only God. And that sets up the triangle — God, the soul, the world.

The wife wants the husband's whole love. Suppose a husband pays no attention to his wife, and we say, "Well, he does not beat you, does he? You should be satisfied that he does not kill you. What are you complaining about?"

It is the same with God. He is not just content that we are not in a state of mortal sin. Mortal sin is the sin of the Pharisee, putting Christ to death in our hearts. Mortal sin, according to St. Thomas, is a turning from God to creatures. We must do more than avoid mortal sin. We must do more than just stay in a state of grace.

[I remember some years ago Father Hugo saying that if a mother had an imbecile child, and someone tried to comfort her by say-

191

ing, "But he has life," she would not find much comfort in that. She wants her child to grow in mind and body. If we say, "But I can get away with this or that; I can do so much and have so much, and still stay in a state of grace," our souls are like the mind of that imbecile child, with no development and no growth.]

The question comes to your mind, then: How can we love our husbands, our children, our mothers?

All other loves I have must be a sample of the love of God. All the world and everything in it must be samples of the love of God. We must love the world intensely, but not for itself. We are human beings; we do not cease to be human beings, but we are baptized human beings. At death we are going to join God with the amount of love we have gathered for Him. What we have when we die we will have for all eternity. "As the tree falleth . . ."

[Outside the chapel where we are having the conferences, the early morning mist has lifted. The hot sun shines through the haze. The birds sing; there is the hot sound of locusts in the trees.]

Two people who are deeply in love are thinking of each other all the time and what they can do for each other. So we must be with God. The love of God is more intense than any human love. Keep asking for this love.

Third Conference

Our heaven starts immediately on baptism. God is most generous in increasing graces, in increasing this heaven within us. Supernatural actions bring with them a reward, an increase. Natural actions bring a natural reward and end at the grave. We must try to amass more and more of God in our hearts. "Our hearts were made for Thee, O Lord, and find no rest until they rest in Thee." We have such a capacity for happiness that nothing here will satisfy it. "Enlarge Thou my heart, that Thou mayest enter in." If we had not heard of God, if we had not been baptized, we could go on looking for happiness here with no fault.

A farmer has a crab apple tree and engrafts a sweet apple tree on it. By baptism we have engrafted the divine on our human tree. If other branches break out, these take nourishment away from the engrafted tree. The farmer keeps lopping them off. We are children of God because we have His own divine life in us by grace. Grace life goes on into eternity. The blood tie ends at the grave. We form part with God because He has given us of His life. We must cultivate divine life, let it get all the nourishment. "Whether you eat or whether you drink, do all for the glory of God." This does not mean that we do not enjoy our spaghetti for lunch. God gives us natural happiness too, in order to help us to love Him. We do not give up spaghetti because we like it. We eat to nourish, to serve God because we love Him.

There are good actions, supernatural and natural, divine and human. There are bad actions — sin. We turn from God, from good to evil, from light to darkness, from heaven to hell. We are going to be saints in heaven to the degree that we are on earth. Natural actions are imperfect actions and lead to venial sin, which leads to mortal sin. So we are separated from God. No one sins to offend God, but to gain pleasure. Natural actions mean a slight turning from God. Sin and purely natural actions show difference in degree. When we commit a mortal sin, it is not a sudden thing. We started to move to that mortal sin a long time ago. The more we go in for purely natural actions, the more we have the tendency to sin. Fight mortal sin? Impossible. Fight venial sin? But natural actions feed tendencies which lead to venial sin, which leads to mortal sin.

[An ad in the *New York Times* some time ago: "I took God into partnership, and after that there were no stoppages, no strikes." How to bring God into business and make it pay! All this and heaven too! Tom Girdler, famous head of Republic Steel, endorses the book advertised in this way. It was in the Republic Steel strike in Chicago in 1937 that the Memorial Day massacre occurred, where twelve were shot dead and a hundred wounded.

Maybe it is since then that God is being taken into partnership by the author of this book and by Mr. Girdler. The natural motive: making the business pay. No wonder that religion is called the opiate of the people.]

The only way to get rid of sin is to get rid of the roots of sin. Going to confession to get rid of the habit of mortal sin is like lopping off the top of the rank weed. The roots remain. Fighting sin is like bailing out a boat without bothering to stop up the leak.

What causes us to commit sin? Because we do not love God. It is not one drop of cold water poured into the barrel of hot water that chills it, but it is many drops. It isn't the one hundredth day of the fast which causes a man to die of starvation, but the days of weakening. Every purely natural motive weakens us.

The battle against mortal sin is a hopeless one. We must attack roots: the natural motive. Then sin will be dried up. The Christian fights on this plane always. Our whole attitude towards the world must be changed (St. Paul). All things NEW (II Cor. 5:17). Like being in love.

Fourth Conference

Why this pull in us? This double attraction? Before the Fall, all our powers were obedient. Now they are in rebellion. They are off balance, unruly, gotten out of hand. To lead a spiritual life we must bring back that obedience. Bring back *pure* nature. Now it is weakened (Rom. 7). The law is spiritual, but I am flesh, sold under original sin. For that which I work, I understand not. For I do not that good which I will, but the evil which I hate, that I do. There is a law of the flesh. All people are essentially good. But there is that which is in them — the law of the members fighting the law of the mind, captivating them in the law of sin against the law of the spirit. Unhappy man that I am — who shall deliver me from the body of this death? The grace of God by Jesus Christ our Lord. It is by denying satisfaction to the flesh that we strengthen the spirit (Rom. 8:13). Wisdom of the flesh is death. Our Adam life and Christ life are like

194

white and black threads all tangled. Gradually and slowly we must take out of our lives all that is of self (Gal. 5:16-17). There is a double attraction. Some lives are a turmoil because people are strengthening both Adam life and the Christ life at the same time.

When we were baptized, a seed was placed in us. It tries to grow into a full-blown tree of holiness. Everyone is given that seed at baptism. It is not too late to begin cultivating this seed [to] the degree of sanctity God intends for us. The burden of the retreat is to uncover that sanctity and let it grow, to start now. The only purpose for which we were made was to become saints. What is to be done? How is it to be done? Continue asking Mary that we be taught.

[It is half-past five, just past benediction. I am sitting by the little statue of St. Anthony by the flowerbed. There are two large, fat robins and three smaller ones. There are two woodpeckers bigger still, with very long bills. There are three tiny birds so small the grass almost hides them. A chipmunk runs across the grass, and a little rabbit, scarcely bigger than the woodpecker, races across the lawn to stand posed under the flowerbed. A typical St. Anthony scene.]

Fifth Conference

What did Christ say about this principle we have been talking about? He condemns our use of the things of the world. All the things we can love outside of God are three: the world[ly] goods, body goods, soul goods. Goods of soul are friendship, love, honor, praise, glory. The goods of world and body are obvious. Every action has an end, a means and a result. He commends their use for God, He condemns their use for natural motives. St. Luke says, *Blessed are you poor; woe to you who are rich.* This is in regard to world[ly] goods.

Blessed are you who hunger now; woe to you who are filled (body goods). Goods of soul: *Blessed are you who weep; woe to you that now laugh. Blessed shall you be when men shall hate you. Woe to you when men shall bless you.* The world is the opposite of Christ. (St. Luke is more the ascetic than St. Matthew.) *Love your enemies; do good to them* that hate you. They can only hate the natural. They cannot hate the grace in you. If we practice these things, then people say we are crazy. Fine. We are then fools for Christ. Then, perhaps, they will leave us alone. People in love wish to be alone, anyway. So God lets these things happen so that we can be alone. *If anyone takes thy goods, ask them not again. If you love them that love you — sinners also do this. Do good, hoping for nothing thereby.*

There are so few saints because they will not act like this (Matt. 6). Justice is good, but if we are rewarded by men, we have then received our reward. The majority of Catholic lives are made up of good actions for natural motives. *"I did this or that for them, and they did not say thanks."* When this happens, be happy. God will give you thanks. If you are disturbed, it shows the natural motive. So many good actions wasted.

[Outside the sun has set; the trees are breathing coolness. Such quiet. Only the locusts again.]

Results? Are we to be as perfect as St. Francis, as St. John, as St. Peter? No, we are expected to be perfect "as our heavenly Father is perfect." Because God wants it. We must aim high because He says so. Lay up [for] yourselves treasures in heaven. What do you think about all day? Worldly things? There is your heart. Are you concerned about health, bodily goods? There your heart is. If one falls in love, all the habits of life are ruled by that love — letters, telephone calls, whatever we do.

Suppose, on getting married, a woman says, *"Are you sure you can supply me with clothes, with food?"* We are in love with God; we will have what we need. "Behold the birds of the air: they neither sow, nor reap, nor gather into barns."

God is a sensitive lover. God will not force you to choose Him. It is an insult to God to worry so about the things of the world.

[Right now, today, as I sit here at this conference, the five-hundred-dollar payment on the mortgage is due at Maryfarm. I haven't the slightest idea how it has been gotten together and paid. For I am sure that it has. If by any chance it is not paid, then that, too, is His will. And we will all take it, whatever happens.

The conferences for the day are over. It is dusk, and a most delightful coolness in the air. We have just finished singing the Salve Regina, and it is almost time to prepare for bed.

Thank God there are such oases as these where one can gather strength and fortitude for the combat, the strong conflict which goes on in one's own soul.

It gets dark as I sit here, and the fireflies add wonderful effects to the flowerbeds. The birds of the air, the flowers of the field — was ever Solomon in all his glory arrayed as one of these?]

These notes are so brief, so abbreviated, jotted down so swiftly. After I make a retreat like this, I carry them around in a little five-cent notebook which can fit into my purse, and I read them over on the subway, while waiting for a telephone message, a bus, or for the lunch bell to ring. There are so many of those brief moments of waiting in our lives. It is wonderful how sweet these notes are to the heart, though often while one is taking them down they seem like commonplaces. But when they are read over again, they have a distilled sweetness. It seems to be God speaking.

One time I was traveling and far from home and lonely, and I awoke in the night almost on the verge of weeping with a sense of futility, of being unloved and unwanted. And suddenly the thought came to me of my importance as a daughter of God, daughter of a King, and I felt a sureness of God's love and at the same time a conviction that one of the greatest injustices, if one can put it that way, which one can do to God is to distrust His love, not realize His love. God so loved me that He gave His only begotten son. "If a mother will forget her children, never will I forget thee." Such tenderness. And with such complete ingratitude we forget the Father and His love!

This morning between conferences I wept, partly for joy and partly for the misery of life, partly at being so overwhelmed with demands made upon me, and partly with fatigue and nerves. It is always a few days before I really settle down in peace and quiet to a retreat. The first day is a delight, but the second is hard. [By] the third I am well into it and beginning to feel firm and sure of the way in which I shall go the coming year.

My troubles are still with me for the first few days. For instance, during the second conference, one of the "friends of the family" came in, stood up in back for a while, sat down, got up again, sat down again. Again at rosary the chapel was crowded, so he, together with half-a-dozen others, had to kneel in the conference room. He chose a huge overstuffed chair to kneel before and, bending over it, buried his face in the depths of the upholstery. It was a heavy August day. These little things would not bother me except that from that same person as well as from a number of others there is a long history of years of such behavior, appealing for attention, coming to bang on my door at midnight, demanding attention, asking to be allowed to go to the farm, demanding it, claiming that I, by the very things I write, must care for them, support them. And the burden gets too heavy; there are too many of them; my love is too small; I even feel with terror, "I have no love in my heart; I have nothing to give them." And yet I have to pretend I have.

But strange and wonderful, the make-believe becomes true. If you will to love someone, you soon do. You will to love this cranky old man, and someday you do. It depends on how hard you try.

My mother was not a Catholic, and how much she had been deprived of back in the time of Henry VIII, when all the bishops but one went wrong! She did not understand this idea of "willing to love"; she knew only feeling. A friend of ours, a Catholic who had made a bad marriage, was living what my mother considered a lie because she still acted as though she respected and loved her husband, still treated him as though he were the head of the house, her friend and companion. "How can she love him?" my mother used to say impatiently. "And she should not act as if she does!"

I used to try to explain that she was a Catholic wife — that on receiving the sacrament, they were "one flesh," and how could she hate her own flesh? She had promised to love and cherish him in sickness and health, for better, for worse, for richer, for poorer, till death did them part.

"It's a good thing something will release her," my mother would add tartly, as though she did not see the point.

Such beautiful words, those of the marriage — no one can bear to give them up even if they do not believe them anymore. Of all the charges made against the Communists these days of congressional investigations, the charge of loose morals is seldom heard, so very loose have become those of *Christian* people.

Recently I have been reading *The Meaning of Love* by Solovyov, and he refuses to accept the idea, so universally accepted, that love is an illusion, a lure, succumbed to so that the purpose of procreation is fulfilled, and then vanishing. Father Farina, in his retreats at Oakmont, used to emphasize the stages love must pass through — all love, whether love of friend, spouse, child, work, or a book one is writing: infatuation, indifference, repugnance, irritation, even hatred itself. I cannot remember the exact order, but all loves, even the love of God, must be purified by being tested, by going through the Garden of Gethsemane, through the Passion, and at whatever stage we stop, we must start again, go over it again, go through it, or rather meet the same situations and perhaps next time with greater courage.

I say I have no love to give, and yet I have to pretend I have. There is a woefully crippled young man who comes into the office, always clean and dapper, well spoiled by his mother and sisters. He is given everything that a small child is given: candy, cigarettes, movies, chewing gum, and he is insatiable for all these things; but of course he wants more. An uncle owns a farm, both the mother and the sisters work, yet he wishes to live with us, live with us on *our* farm; and of course there is no question of payment for board. No, are we not running a hospice, a retreat house, on a farm? Are we not supposed to be taking care of the poor? And is he not one of the poor? Poor in spiritual and mental and physical resources, it is true. So why do I worry about "being taken advantage of"? That is the attitude of the world, of those who give to us to give to others. "You are contributing to people's delinquency. You are taking care of those who do not need to be taken care of. We will not help you any longer to take care of such as he."

Of course I can go and ask his mother to pay something towards his board. If he were living at home, it would cost her to feed him. If she refuses to pay, to make a contribution, am I still to refuse him, when we have such richness — Holy Mass every morning, a priest living with us, a way of life and instruction? We talk about our poverty, and we are indeed poor in money, but we have a house, a farm, a library, music, comfortable, clean beds, health of mind and body, and also a capacity to enjoy. Of course we share these things. The farm has come to us both in contributions and in our own hard work. The men work from morning until night with no pay. They ask with humility, not as of their right, for such things as underwear, shoes, tobacco to roll their cigarettes. They are working men who originally came to us for help, and they stayed to help us, year after year, serving a Cause, [doing] carpentering, plumbing, electrical work, farming, and cooking. And are they to work for such as this whining, spoiled cripple? they ask. His very crippled state should make him an object of our pity and our love. Mental cases, mental illness, and physical illnesses, as well as poverty, are calls upon our compassion, because we must see Christ in them, but it is so hard to see Christ in anyone who is whining, resentful, self-indulgent, demanding, hating! "The venom of asps is under their lips." I have often thought of this verse from the psalms. And how to love these, how to see Christ in them!

There are two women at this moment, as there have been many more through the year, who accept for months our ministrations, our help and lovingkindness, only to turn and rend us. Lies, scandal, accusations roll from their lips in a torrent and a flood of poison.

Last week a woman came in with a policeman. She was a very difficult alcoholic whom Irene, who has charge of the women's house, had tried to help for the past six months. Over and over again she had cleaned Ann up, had tried to get her on her feet, had helped her to jobs, had forgiven her seventy times seven rather than put her out on the streets. The last time she was drunk, she had lost ten dollars in the house and we found it. Tom has charge of the money of the house, and it was turned over to him and used for "flop money" for others, for beans for the soup, or whatnot. When she next came in, sober, with a job, and asked for her money, we told her that we had found it but used it. We live often from day to day, so there was nothing at that moment in the house to give her. We did not say that she owed us far more for her six months' stay with us. And now here she was, coming in threateningly with a policeman, demanding we give her the ten dollars.

"Give her your cloak, too," Bob said.

How to love! How to turn the other cheek, how to give your cloak and your trousers and your shoes, and then when you are left naked, you are beaten and reviled besides.

"You never get a lick amiss," my mother used to say wisely, and I suppose it is true. But sometimes the blows come too thick and heavy. From morning till night they seem to be descending. Just before the retreat, another woman, mother of a small child who had been with us several years, pulled a terrible scene, drew a knife on one of our Italian neighbors, and there was screaming, hair-pulling, one woman . . . stripped half-naked. A mob of the neighbors gathered, the police came, and the riot not only happened once but was repeated again during the day. And with the neighbors standing guard so that the woman did not return, the end of the day saw us with one less woman in the hospice, the woman . . . evicted who had long been troubling us, abusing us, stealing from us, even inflicting violence upon us in her rages.

There was a sense of relief that she was gone, that she had met her match, that a difficult situation had been handled, but not by us — that she had been gotten rid of. But where has she gone? She is one of our many failures.

The same at the farm. A young prostitute with amnesia, so she told the police, had been picked up at four in the morning, wandering in the streets of a small town along the Hudson. She was kept in the hospital for two weeks, and then a priest and a welfare worker tried to find a place for her. None would take her. The House of the Good Shepherd refused unless the court would commit her. The court refused to commit her. No convent, no hospital, no charitable family in the parish would have her. (And one could scarcely wonder, since she would seduce any man she came in contact with, if she had her way, and she had a different tale each day of the week in her bid for sympathy.)

So she was brought to us, though over our protests. She came in

201

drunk, early hours in the morning. She begged and stole from our visitors. She lied and got much sympathy. She was taken to a job by the welfare worker and ran away from that, and now we do not know where she is. Another one of our failures. She was kicked around until she got lost. That is probably the history of her life, or perhaps I am overly pitiful, overly compassionate. I cannot get over the feeling that if we loved enough, if we were patient enough, if we were saintly enough, if we prayed enough, we would move hearts, effect conversions, and would save the lost, in other words.

Failures. It is these things that overwhelm one. Physical sickness like epilepsy, senility, insanity, drug cases, alcoholics; and just the plain, ordinary poor who can't get along, can't find a place to live, who need clothes, shelter, food, jobs, care, and most of all love — these are the daily encounters.

So it is wonderful that this retreat comes in the middle of summer, when one can stop and think in his heart about these things. I have made this retreat eight times, and always there is something new, always there is something to learn about how to progress in the love of God and one's neighbor. How can we ever give up thinking and longing for love, talking of it, preparing ourselves for it, reading of it, studying about it? It is really a great faith in love that never dies. We hope against hope, as Abraham did in the promise, and we know with something that bears witness in us that this love is true, and that the promise is there.

I am speaking of heavenly things, but heaven and earth are linked together as the body and soul are linked together. We begin to live again each morning. We rise from the dead, the sun rises, spring comes around — there is always that cycle of birth and growth and death, and then resurrection. And the great study of how truly to become the sons of God, to be made like God, to participate in the life of God — this is the study of the retreat. It is a painful study, and one can make it over and over again, and always we need to straighten our course, adjust ourselves to this upside-down way of looking at things, which is the Christian way and which seems so often to be not common sense, not natural. It is breathing rarefied air; one must get used to this air of the mountains, so clear, cold, sharp, and fresh. It is like wine, and we have prayed to Mary and said, "We have no wine," and she has given us wine, the body and blood of her Son, the life of her Son, the love of her Son.

About these two books which I have come across recently, *The Mind and Heart of Love* by Father D'Arcy, the English Jesuit, and *The Meaning of Love* by Vladimir Solovyov, the Russian theologian of the last century, called the systematizer of Dostoyevsky's thought. I have always found Dostoyevsky's message for me was love and compassion, so I was much interested in this book, *The Meaning of Love*.

My whole life so far, my whole experience has been that our failure has been not to love enough. This conviction brought me to a rejection of the radical movement after my early membership in the Socialist Party, the Industrial Workers of the World, and the Communist affiliates I worked with. "Youth demands the heroic," as Claudel said, so the work of these militant minorities had appealed to me. One could not read such books as Sinclair's *The Jungle* and not want to do something, join with someone to do something about it. And who else was doing anything? Employers, landlords, political bosses, all professed Christians, were corrupt and rotten to the core, I felt. What was there to love in them? Certainly it seemed madness to think of reforming them, converting them. Such an Augean stable was beyond cleaning up; it needed flushing out. So I reasoned. Youth certainly is always looking for a "strong conflict."

It was not that I was ever disillusioned. My conviction that there was a work to be done never wavered. Things did not need to be as bad as they were. There was a possibility of change.

Certainly, too, there was always an inward conviction that we were but dust. Alone by ourselves, we could do nothing. Probably all my early religiousness as a child was still with me, and that religiousness included a conviction of sin, of the depravity that was in us all. The argument of conscience was always there. I was "bad" or I was "good." I was bad when I hated and quarreled with my brothers and sisters, when I stole from a neighbor's garden, when I was impure (and I felt that "dark fascination" of sex, of the physical forces in my own body, very early).

This reminds me of St. Augustine's *Confessions* and his story of childhood wickedness, stealing for the sake of stealing, deliberately giving way to evil, to the dark forces within one. *The Turn of the Screw* is a story of childish evil. Jesus Christ knew what was in man. I was not baptized until I was twelve, but I had a conscience. I knew what was in man too. But I had too a tremendous faith in man as a temple of the Holy Ghost, in man made [in] the image and likeness of God, a little less than the angels. Truly I did not want to know good and evil. I wanted to know, to believe only the good. I wanted to believe that man could right wrongs, could tilt the lance, could love and espouse the cause of his brother because "an injury to one was an injury to all." I never liked the appeal to enlightened self-interest. I wanted to love my fellows; I loved the poor with compassion. I could not be happy unless I shared poverty, lived as they did, suffered as they did.

Well, now at fifty, I cannot say that I have been disillusioned. But I cannot say either that I yet share the poverty and the suffering of the poor. No matter how much I may live in a slum, I can never be poor as the mother of three, six, ten children is poor (or rich either). I can never give up enough. I have always to struggle against self. I am not disillusioned with myself either. I know my talents and abilities as well as failures. But I have done woefully little. I am fifty, and more than half of my adult life is past. Who knows how much time is left after fifty? Newman says the tragedy is never to have begun.

I have been disillusioned, however, this long, long time in the means used by *any* but the saints to live in this world God has made for us. The use of force, the use of diplomacy in foreign affairs, the use of anything but the weapons of the spirit seems to me madness. Especially now since the atom bomb. This means the weapons used by either Communist or Christian, who today seem to me in both political [and] economic life to be Marxist also. The Communist believes in force, in espionage; so do the press and the pulpit of the Christian churches.

The Communist does not believe in God; he does not see Christ in his neighbor. Nor do we in the poor, the lame, the halt, the blind, the prodigal, the sinner, the harlot; nor in those of another race — the Filipino, the Japanese, the Chinese, the Mexican, the Negro. (It is only *atheistic* communism that is condemned by the Pope, we should remember.)

We too have done away with property, the land, the ownership of small shop and business, with our monopolies and trusts, chain stores, hotels, gas stations, everything on a colossal scale, wiping out the dignity of man, who has hands and needs to use them, who has a body and needs shelter, food, and clothing, who needs to live in dignity with his children and enjoy the abundant life.

What should really set us apart from all other men is our love. "See how they love one another." In the Bible which is still, after all, the Book for all who have faith, the relationship between God and man is described as that between animal and master (the Good Shepherd), between servant and lord, between child and father, and between husband and wife. Right now, by our baptism we have been made sons of God. But who does not aspire to the joys of marriage, that love which makes all things new? Who does not long to dissolve and be with Christ? The pleasures of the beatific union are described as those of a wedding banquet or an embrace. "He will overshadow me with his shoulders." "He will kiss me with the kisses of his mouth."

And strange and wonderful to think of, we should have something like this love for all creatures — for mate, for friend, for child, for enemy too — the kind of love that makes all things new. For God first. "My heart and my flesh cry out for the living God." The love of the will, the memory, the understanding, and the love of the flesh. The tenderness of a mother for her child, the physical love and joy she feels in caressing it, contemplating it, nourishing it at the "breasts of her tenderness." "If a mother forgets her child, never will I forget you, O Jerusalem." "If a son ask of his father bread, will he give him a stone?"

How much there is to learn of love, that feeling of the body and soul, that teaches us what God is, that He is love.

I suppose one reason why people know so little of love is that the attitude has been that love is implanted in the human breast to facilitate the job of bringing children into the world and bringing them up.

"What a terrible force this is," I said to my daughter once, "this love of children, of grandchildren. And it is just as strong for the grandchildren as for the children." I had thought that such joys were finished for me. And such pains too, since all love means suffering, the sufferings of parting, separation, and loss; and of course the suffering because all relationships are not as they ought to be — we never can get enough of the other person. You love your own so much that you want to be one with them, live their life, be inside their skins, as it were.

My daughter answered me that the instinct, the love *had* to be strong, so great was the struggle sometimes, what with illness or refractoriness.

So many mothers run away from their children or put them in nurseries or go out to work because they can't stand the "pruning," the cutting, the suffering that such love entails. The more exuberant the growth, the more vigorous the cutting. And yet of course we should love all other children with something of this love, this aching longing to cherish and protect and save them from physical and moral dangers.

"Love can die," people say about marital love. "It is sentimental to think of it as enduring. Once the work of procreation is done, the glamour, the freshness, the alluring charm of love is gone. It is an illusion."

People want the ending "happy forever after." They desire it as they desire God, but they will not journey like Pilgrim towards it. They are children and will not grow.

There is much to be thought and studied about love. The marriage act, for instance, as a sacrament for the mutual sanctifying of husband and wife. It is not the promises that make the marriage. The vows are exchanged at the altar; the marriage is the embrace itself. "I've heard it called many things," a seaman said to me once, "but not a sacrament."

For a husband to withdraw from his wife or a wife from her husband on the ground that they wish to be detached is false piety. Such a withdrawal should be by mutual consent, for the sake of seeking a still higher path. The marriage act is a sacrament. It is also a "debt" which each party owes the other, St. Paul says. Love is an exchange of gifts, St. Ignatius said. To fast, to abstain from the marriage embrace (by mutual consent) is certainly for the health of that love too, just as fasting from food can be for the health of the body. It is a way to increase it also.

September

TO GO on picket lines to protest discrimination in housing, to protest the draft, is one of the works of mercy, which include "rebuking
the sinner, enlightening the ignorant, counseling the doubtful." But
I confess I always do these things with fear and trembling. I loathe
the use of force, and I remember how Peter used to react to violence.
On one occasion when two men fought in the office over on Charles
Street, he threatened to leave the work forever if it ever happened
again. In a collection by Federov, . . . *Russian Spirituality,* there is the
story of St. Sergius, who left his monastery for two years rather than
impose his authority by force. On another occasion years ago at the
Easton farm, one man knocked down another over a dispute about
an egg (it is horrible to think of people fighting physically over
food), and for the rest of the summer Peter ate neither eggs nor milk
in order that others might have more. That was his idea of justice.

On a picket line there is always the threat of violence. A picket
line may be called the use of force, compelling others to hear your
point of view through the medium of the poster and the placard,
but I prefer to list it as a work of mercy.

Picket lines are too often associated with violence, and it is true
that as in Boston, an opposing party may suddenly spring in among
you, wrest the signs from your hands, and by the use of force, induce

others to use force. The very effort to hold on to signs, to resist being choked to death when the sign hangs around your neck, gives the appearance of participation in violence, and the police enter in then and contribute their share. From a peaceful, orderly demonstration I have seen a picket line become in one second a rioting mob. There is always the feel of it in the air, the threat of it. There is always the passerby who contributes his share — "Why don't you get in there and rough 'em up!" — to the crowd gathered on the other side of the street watching for trouble. And of course we were all accused of being Communists and socialists.

But the picket line went on, and the papers were distributed for three hours, through the hot noonday, and there was no trouble, nor has there been since in New York. In Boston and Philadelphia there has been evidence of the mob spirit on picket lines, but only at a few meetings in New York was there threat of trouble.

The picketing will continue every week until all the registration is complete.

At the farm we had just finished a retreat, and there was much work of cleaning up after one and getting ready for the Labor Day retreat for families. We have a permanent summer staff of a score or more, and expect an influx of another fifty over the weekend, so we are using a neighboring farm to help house the older boys.

During the spring we planned only one retreat a month for the next six months, and then, as things worked out, other groups found their way in, and one cannot refuse the emergency calls made on us. In this way there were a number of extra retreats and weekends this summer which we had not counted on at all. There were a dozen young Puerto Ricans, for instance, who came up with Joe Gil one weekend, and they brought goatskins, which they stretched over drums and made into tom-toms. And they caught snakes and skinned them and cured the skins and made bracelets. There were three conferences a day and hearty eating and swimming, and two seminarians and a priest had their hands full answering questions.

And then there are what Hans Tunnesen calls "proyects," and they certainly are coming on apace what with extra help like George Collins from Pittsburgh, Ed Gibson from the Catholic University, Joe Sweeney, Bob Campbell, and others. The root cellar was dug over two summers, right through rock and shale, and during this last month they cemented up the side walls and cut down oaks in the woods which John Filliger snaked in with the tractor and worked into place. (He is getting to love that tractor as he does his horses.) It is such a foundation as the Empire State building might rest on, we all say, and though we will cover it over with tons of rock and dirt this year, it stands there, a completed foundation for a future house. The potatoes are coming in, and turnips and beets and enormous carrots, and string beans and salads and tomatoes, and now the cannery is underway, and Dave Mason and Joe Carter are busy in that from morning till night.

September 10
Stottler's Crossroads

AFTER A MONTH of drought, rain has come, and I arrived at Dave's and Tamar's between heavy thundershowers that settled down to an all-night and all-day downpour. It is too late to do the garden any good. It is all burned up now, and there is nothing left to can. The early crops were good, however. The best milk goat died in the middle of the heat wave, and now there is only one giving a couple of quarts of milk, and three kids. Tamar nurses the baby, drinks a quart of the goat's milk herself, and the other two children and David have the remaining quart and additional canned or powdered milk. One of our visitors at the Catholic Worker this summer was a woman who has run a dairy farm for years. She says that the time is coming soon when everyone will be using powdered milk, the costs of shipping fresh milk have become so high.

Expenses are not great down here. The farm, which cost twelve hundred dollars, is all paid for. There is no gas, no electric, no water bill. Taxes are very low and spaced out over the year, the poll tax coming in April, personal property tax in October, real estate tax (three dollars) some other month. They don't know what the buildings are taxed for yet. No money goes out for ice. The children and Tamar go barefoot all summer. She makes all their clothes. The one expense is food, and they certainly eat very simply. The lunch today was fishcakes made from a fifteen-cent can of sardines mixed with whole-wheat breadcrumbs, homegrown tomatoes and beans, boiled barley, and applesauce for dessert. For supper, Spanish rice, using the leftover beans and tomatoes.

David is working in the tomato cannery a mile down the road, and his wage is sixty cents an hour. The women make more on piece-work, some of them getting ten dollars a day. They started today at eight, and Dave did not get home until six, but he worked only five hours, as the machinery was always breaking down.

Mrs. Fearnow, our sixty-seven-year-old neighbor, works every day, standing on her feet at the job, and her grandson Willard too. A married woman with a two-year-old boy was there, and while she was working he was tied in a stroller all the day. The canning season is at its height now and will last until frost. Last year frost came October first. People who work in the canneries sell their tomatoes there, too, so they take some days off to pick them. The cannery owner also has a store, and he would like always to do business by barter, his customers bringing him their cash crop and eggs and he giving them gasoline and dry goods, hardware and staples. He does not have much in the way of foodstuffs, only what people can't raise. People make sort of a holiday out of the cannery season — a change of work, a getting away from the farm for a while, visiting with others.

The Fearnows are picking tomatoes Monday, and Dave will help them. There is much working together, the boys helping on our place to get the hay in, and each helping the other with the wood.

Roy, the fourteen-year-old grandson, has had to go back to school, but he can work after school and do the chores besides. Becky has a great admiration for him and imitates his way of speech and his deepening voice. Already at three, she has a West Virginia accent.

It is so wonderful to have these weeklong visits every few months, to see how the children are growing and learning. Six weeks ago when I was here, they were having such a good time out of doors that they didn't want cuddling, but this time, what with the rain, they were only too anxious to sit on my lap and rock and be read to and sung to. We had "All ye works of the Lord," of course, and included the fifty new chickens, the young goats, all the neighbors they have become better acquainted with, as well as all the relations. We said our morning prayers, a Hail Mary and a Morning Offering, and they were very good about grace at meals.

Toward late afternoon the weather cleared, and we got a few lines of wash out and a few more tubs-full put to soak. Tamar got some weaving done — she is making rag rugs to sell — and baked a cake, besides driving to and from the cannery twice for practice in driving. She has no license yet.

It is a full day, with animals to feed and re-tether, and three babies and a seven-room house to look after. Nothing ever gets done thoroughly, but that's the way things have to be with children. A mother has to keep her mind on a number of things at once, on the cake in the oven, on Becky, Susie, and Eric, planning and replanning what she wants to do and what she has to do, and what she *can* do. There is not much time wasted.

Now it is eight-thirty, and Tamar is reading *Kristin Lavransdatter,* and David, *Blackfriar's,* and I am adding these few pages to my notebook.

So many pages are given over to ideas, theorizings, figuring things out, setting things down, for my own benefit as well as my readers', that it is good to write about just facts — the account of a day.

And I must say I feel good, physically and mentally refreshed, to have had this day with babies after weeks of seeing and talking to people in the office, in the house of hospitality, at the retreat house; writing, answering letters, going to meetings. It is living, not just talking about it.

Sunday
Feast of the Holy Name of Mary

A BEAUTIFUL DAY, and we all went to the nine o'clock Mass. The children were very good through a twenty-minute wait before Mass while Father Kealy heard confessions, then during a long, leisurely

Mass which included the reading of the epistle and gospel, a letter from the bishop urging the parishioners to support the home missions, a sermon explaining the gospel, and all the announcements about a garden party, a chicken supper, and the coal needs of the church for the coming winter. They were good though restless, and of course we were conscious of them and fearful of what they would do next all through the Mass, as were all the other parents. It was a happy morning. By the time we got back, having traveled twenty-four miles to and from Mass, it was time to prepare the traditional Sunday dinner, which meant killing two roosters, plucking them, cleaning them, and having them in the pan an hour after the work started. That with carrots, onions, tomatoes right out of the garden, whole-wheat bread, and peaches and goats' milk made a wonderful meal, and no worrying about the grocery bill.

The children had their naps while we read the paper, which we get once a week after Sunday Mass. There was a review of Gandhi's *Autobiography* by Vincent Sheehan, and he said in it, rebuking Toynbee, that Gandhi's great love for his brothers in their poverty led him to turn to the spinning wheel; that it was not an attack on industrialism but a move to clothe his people who had not been clothed by industrial capitalism.

As I write, Tamar's spinning wheel is in one corner of this guest bedroom, and there is a bag of wool up at Maryfarm, Newburgh. We washed and cleaned it of weeds and seeds this summer, and it is all ready to be carded and spun and knit into socks and sweaters. (Right now there are the rag rugs on the loom, and Tamar still has spun wool for dyeing and weaving.) We will send the wool down here after we have carded it for spinning there.

When the children woke up, we went down to the brook for a swim. There is a most wonderful scent in the air these days, a mixture of pine and an odor of flowers I cannot identify, like the smell of mignonette or heliotrope. Goldenrod has a distinct fragrance which one only notices when you get the plant in the house. People have such a prejudice against it on account of hay fever that they are wary of smelling it. The brook was full and cold in the deeper parts. We had a good swim, and Becky and Susie paddled happily around, collecting stones.

Coming back across the sunny meadow, which is no longer harsh stubble but as soft as it looks to walk upon, we could not resist the temptation to lie out there in the cropped field under the sky. The hay from that field was in the barn; the goats stood out snowy white against the green. The children wandered away to play with them and left us there to bask in the sunlight. It is almost the time of the equinoctial storms, and we are thanking God for this weather while we have it.

Right after supper Peter Yost drove by with a truckload of equipment from Leslie's farm. He bought him out last week for twenty-one hundred dollars, and Leslie, the near neighbor, now intends to go back to school on the GI bill.

Yost's trade slogan is that he buys anything from a baby chick to a grain of corn. He has great sales every month down on the Martinsburg road, and Tamar and I went to one on a cold, drizzly day last winter. As he passed us this afternoon, he wanted to know if Dave could use a team of horses — he could have them for fifty dollars, harness included. Those same horses had cost Leslie one hundred and fifty last November when the Michaels had their sales.

Mr. Yost will fence in the place, he says, and after he has harvested the corn, he will fatten stock on the farm, sell the lumber on it, and rent the house for five dollars a month.

Tuesday, September 14

YESTERDAY WE canned sixteen quarts of peaches and today twenty quarts of tomatoes. In the afternoon we went down to the brook and bathed. Today we saw three large turtles swimming underwater and any number of striped fish about eight inches long. While we sat on a gravelly bank collecting pieces of stone with the imprint of shells and leaves on them, of which the brook bed is full, Susie caught sight of a slim little garter snake the color of a twig, coiled out on a branch sunning himself. No matter how close the pebbles we threw came to him, he would not move. Now we will be adding more verses to our "all ye works of the Lord" song.

No work at the cannery these last two days, but tomato-picking and corn-cutting [are] going on all over the neighborhood, and both Fearnows and Smiths asked for David's help. There is no dearth of work of such kind right now. Smith works all the way over in Hagerstown at the airplane factory for ten dollars a day and counts on his sons to help with the farm. But the young men in the neighborhood, his sons among them, who missed the last war are enlisting, and the young ones are having a good time outside school hours.

Feast of the Sorrows of BVM,
September 15

HOW ONE does work in the country! Washing, making chili sauce, feeding the children, baking. And today we had to go to town so Tamar could take a test for her driver's license. That is why I am here, to be with her. We had to have the lights and the horn fixed, and that took two hours. And then she didn't pass her test. There was a substitute state trooper because one of our two district troopers had a sick wife in the hospital (she had just had twins and they died) and the other was moving. Our substitute friend said Tamar seemed to lack confidence and that she should practice more. So her test is held up another three weeks until the first Wednesday of next month. (She will drive to Mass anyway.)

On the way home we stopped at the cannery, where David [had been] working since eight o'clock. Our neighbors Mrs. Fearnow and Willard, her grandson, were there too, so we drove them home at five-thirty. There were twenty-eight girls peeling tomatoes, a number of men unloading them off a truck and scalding them, three women filling the cans, scooping them up from a deep wooden trough and putting them on a conveyor belt which delivered them to a machine which capped them and sent them into another trough to David, who stacked them in a huge basket which later is lifted by a crane and deposited in one of three tanks of water, where it bubbles away under water for thirty-five minutes. Willard, general handyman, had the job of unloading and restacking the cans ready to be labeled and shipped. They are all the same tomatoes, but all kinds of labels are affixed to the cans, according to which stores sell them.

The women are of all ages working in these little canneries which dot the countryside hereabouts. There are teenage girls and grandmothers, and some young mothers bring their young children. I saw the two-year-old again in his stroller, at five. He had been there most of the day, aside from a nap morning and afternoon outside in a car. He was yawning and crying alternately at the end of his long day. There is an hour for lunch and ten minutes off morning and afternoon, and also an occasional cessation from work when some part of the machine breaks down. They are pretty ramshackle affairs, these canneries, in old barn-like structures, open to the weather, sloppy underfoot. But everybody seems to be glad of the chance at this irregular and neighborly work. Again there will be no work till Friday because the nights are too cold to ripen the tomatoes properly. Green tomatoes cause the cans to burst.

Tomorrow Dave will go to cut corn for the Smiths. One of his young lads came by at suppertime on a skittish horse, and Becky and Susie stood in stunned admiration watching him. What a paradise this is for children. This same boy with his brothers and a neighbor's boy had been sneaking out of what chores they could to play cowboys and Indians up and down the creek all afternoon after school. And Susie and Becky are happy and singing the long day through.

A letter came from Walter from the steel mills at Sparrows' Point today. He is working there for the time being (many of his relatives are in the mills), but he has his name in for a truck and wants to go into the trucking business.

Today we got a paper, and on the front page the headline was "Scientists Warn that the Population Outgrows Food." The occasion was the centenary meeting of the American Association for the Advancement of Science.

"Scientists took stock today of what science had wrought in the past hundred years and visioned a dark outlook for the human race in the next century. They linked this outlook to overpopulation and the dwindling of natural resources, both of which are the direct consequences of progress of science and technology."

The conclusion seemed to be the usual upside-down one of limitation of population rather than limitation of all the unnecessary things so that basic needs could be cared for. Dr. Edmund Sennett of Yale, [a member] of the Association, said, "Man, not nature, is the great problem today. These vast new powers in the hands of selfish or arrogant men simply increase their power to dominate their fellows. If modern technology enables greedy exploiters to destroy our patrimony or natural resources, we would be better off to go back to the horse and buggy age. . . . Man wants to be much more than a well-kept beast," he said. And then, astoundingly enough, he added, "Unless we give him ample opportunity and encouragement to cultivate the higher side of his nature fully and can *free him from the restraints of dogma and compulsion,* he will never be satisfied, and there will be no real hope for him."

Lewis Mumford was an interesting speaker. "The whole process of mechanization may be defeated unless we engage every part of the human personality. Otherwise we may bring about a revolt against the machine like that Samuel Butler jokingly predicted in *Erewhon.* To overcome the present crisis both in techniques and in Western civilization, there must be a changeover from mechanical to living criteria. We must concentrate on the repressed and dwarfed elements in the personality and the community. . . . Not the power, not the profit man, nor the mechanical man, but the *whole man* [Eric Gill would say "holy" man] must be the central actor in the new civilization."

Saturday, September 19
St. Januarius

IN NEW YORK these last few days, around the corner from us on Mulberry Street, there is a fiesta, a feast, celebrated every year with bands and processions [and] feastings around open charcoal fires, where sausages are roasted on spits, huge pots of grease in which pieces of dough wrapped around pot cheese are French fried, corn is boiled.

There have been several other feasts this summer — Our Lady of Grace, Our Lady's Assumption, St. Rocco — and now there is this last feast of the summer. The noise is tremendous, and people drag out benches and chairs and tables and live on the sidewalks night and day.

There we are in the most congested section of the largest city of the world, if you speak of greater New York. Half a block down the street is the wide stream of traffic on Canal Street, which separates Little Italy from Chinatown. Two blocks east is the Bowery — with its elevated railroad, which makes din enough, though the clanging streetcars have been replaced by buses, and the truck traffic dies down at night. Noise of traffic, noise of radios, jukeboxes, of humans.

And down here in West Virginia, only a few hours out of the capitol, Washington, D.C., and one mile from Stottler's Crossroads, there is silence.

That is, comparative silence. Crickets outside make the night alive, and Susie upstairs has kept up a conversation and a singing with herself for an hour and a half. She is tireless. (Right now a plane flies overhead.)

Becky, who is three, goes to bed quietly, insists upon having her covers arranged tidily, composes herself quietly, turns her face to the wall, and that is all from her for the night. Susie, just two, on the other hand, acts as though wound up. Constant motion, constant noise. She wanders in and out of bed, makes a wreck of her covers, drags everything out of bureau drawers, dresses and undresses herself, until finally in the midst of reading or conversation downstairs, we realize that there is *silence*. The great silence has then descended on the house. Susie has run down.

Eric, seven months, presents no problems as yet. He is suckled, he sleeps. He awakes, eats applesauce or cereal, plays, laughs, practices crawling, and again is suckled and sleeps. A bright, responsive, adorable baby with a close cap of curling golden brown hair, deep blue slanting eyes, and a curly mouth, always smiling.

This last week there have been Ember Days, but there is no problem feeding the man of the house here. He likes simple meals: bread and cheese, a bowl of soup, a cup of tea for one meal; spaghetti or Spanish rice for the other. There have been tomatoes, cucumbers, string beans, applesauce. Always we seem to be low on food, but there is always something in the pantry or garden. And Tamar has put up a great deal in jars for the winter.

Most certainly we miss [daily] Mass and Communion, being twelve miles from Mass. But how much the more do we look forward to Sunday. Even the children, tiny as they are, started getting ready today, getting out their shoes, dresses, scarves, little pocketbooks that Marge sent for an Easter present. The pocketbooks represent something to carry their offering in.

Certainly when one cannot get to Mass in the morning, one feels the need much more to stop at times during the day to pray. Thank God for Father Frey's little prayerbook of the Psalms, beautifully printed and arranged as the breviary is, so that one can pray "seven times" during the day.

Today the *Commonweal* came with a chapter from Thomas Merton's book in it about his entrance into the Trappist monastery at Gethsemane, Kentucky. He mentions the need we have in our religious life for a formal observance of prayer, the need for ritual.

And I remember reading in Father Faber's *At the Foot of the Cross* how our Blessed Mother in Egypt, a pagan land, must have surrounded herself with articles and customs which reminded her of her country and her people and their faith.

David has a crucifix in every room, even on the porch, and it brings me a great sense of comfort when I see it, black against the whitewashed porch.

There is a wonderful calendar compiled by the Maussolff and von Trapp families and published by the Society of St. Paul, 2187 Victory Blvd., Staten Island, N.Y., which has short biographies of the saints of the day, which is perfect to read aloud every morning.

The children love their morning prayers, and even when I am rocking them and singing "All ye works of the Lord," they fold their tiny hands reverently.

When the Church is not near at hand, one is forced to see that there is religion in the home.

We are all sitting around the Aladdin lamp, which gives just as good a light as electricity, and Tamar is reading a geological survey of Morgan County, and David is reading a book on rural sociology, describing the dismal condition of the farmer.

Tamar gets very impatient sometimes at the lack of such facilities as running water, but there is the possibility later of getting a well drilled outside the back door, thanks to the generosity of relatives. Until then, she must leave it to David to cart pails of water from the spring five hundred feet away. Sometimes they arrive with little fish swimming in them. Today during a thundershower, while the children danced in the downpour, we filled pails and tubs and a hogshead with water, which will simplify the washing problem Monday.

Tomorrow I must leave, after this brief week's visit, and it is so beautiful, so peaceful here, far from noise and traffic and the world.

There are good books here to be read and studied — Gill and Belloc and Chesterton, sociologists, historians, and philosophers. There are the Scriptures to be studied. There is God's beautiful world, the world He loved around us, with its simple people, hardworking people, poor people. Life is beautiful here, and I hate to go.

But it is only a day away from New York, and we will visit again soon.

It is so good to have such beginnings as this to come to, for "refreshment, light, and peace."

As Gill says in one of his letters to Graham Carey, "I am sure that all attempts to create cells of the good life in the form of small communities are not only much to be encouraged but are the only hope. . . . It is to me perfectly clear that communities of layfolk religiously cutting themselves off from the money economy are an absolute necessity if Christianity is not to go down, either into the dust or the catacombs. . . . There are lots of little attempts going on in England today in spite of everything. But of course they are pretty hard up against it, and they get jolly little encouragement from the ordinary population, and still less from the Catholic."

There are lots of little attempts in the United States too, but in all I have visited, there is still a hankering for the "fleshpots," and strangely enough, pots are in this case modern plumbing. The men

219

as much as the women insist on having it, and it is ridiculous to think that so many are deterred from achieving freedom because of this.

Father Gindler, who is a parish priest in the coal regions and an editor of the *Sunday Visitor,* once said to me, "Do you have to always mention outhouses?"

I feel like the Meagles family in *Little Dorrit,* who are always talking about how *practical* they are. A place with an outhouse costs between twelve hundred and twenty-five hundred dollars. A place with plumbing begins at eight thousand dollars. What a difference to pay!

It is late, ten o'clock, and time for sleep. Tamar has been reading *Kristin Lavransdatter* this last hour, and David is closing all the downstairs windows to keep out the morning damp. The house is heavenly quiet. When I write again in my notebook, it will be from Harrisburg, where I will stop off for a few days on my way back to New York.

October

THERE IS Käthe Kollwitz, mentioned often in the art world, who died recently. [She] spent her life drawing pictures of the poor. She felt it was her job to arouse the consciences of those who looked at her pictures, and since she was the wife of a doctor and saw a great deal of human suffering, she had many a model for her work. I have only seen reproductions of a few of her things, but I was reminded so much of her this month when I visited Mary Frecon in Harrisburg at her Martin de Porres House of Hospitality at 1017 N. Seventh Street.

It has been about ten years now, maybe more, that Mary has worked there in Harrisburg, combating the indifference of the whites to the tragedy of the blacks.

No use talking. Aside from a tiny few more privileged ones, the majority of the colored are the poor of this country.

I arrived in Harrisburg one Sunday evening last month before the weather had turned cold, and it was a good time to be there, because the night was alive with dark faces and bodies, sitting on the steps of the ramshackle houses, nursing their babies, watching their children, listening to the music, the rhythm of tambourines, the clapping of hands, the singing from the tabernacles, churches of the Lord, or Pentecostal churches on every corner.

Around one corner was a tent with the flap open in the front, and on a platform was a beautiful young light-brown girl, slim and graceful, swaying to the music, all dressed like a bride or an angel in white satin — three men, well-dressed, preaching at intervals and saying nothing, punctuating every phrase, every sentence with Amen, Amen. And the music kept beginning again, and more and more of the congregation got up and swayed and sang, and people were waiting, waiting for something to happen. You felt that in the air, that waiting, that tenseness, that excitement. The rhythm of the singing [and] the clapping went on and on, staccato, sharp, till the breath quickened and the heart beat faster, and the excitement rose again and again, and again and again fell exhausted.

Someday, something will happen; someday there will be the climax, the glory, the fullness of life, release, joy, and freedom. You felt it in the air.

Meanwhile, across the street from 1017, the open windows of another church of God gave us a view of a young, sturdy Negro with seemingly inexhaustible voice who shouted, who groaned, who cried out, who kept saying over and over, "God has taken my children. He has killed them all. The Lord gave; the Lord took away. God help us all. We got misery. Everyone got misery. God killed my children. He burned my house. Oh God, God. Oh my God. But I say Amen. Amen. All right then, God killed my children. God burns my house. Amen, God. Amen."

It went on and on, and it was only when he stopped for breath and a woman on a bench near him took up the reading of the book of Job from a Bible, that we realized that he was acting out his concept of the suffering Job. He groaned; he tore his hair; his knees buckled under him; he roared in anguish. And then, after a long, long time, when the nerves were taut and could not stand any more, suddenly he stopped, and the singing began again, a single tune which was barbaric, horrible, monotonous, always the same tune, here and around the corner, down the street, the rhythm the same, the beat the same, until the pulse quickened again and the breath came short.

All through the warm night there was the smell of rats. The smell of dead things; the smell of rotting garbage. If you have ever been in a town where there are stockyards, fertilizer factories, [or] paper mills, you know the peculiar odors of our industrial system. They are not sweet.

I have smelled them in Bayonne, in Chicago, in Mobile, and they are the smell of death. I have also lived in a tenement where a rat died in the walls, and it was winter, and to live you had to leave your windows open to breathe. You could not get the rat out; you could not locate it without tearing down the house. It was a torture. And all that evening as we walked through that slum district of Harrisburg, there was that odor of dead rats coming from windows and doors, from alleys and the holes in the sidewalk.

The night was soft and alive. There was a velvety feeling in the air. The children were playing and dancing. Mothers nursed their babies. There was a hunger for beauty there, and it expressed itself in song and music and the movements of the bodies of the young.

I stayed for three days after that, and the neighborhood was something else again. When we got up to go to Mass at the cathedral which is the nearest church, and that ten blocks away, men were going from the houses with paper bags of lunch — young men, family men — [and] women going out to housework. Later on, children were on their way to school. The street had the weekday aspect. No one sat out, no one was idle save a few little ones too young for school who played in the playground that Mary [had] built with her own hands across the street, playing on the swings, the slide, and the sandbox.

The night before, the street had been for the humans. Now trucks and cars roared and raced by all day. It is a dangerous street and full of [the] noise and dirt of traffic. Directly in back are the Pennsylvania railroad tracks; down the street are gigantic junkyards, fencing in with ten-foot fences all other vacant spaces where the children used to play. Down the street on the other side is Swift's.

What do these people eat? Beans cooked up in bacon rind. Beans and oxtail broth. Swift sells them all the trimmings at top prices. Swift smells.

An ordinary journalistic device is to paint a picture with contrasts. It is an emotional way of making a point. Our aim is to move the heart, stir the will to action; to arouse pity, compassion; to awaken the conscience. We want to do such work as Käthe Kollwitz, and so does Mary Frecon. *Compassion* — it is a word meaning "to suffer with." If we all carry a little of the burden, it will be lightened. If we share in the suffering of the world, then some will not have to endure so heavy an affliction. It evens out. What you do here in New York, in Harrisburg, helps those in China, India, South Africa, Europe, [and] Russia, as well as in the oasis where you are. You may think you are alone. But we are members one of another. We are children of God together.

Contrast Ana Pauker, whose picture appeared on a *Time* cover a few weeks ago, and Mary Frecon. It was a fearful picture. The story described her as "the most powerful woman alive," [and said that] "millions depended on her for life, bread, and spiritual guidance. . . . Ana Pauker, Communist and key figure in the struggle for the world. . . . Leading Communist in Russian satellite states from the Baltic to the Adriatic." (We notice that Finland is never listed as a satellite state. Small as she is, powerless as she seems to be, she keeps her integrity.) Ana is described as "fat and ugly, cold as the frozen Danube, bold as a boyar on his own rich land, and pitiless as a scythe in the Moldavian grain." A poetic description indeed. The magazine went on to describe a series of women, once idealistic, warm, full of pity, and now they are Amazons, fiends, ruthless, etc., etc. I cannot begin to match the invective of the capitalist press. It is better even than the Communist.

We have many a woman in politics or in the trade-union field in this country who is just as hard, bold, brazen, and ruthless.

On the other hand, you have Mary Frecon, making crab apple jelly in the little kitchen of her house on Seventh Street from the fruit sent to her by one of her sons, both of whom have fruit farms. (She does not need to live on Seventh Street.) Mary, nursing a diabetic swollen, heavy with water, holding her up at night so she could breathe, bringing the priest to her, looking after her body and soul, materially and spiritually. Susie, burned by a jealous rival, oozing pus from her infected shoulders cut by glass from broken windows when she tried to escape, nursed back to health of body and soul. Katie, dying of cancer, tuberculosis, and syphilis, her body dung now indeed, but once a thing of beauty, strung taut with life and pleasure, and now overwhelmed with torrents of pain. Lucille Pearl, dying in an alley, flies and worms feasting on the open sores of her flesh — these women dying and yet alive today in heaven, literally dragged into the wedding feast, dying happy and sure, and already before their death given a foretaste of the life to come.

And those Communist women — Pauker, Vermeersch, Bloor, Knusinen — have they so changed? We are given a horrible picture of brute strength, all softness and tenderness gone. We know there is evil, cruelty, disease, vice; it is all around us in these slums in which we live. Graham Greene in all his books is haunted by the violence, the sin of the world. It is a fearful picture he draws too.

How to draw a picture of the strength of love! It seems at times that we need a blind faith to believe in it at all. There is so much failure all about us. It is so hard to reconcile oneself to such suffering, such long, enduring suffering of body and soul, that the only thing one can do is to stand by and save the dying ones who have given up hope of reaching out for beauty, joy, ease, and pleasure in this life. For all their reaching, they got little of it. To see these things in the light of faith, God's mercy, God's justice! His devouring love! I read one story of the death of the Little Flower, and her death just as harrowing in its suffering as that of Mary's Katie. Her flesh was a mass of sores; her bones protruded through her skin; she was a living skeleton, a victim of love. We have not such compassion, nor ever will have. What we do is so little.

The stink of the world's injustice and the world's indifference is all around us. The smell of the dead rat, the smell of acrid oil from the engines of the Pennsylvania railroad, the smell of boiled bones from Swift's. The smell of dying human beings.

Souls! But we are living in the flesh, we are very much in our bodies, and we want to know whether it is too late to do anything but save souls. No use in talking about how many *souls* there are in the neighborhood of West Seventh Street. God has made us creatures of bodies and souls, and what we know of Him we learn through our senses, exterior and interior. It is good to be able to tell that Mary saves bodies too. She feels she does so little; the years are long, and everything seems the same. But there is the story of the twins which we could tell, who were locked for a year and a half in a room and starved and beaten, and whom Mary rescued and put away in a school. And Susie is still alive, and at present in a state of grace.

But here is the story of one she did not save. Did I say in the beginning of this story that there was that feeling of waiting? That sense of violence? It came to a climax in the murder of a young woman around the corner. It happened when Mary was away, and 1017 is out of earshot of the place anyway, so she might not have known it was going on, [even] if she had been home. A few blocks away a man of thirty beat his twenty-six-year-old wife to death with a broken chair. He had been blinded in one eye some years before when a beer bottle flung from a tavern hit him as he passed by, and he was a melancholy man who drank sometimes himself and did not talk to his neighbors. He worked every day, and he and his wife were considered respectable people. They never came to Mary for help in the way of clothes, as others in the neighborhood did. There had been one scene of violence between them before, and they had separated for a few days, but then they were seen walking down the street hand in hand.

And then this other fight had come about, and with the neighbors standing outside waiting for the police and listening to the violence within, he had beat his wife [in]to unconsciousness behind his locked door so that she died three hours after she was taken to the hospital.

And Mary faces all this misery pretty much alone. Dr. Clark helps her with the sick. The Johnsons next door are her able assistants in many a work of mercy. Young people from the Catholic high school come every week and help with the children.

Out in the backyard there is a little garden with sunflowers, marigolds, petunias, and ice plant. Out in front there is one tree.

How little it all is, as obscure as the life of the Blessed Mother and as "little" as the life and sufferings of the Little Flower!

Someday, something will be done. There will be decent places to live. Instead of a tent tabernacle with the rhythm of the jungle, there will be a church with the Mass, with Christ Himself in the Blessed Sacrament.

Yes, the nearest Catholic church is ten blocks away, but just the same, Christ is there, most surely there, in the least of His children. He has said it Himself.

~

The only answer to this mystery of suffering is this. Every soul seeks happiness either in creatures (where it cannot be satisfied in the long run) or in God.

God made us for Himself.

We must die to the natural to achieve the supernatural, a slow death or a quick one. It is universal. "Unless the grain of wheat fall into the ground and die, itself remaineth alone, but if it die, it beareth much fruit." All must die; it is a universal law very hard for us to realize.

If this mind or this flesh is an obstacle, we will suffer the more when this tremendous Lover tries to tear from us all veils which separate us. Some suffering is more visible, some hidden. If we long for beauty, the more our faith is tried, as though by fire, by ugliness. The more we long for love, the more all human love will be pruned, and the more we will see the venom of hatred about us. It is a pruning, a cutting away of love so that it will grow strong and bear much fruit. The more we long for power, the more we will destroy and tear down until we recognize our own weakness.

But still, suffering is a mystery as well as a penalty which we pay for others as well as for ourselves.

How gigantic was that first Sin, that turning from God! All nature travailleth and groaneth even until now because of it, St. Paul says. The blackness of it, the peculiar hideousness of it, the loathsome perverseness of it, the empty, sterile, grotesque horror of it can scarcely be realized except as we see an echo of it in every sin and crime around us.

Some years ago a terrible crime was committed. A little girl was dragged behind a movie screen while a comedy was on the screen, and while the audience howled with mirth, the child was raped and murdered within a few feet of the audience. But why do we think of a sex crime, as though there were only one commandment! It is be-

227

cause our Lord Himself is likened to a lover. It is because sex is "the most deeply wounded of all our faculties" since the Fall. Because in sex, body and spirit are so interwoven, so attuned, so single-minded, so concentrated, and so alive. It is in sex love that people catch glimpses of harmony and peace unutterable. That is why thwarting sex, unfulfilled marriage, is a tragedy often dealt with by physicians and psychiatrists. If the act, which is called by St. Paul "the marriage debt," is not paid generously and to the full, people are warped and nerve-racked, curiously askew.

The prevention of conception when the act which one is performing is for the purpose of fusing the two lives more closely and [to] so enrich them that another life springs forth; the aborting of a life conceived — these sins are great frustrations in the natural and spiritual order.

So are the lives not directed to God, flowing toward him freely, eagerly, with hunger and thirst desiring Him, the very glimpse of Him like an attaining to Him, so that all suffering is as little noted as the tearing aside of the virginal veil or the budding forth of new life. In gross material reality, it is a bloody, anguished racking of body in which the soul can even exult. "With desire have I desired to eat the Pasch," Christ said.

The mystery of suffering. I feel presumptuous in writing of so high and lofty a thing. It is because I am not now suffering that I can write, but it is also because I have suffered in the past that I can write.

I write to comfort others as I have been comforted. The word *comfort* too means to be strong together, to have fortitude together. There is the reminder of community. Once when I suffered and sat in church in a misery while waves and billows passed over me, I suddenly thought, with exultation, "I am sharing suffering," and it was immediately lightened. But usually it is as the Little Flower said: "Let us suffer if need be with bitterness and without courage. Jesus truly suffered with sadness. Without sadness, would the soul suffer? And we would suffer generously, grandly; what an illusion!"

WHEN WE went to press last month, we had only the day before finished the Labor Day family retreat, and it was too late to write about it. Now it is hard to write without boasting about it. We are the only Catholic retreat house in the United States where mother and father and all the children can come and camp out with us for a few days to partake of refreshment for body and soul. Over the Labor Day retreat there were twenty-two children and eleven couples. Some families had left a child or two at home or with relatives. Some brought two or three or five. There were three babies around five months old. They were easy to care for, since they stayed in their cribs and were quite content to be left alone. The hardest to care for were the two-year-old ones, who could not understand why at arbitrary times their mothers answered a bell and rushed away, regardless of their very important needs, which they felt could be satisfied by no one but the mother. Of course, Julia Purcelli made a very good substitute for mother for all of them, but the two-year-olds did not appreciate that. They were not to be reasoned with. At the risk of being untheological, I'd say that the four-year-olds had achieved the use of reason. They were very well-behaved indeed.

I am tempted to write only of the children, how they slept in the long barn which housed all the children and the mothers of the young babies (except a few older youngsters, who went to a neighboring farm for the long weekend). How they ate outside at a long table; how they built a little shrine to our Lady under a wild cherry tree. How they drew pictures, some of them very strange indeed, and not only had an outdoor exhibit but brought them in procession to the chapel to give them to God in exchange for a blessing. They brought pretty stones, too, and fruits and leaves and bunches of flowers. One baby ate half its bouquet before reaching the altar.

Of the picnic which we all shared with the children on the last day and to which neighbors came from a nearby farm and from the town of Newburgh. Julia says next year the girls who helped her must come a few days early to learn a few fundamentals about the care of babies, such as pinning diapers and cutting up food, not to speak of singing songs, telling stories, arranging dances and little plays. A mother has to be all these things — singer, artist, sculptor, storyteller, dancer, impressario, toy maker, inventor, cook, laundress, and nurse. What a full life! What talents to develop! It would be hard indeed even to get a smattering in a few days.

As for the adults, I'm sure they did not have such a good time as the children. Next time we will arrange it so that the mothers of the very young ones, those who lie in the cribs and do not try to climb out, will have their infants in a dormitory with them. The mothers of the older ones will be separated entirely from the rest of their brood. Then there can be silence indeed.

Father Schott, with whom I talked in Harrisburg this month, who arranges Cana conferences for the diocese, said that on their days of recollection they have what they call a Cana silence, where the husband and wife talk only to each other but to no other families. Then they find they have not been really talking to each other for a long time, but to their children or about their children.

There are many things we will do differently next year, and we hope the parents will send us suggestions as to what to do. Mr. Rudzick, who came not once but twice during the summer with his five children, wife, and mother-in-law, is by now a charter member of our retreat house, and I am sure can help us a lot with his ideas. He has made three retreats with us, and while he would have found it more enjoyable, I am sure, to go away alone by himself, he wanted to share things with his family. His wife could not get away, and he would not go without her.

What a wonderful staff we have, growing food, building, repairing, canning outside the big house and cooking, dishwashing, and generally running the place and the retreats. Jane O'Donnell is in charge. Thank God for them all. But of course we did not make ends meet, and since half those who came could not pay anything for their visit and just managed to get there themselves, we have a bill for staples, another for more lumber, and what with invalids to care for this winter, we need to do things to the inside of the house in the way of putting up wallboard and buying coal. Our family only amounts to a dozen or fifteen people now, but we never know who is going to walk up the road and pay a call which lasts anywhere from a week to six months. (Some stay forever.) We have sent out our appeal from New York, and we are hoping enough comes in to take care of our farm bills too.

Everyone always asks whether the farm is self-sustaining. It is one of those questions which always come up when you talk about farming. How hard it is to explain that though we raise three hundred bushels of potatoes, we use a bushel a day in New York, and we try to ship in as much as we can whenever a car is going down to the city. (No one has offered a truck yet.) Although we put up a few thousand cans of applesauce and tomatoes, still that is a drop in the bucket when you count the breadline. Just this morning as I came from seven o'clock Mass, I counted the men from Canal Street up to the house, and there were at that time one hundred and five on the street waiting and fifty inside the coffee room having their breakfast. Slim has been "on the line," serving the men year in and year out, and although he calls me "Führer-ess," he is the big boss of the line. He is beginning to talk of a vacation, "and not on the farm either, to help bring the crops in."

He thinks of long sleep in the morning and a leisurely breakfast, unrushed by the demands of two hundred or so guests.

Maybe the farm would meet expenses if we would limit our family and think of it in terms of a family-sized farm. There was never such a family as ours. Once, when the board of health was objecting to our line, we talked to their representatives about the household as being a family. "We are quite ready to regard the people living in the house [only about sixty or so] as a family, but the breadline is the *public.*"

Quite a few of the public creep in.

This month Tony de Falco, our corner grocer, who is also a college graduate and a lawyer, and to whom we owe two thousand dollars, got married. [Given] his new state, we are sure that an early payment of his bill would be welcome. So we are asking St. Joseph, the head of our family, to take care of it.

As for other vital statistics, there are the twins, the youngest members of our household, a month old now, and gaining rapidly. Big appetites, both of them. So how in the world can we make ends meet?

November

THERE IS a character in *The Plague,* by Albert Camus, who says that he is tired of hearing about men dying for an idea. He would like to hear about a man dying for love for a change. He goes on to say that men have forgotten how to love, that all they seem to be thinking of these days is learning how to kill. Man, he says, seems to have lost the capacity for love.

What is God but Love? What is a religion without love? We read of the saints dying for love, and we wonder what they mean. There was a silly verse I used to hear long ago: "Men have died from time to time, and worms have eaten them, but not for love." It comes from *As You Like It.* And nowadays in this time of war and preparing for war, we would agree, except for the saints. Yes, they have died for love of God. But Camus's character would say, "I mean for love of man." Our Lord did that, but most people no longer believe in Him. It is hard to talk to people about God if they do not believe in Him. So one can talk and write of love. People want to believe in that even when they are all but convinced that it is an illusion. (It would be better still to love rather than to write about it. It would be more convincing.)

In the Old and New Testaments there are various ways in which the relationship of God and men [is] mentioned. There is the shepherd and his sheep. "The Lord is my shepherd." "I am the Good Shepherd." The animal and the man. There is the servant and the master, there is the son and the father, and there is the bride and the bridegroom. "Behold, the bridegroom cometh." The Song of Songs, the Canticle of Canticles, is all about love. "Let Him kiss me with the kisses of His mouth."

It is hard to believe in this love. In a book by Hugh of St. Victor, which I read once on the way from St. Paul to Chicago, there is a conversation between the soul and God about this love. The soul is petulant and wants to know what kind of a love is that which loves everyone indiscriminately, the thief and the Samaritan, the wife and the mother and the harlot? The soul complains that it wishes a *particular* love, a love for herself alone. And God replies fondly that, after all, since no two people are alike in this world, He has indeed a particular fondness for each one of us, an exclusive love to satisfy each one alone.

It is hard to believe in this love because it is a tremendous love. "It is a terrible thing to fall into the hands of the living God." If we do once catch a glimpse of it, we are afraid of it. Once we recognize that we are sons of God, that the seed of divine life has been planted in us at baptism, we are overcome by that obligation placed upon us of growing in the love of God. And what we do not do voluntarily, He will do for us. Father Roy, our dear Josephite friend who worked with us at Easton and who has been these past two years in a hospital in Montreal, learning what it is to be loved, used to tell a story of a leper he met at a hospital up on the Gaspé peninsula. The leper complained to him, How could he believe in the love of God?

Father Roy proceeded to tell his favorite story. First of all, there is dirt, the humus from which all things spring, and the flower says to the dirt, "How would you like to grow and wave in the breeze and praise God?" And the dirt says "Yes," and that necessitates its losing its own self as dirt and becoming something else. Then the chicken comes along and says to the flower, "How would you like to be a chicken and walk around like I do and praise God?" And the flower assures the chicken that it would like it indeed. But then it has to cease to be a flower. And the man comes to the chicken and says to it, "How would you like to be a man and praise God?" And of course the chicken would like it too, but it has to undergo a painful death to be assimilated to the man, in order to praise God.

When Father Roy told this story, he said with awe, "And the leper looked at me, and a light dawned in his eyes, and he clasped my hands and gasped, *'Father!'* And then we both cried together."

Father Roy is a childlike man, and the Russian leper up in the Canadian peninsula was a simple sufferer, and he saw the point that Father Roy was trying to make, and he began to believe in this love and to see some reason for his sufferings. He began to comprehend the heights and the depths and the strange mystery of this love. But it still takes the eyes of faith to see it.

The love of God and man becomes the love of equals, as the love of the bride and the bridegroom is the love of equals, and not the love of the sheep for the shepherd, or the servant for the master, or the son for the father. We may stand at times in the relationship of servant, and at other times in that of son, as far as our feelings go and in our present state. But the relationship we hope to attain to is that of the love of the Canticle of Canticles. If we cannot deny the *self* in us, kill the self-love, as He has commanded, and put on the Christ life, then God will do it for us. We must become like Him. Love must go through these purgations.

Unfortunately, when we speak of the human love of man and woman, most people, though they hope against hope, still regard it as an illusion, a great and glowing experience, a magic which comes into their lives for the sake of the procreation of the race. They assume and accept the fact that it will die, that it will not last, and in their vain clutching at it, they will put off one partner and look for it in another, and so the sad game goes on, with our movie stars going from the fifth to the sixth bride and swearing the selfsame promises to each.

The Best Years of Our Lives had a sad and cynical ending. While one young couple plighted their troth, exchanged their promises, another young couple disregarded promises already made and fell into each other's arms to try to regain, to recapture love once more. Illusive love!

Vladimir Solovyov writes in *The Meaning of Love* about the need to study this problem, to seek the growth of this love, so that the force of love may be set loose in the world today to combat the terrible force of hate and violence that we have unloosed. Father

D'Arcy deals with the problem in *The Mind and Heart of Love.* De Rougemont, in *Love in the Western World,* writes also about this work of love. These books may be hard reading for those who seem to learn of love by reading best-sellers and seeing the prize movies. But the very fact that all best-sellers and prize movies deal with this very theme of love should make the man of today turn to such books as these and get down to a study of what is most vital in our lives.

That most people in America look upon love as an illusion would seem to be evidenced by the many divorces we see today — and the sensuality of despair that exists all around us. But all these divorces may too be an evidence about love. They hear very little of it in this war-torn world, and they are all seeking it. Pascal said of love, "You would not seek me if you had not already found me." Just so much faith is there, at any rate. A faith in love, a seeking for love. It is something, then, to build on, amongst the mass of people who have lost God, who do not know in what they believe, though they believe [in] and seek for love.

And where are the teachers to teach of this love, of the stages of this love, the purgations of this love, the sufferings entailed by this love, the stages through which natural love must pass to reach the supernatural?

We would all like to hear of men laying down their lives for love for their fellows, and we do not want to hear of it in the heroic tones of a statesman or a prince of the church. We all know that such phrases used in wartime mean nothing. Men are taught to kill, not to lay down their lives if they can possibly help it. Of course we do not talk of brothers in wartime. We talk of the enemy, and we forget the Beatitudes and the commandment to love our enemy, do good to them that persecute us. "A new commandment I give you, that you love one another as I have loved you." One said that who did lay down His life for all men.

Youth demands the heroic, Claudel said, and youth likes to dream of heroic deeds and of firing squads, of martyrs and of high adventure. But bread means life too; and money, which buys bread, for which we work, also means life. Sharing and community living mean laying down your life for your fellows also, and it was of these things that Father Perrin, S.J., the workman priest in Germany, wrote in his moving book.

We have repeated so many times that those who have two cloaks should follow the early Fathers, who said, "The coat that hangs in your closet belongs to the poor." And those who have a ten-room house can well share it with those who have none and who are forced to live in a municipal lodging house. How many large houses could be made into several apartments to take in others? Much hospitality could be given to relieve the grave suffering today. But people are afraid. They do not know where it all will end. They have all gone far enough in generosity to know that an ordeal is ahead, that the person taken in will turn into "the friend of the family," most likely, or "the man who came to dinner." No use starting something that you cannot finish, they say. Once bitten is twice shy. We have all had our experiences of ingratitude, of nursing a viper in our bosom, as the saying goes. So we forget about pruning in the natural order in order to attain much fruit. We don't want to pay the cost of love. We do not want to exercise our capacity to love.

There are many stories one could tell about Catholic Worker life, but it is always better to wait until years have passed so that they become more impersonal, less apt to be identified with this one or that. There is the story of the sorcerer's apprentice who took over the kitchen this last month at the farm. There is the story of a "friend of the family" who tried to stab a neighbor and was evicted by the neighbors. Too bad we cannot write these stories for the edification and instruction of those who are starting new houses of hospitality today.

There is a story now, however, about a reader of the paper — and this happened long enough ago so that we can tell it — who adopted a young girl and educated her, and the young girl proved to be a great joy and a comfort. Now she has entered a contemplative order to spend her life in prayer and work. The same reader then took in another young woman, who brought home a fatherless baby, and when that was forgiven her, went out and brought in still another, and there was apt to be a third, and our friend wrote and begged us for advice and help as to what to do. Was she contributing to the delinquency of this girl by forgiving seventy times seven, and was she perhaps going to have seventy times seven children to take care of?

It is good to think of the prophet Hosea, whom I have mentioned before in writing on love. He was commanded by God to take a harlot to wife, and she had many children by other men. He was a dignified, respected teacher of his people, and he was shamed and humiliated by the wife of his bosom. Yet he was to go down in history as [exemplifying] the love of God for His adulterous people.

Love must be tried and tested and proved. It must be tried as though by fire, and fire burns. "It is a dreadful thing to fall into the hands of [the] living God."

In times of catastrophe we are all willing to share. In an earthquake, hurricane, war, or plague, people begin to love one another. Of course, the wife must consider her husband, but it is not so necessary for the husband to consider the wife. As head of the household, it is his job to lead the wife in hospitality, and if he is willing to support others in need, he should induce his wife to go along with him. He should share all but his intimate love with others, and that is for her alone. If he should withdraw that tenderness, that embrace, then he would be guilty indeed.

What kind of a love was that of Scobie, the Major in the current best-seller of Graham Greene, the love which had turned to indifference, if not to loathing at times, and which the author felt to be redeemed by the pity and compassion of Scobie for his nagging wife? How to love truly a woman after the *illusion* has passed and that woman becomes a climbing, snobbish, petty, self-conscious *inferior,* and not an equal, with whom there is no longer any possibility of the love of equals, which is the love of the Canticle of Canticles?

Here are some excerpts from Solovyov that perhaps are pertinent:

It is well known to everyone that in love there inevitably exists a special idealization of the beloved object, which presents itself to the lover in an entirely different light from that in which outsiders see it. I speak here of light not merely in a metaphorical sense; it is a matter here not only of a special moral and intellectual estimate, but moreover of a special sensuous reception; the lover actually sees, visually receives what others do not. And if for him too this light of love quickly fades away, yet does it follow from this that it was false, that it was only a subjective illusion?

. . . The true significance of love consists not in the simple experience of this feeling but what is accomplished by means of it, in the work of love.

For love it is not enough to feel for itself the unconditional significance of the beloved object, but it is necessary effectively to impart or communicate this significance to this object. . . .

. . . Each man comprises in himself the image of God. Theoretically and in the abstract, this Divine image is known to us in mind and through mind, but in love it is known in the concrete and in life. And if this revelation of the ideal nature, ordinarily concealed by its material manifestation, is not confined in love to an inward feeling, but at times becomes noticeable also in the sphere of external feelings, then so much greater is the significance we are bound to acknowledge for love as being from the very first the visible restoration of the Divine image in the world of matter. . . .

A woman wants compassion, not pity, and Major Scobie did not work very hard at communicating the significance of his love to his wife. Even two of the characters in *The Best Years of Our Lives* had gone a bit farther along the path of love when they told their daughter, who was falling in love with a married man, "How often have we hated one another!" In other words, what a purgation, what a working out we have been through together!

(I am consciously and purposely writing with these allusions so that those who are not able to read Solovyov but who do go to the movies will also know what I am writing about.)

True love is delicate and kind, full of gentle perception and understanding, full of beauty and grace, full of joy unutterable. Eye hath not seen, nor ear heard, what God hath prepared for those who love Him.

And there should be some flavor of this in all our love for others. We are all one. We are *one flesh* in the Mystical Body, as man and woman are said to be one flesh in marriage. With such a love one would see all things new; we would begin to see people as they really are, as God sees them.

We may be living in a desert when it comes to such perceptions now, and that desert may stretch out before us for years. But a thousand years are as one day in the sight of God, and soon we will know as we are known. Until then, we will have glimpses of brotherhood in play, in suffering, in serving, and we will begin to train for that community, that communion, that Father Perrin talked so much about in his story of the workman priest in Germany.

This last month there was an article by John Cogley in *America* about his experiences in the Chicago House of Hospitality. He writes of it as in the dim and distant past, and tells of the "mushroom growth" of such houses back in the thirties. In the present there are a few still struggling along, he writes, and a few farms existing in dire poverty.

Yes, the problems have become intensified; a great many have left the running. Where there were thirty-two houses of hospitality and farms, there are now eleven. But in those eleven we are still trying to work out a theory of love, a study of the problem of love so that the revolution of love, instead of that of hate, may come about, and we will have a new heaven and a new earth wherein justice dwelleth.

POEM FOR FALL

All around are the irregular fields.
Irregular because woodlots space the scene.
The fields are colorful with red and purple cabbages, pale
      carrots, green turnips, feathery dill, and dark red beets.
The harvest is not yet in, and far in the hundred-acre field are
      the bent figures of a dozen workers dressed in denim.
The trees — the oak, the maple, the elm and sassafras —
Are decked out brilliantly,
Dying gloriously
With joy,
With thankfulness.

Hope springs in my heart like a refreshing fountain.
This is the season of hope,
This, the month when we pray for the dead.
And I, whom "the certainty of dying afflicteth,
Am consoled by the promise of future immortality."
"Life is changed, not taken away."
Life is still there.

And as I walk these wagon tracks between fields,
Through the bright November air, sharp with impending frost,
But with the caress of the sun still on it,
Still as only November days can be still, expectant, breathless,
It is easy to think on death and life and their embrace.

For it is long since that my dying has begun.
So long that one gets used to it.
And long since, and yet how short a time
That I began to live.
The life increases with my dying.
That life becomes the more abundant life.
Life that is the beginning of our heaven here and now.

Some fields are bare and brown amid the green,
And striding through the harrowed field
Comes the sower.
His arm swings with long rhythms;
He strides freely.
He flings the seed.
Overhead wheel the swallows,
Swooping and dancing in the sun.
Another field far distant
Already shows its cover crop
Of tender rye,
And as I watch, I think of St. Paul's words:

> But some man will say:
> "How do the dead rise again?
> Or with what manner of body shall they come?"

Senseless man! That which thou sowest is not quickened,
Except it die first.

And that which thou sowest,
Thou sowest not the body that shall be,
But bare grain,
As of wheat, or of some of the rest.
But God giveth it a body as He will,
And to every seed its proper body.
All flesh is not the same flesh;
But one is the flesh of man,
Another of beasts,
Another of birds,
Another of fishes.
And there are bodies celestial
And bodies terrestrial;
But one is the glory of the celestial
And another of the terrestrial.
One is the glory of the sun,
Another the glory of the moon,
And another the glory of the stars.
For star differeth from star in glory.
So also is the resurrection of the dead.

It is sown in corruption;
It shall rise in incorruption.
It is sown in dishonor;
It shall rise in glory.
It is sown in weakness;
It shall rise in power.

It is sown a natural body;
It shall rise a spiritual body.

Behold, I tell you a mystery.
We shall all indeed rise again.

Deo gratias.

THIS MONTH I think of my mother, who died a few years ago on the feast of St. Raphael, the patron of travelers.

"My soul hath thirsted after the strong living God; when shall I come and appear before the face of God?"

But the psalmist also says, "In death there is no one that is mindful of thee." So it made me happy that I could be with my mother the last few weeks of her life, and for the last ten days at her bedside daily and hourly. Sometimes I thought to myself that it was like being present at a birth to sit by a dying person and see their intentness on what is happening to them. It almost seems that one is absorbed in a struggle, a fearful, grim, physical struggle, to breathe, to swallow, to live. And so, I kept thinking to myself, how necessary it is for one of their loved ones to be beside them, to pray for them, to offer up prayers for them unceasingly, as well as to do all those little offices one can. When my daughter was a little tiny girl, she said to me once, "When I get to be a great big woman and you are a little tiny girl, I'll take care of you," and I thought of that when I had to feed my mother by the spoonful and urge her to eat her custard. How good God was to me, to let me be there. I had prayed so constantly that I would be beside her when she died; for years I had offered up that prayer. And God granted it quite literally. I was there, holding her hand, and she just turned her head and sighed. That was her last breath, that little sigh; and her hand was warm in mine for a long time after.

It was hard to talk about dying, but every now and then we did. But I told her that we could no more imagine the life beyond the grave than a blind man could imagine colors. We talked about faith, and how we could go just so far in our reasoned belief, and that our knowledge was like a bridge which came to an end, so that it did not reach the other shore. A wonderful prayer, that one. "I believe, O God. Help Thou mine unbelief."

The beautiful flowers around her bedside were like a gorgeous promise of the new life to come. In winter everything seems so dead — the ground, the trees, and all the shrubbery around the house — and then in a few short months things begin to stir, palpably, and life bursts forth again. Mother had seen seventy-five autumns. Seventy-five times had she seen those promises fulfilled.

Life is changed, not taken away.

In Him there hath shone forth upon us the hope of a happy resurrection, so that we, saddened by knowing that we must one day die, are comforted by the promise of immortal life to come. From Thy faithful, O Lord, life is not taken away; it is but changed, for when their dwelling place in this earthly exile shall have been destroyed, there awaiteth them an everlasting home in heaven.

But some man will say: "How do the dead rise again? Or with what manner of body shall they come?" Senseless man! That which thou sowest is not quickened, except it die first. And that which thou sowest, thou sowest not the body that shall be, but bare grain, as of wheat.

These were comforting things to talk about and to think about, those all-too-short afternoons by mother's bedside. Outside, the maple trees blazed, cast their leaves about them, and stood gaunt and clean against the sky. Asters and chrysanthemums still bloomed in the garden.

One morning I prayed to the Little Flower, whose picture is over the foot of my bed, that she would especially look after my mother. I reminded her of her own grief at her father's long dying. That night Julia Porcelli brought me in some dried blessed roses. The next day, a friend brought a tiny bouquet with lace paper about it made up of roses and carnations, and my mother greeted it with a smile and held it in her hands a few times that afternoon. And it was that evening that she died, so quietly, so gently, saying but a few moments before to my brother, "Kiss me goodnight and run along, because I want to go to sleep."

A week later, when I went to Poughkeepsie to visit my three aunts, one of whom is a Catholic, and to go with them to offer up a Mass of thanksgiving for my mother's most peaceful death, we came out of St. Peter's Church that misty morning to be greeted by a brilliant rose in the garden next to the church. And when we arrived

244

home for breakfast, there was a bouquet telegraphed to us from Florida, and in the center of the fall flowers were two lovely roses. The Little Flower was prompt and generous indeed in her message.

I wrote the account because I like to show my gratitude by telling others of such favors. Perhaps, too, it may comfort others who have sore and lonely hearts over the approaching death of a near one. "Life is changed, not taken away," and what a glorious change in these sad times, after a long and valiant life.

Look down with favor, we beseech Thee, O Lord, upon the offering we make for the soul of Grace, thy servant; from heaven send healing to it, and bid it rest in the certainty of Thy love.

O Lord, the God of mercies, grant to the soul of Thy handmaid a place of solace, of peaceful rest and of glorious light.

December

FOR THE LAST month I have meditated on the use of spiritual weapons. In Father John J. Hugo's pamphlet "Weapons of the Spirit," he advocates as weapons devotion to the Sacred Heart and the Rosary. The love of the humanity of our Lord is the love of our brother. The only way we have to show our love for God is by the love we have for our brother. "Inasmuch as you have done it unto one of the least of these My brethren, you have done it unto Me." "You love God as much as the one you love the least."

Love of brother means voluntary poverty, stripping one's self, putting off the old man, denying one's self, etc. It also means nonparticipation in those comforts and luxuries which have been manufactured by the exploitation of others. While our brothers suffer, we must compassionate them, suffer with them. While our brothers suffer from lack of necessities, we will refuse to enjoy comforts. These resolutions, no matter how hard they are to live up to, no matter how often we fail and have to begin over again, are part of the vision and the long-range view which Peter Maurin has been trying to give us these past years. These ideas are expressed in the writings of Eric Gill. And we must keep this vision in mind, recognize the truth of it, the necessity for it, even though we do not, cannot, live up to it. Like perfection. We are ordered to be perfect as our heavenly Father is perfect, and we aim at it, in our intention, though in our execution we may fall short of the mark over and over. St. Paul says, it is by little and by little that we proceed.

If these jobs do not contribute to the common good, we pray God for the grace to give them up. Have they to do with shelter, food, clothing? Have they to do with the works of mercy? Father Tompkins of Nova Scotia says that everyone should be able to place his job in the category of the works of mercy.

This would exclude jobs in advertising, which only increases people's useless desires. In insurance companies and banks, which are known to exploit the poor of this country and of others. Banks and insurance companies have taken over land and built huge collective farms, ranches, plantations, of 30,000, 100,000 acres, and have dispossessed the poor man. Loan and finance companies have further defrauded him. Movies [and] radio have further enslaved him. So that he has no time nor thought to give to his life, either of soul or body. Whatever has contributed to his misery and degradation may be considered a bad job and not to be worked at.

If we examine our conscience in this way, we would soon be driven into manual labor, into humble work, and so would become more like our Lord and our Blessed Mother.

Poverty means nonparticipation. It means what Peter calls regional living. This means fasting from tea, coffee, cocoa, grapefruit, pineapple, etc., from things not grown in the region in which one lives. One day last winter we bought broccoli which had the label on it of a corporation farm in Arizona or Texas, where we had seen men, women, and children working at two o'clock in the morning with miners' lamps on their foreheads, in order to avoid the terrible heat of the day, which often reached 125 degrees. These were homeless migrants, of which there are some million in the United States. Carey McWilliams' *Factories in the Fields*, which you can get at any library, tells of the conditions of these workers. For these there is "no room at the inn."

We ought not to eat food produced under such conditions. We ought not to smoke, not only because it is a useless habit but also because tobacco impoverishes the soil and pauperizes the farmer, and means women and children working in the fields.

Poverty means having a bare minimum in the way of clothes and seeing to it that these are made under decent working conditions, proper wages and hours, etc. The union label tries to guarantee this. Considering the conditions in woolen mills, it would be better to raise one's own sheep and angora goats and rabbits, and spin and weave and make one's own blankets and stockings and suits. Many groups are trying to do these things throughout the country, both as a remedy for unemployment and for more abundant living.

As for the dislocation in employment if everyone started to give up their jobs? Well, decentralized living would take care of such a situation. And when we look at the dirty streets and lots in our slums, the unpainted buildings, the necessity of a nationwide housing project, the tearing down that needs to be done (if we do not in the future wish to have it done in the hard way and have them bombed down), then we can see that there is plenty of employment for all in the line of providing food, clothing, and shelter for our own country and for the world. We should read Eric Gill, A. J. Penty, and Father Vincent McNabb on the machine.

Poverty means not riding on rubber while horrible working conditions prevail in the rubber industry. Read Vicki Baum's *Weeping Wood* and André Gide's *Congo Journey*. Poverty means not riding on rails while bad conditions exist in the coal mines and steel mills. Poverty means not accepting that courteous bribe from the railroads, the clergy rate. Railroads have been built on robbery and exploitation. There are stagecoaches, of course, and we are only about a century past them. But pilgrims used to walk, and so did the saints. They walked from one end of Europe and Russia to the other. We need saints.

Father Meus, the Belgian who is a Chinese citizen since his missionary life began in China, has walked thousands of miles. He said he would dearly love to walk from one end of the United States to the other. Of course, we are not all given the grace to do such things. But it is good to call to mind the *vision*. It is true, indeed, that until we begin to develop a few apostles along these lines, we will have no mass conversions, no social justice, no peace. We need saints. God, give us saints!

How far we all are from it! We do not even see our infirmities. Common sense tells us, "Why live in a slum? It is actually cheaper to live in a model housing project, have heat and hot water, a mauve or pink bath and toilet, etc. We can manage better; we have more time to pray, to meditate, study. We would have more money to give to the poor." Yes, this is true according to the candlelight of common sense, but not according to the flaming heat of the Sun of justice. Yes, we will have more time with modern conveniences, but we will not have more love. "The natural man does not perceive the things of the spirit." We need to be fools for Christ. What if we do have to buy coal by the bucket instead of by the ton? Let us squander money, be as lavish as God is with His graces, as He is with His fruits of the earth.

Let us rejoice in poverty, because Christ was poor. Let us love to live with the poor, because they are specially loved by Christ. Even the lowest, most depraved — we must see Christ in them and love them to folly. When we suffer from dirt, lack of privacy, heat and cold, coarse food, let us rejoice.

When we are weary of manual labor and think, "What foolishness to shovel out ashes, build fires, when we can have steam heat! Why sew when it can be better done on a machine? Why laboriously bake bread when we can buy so cheaply?" Such thoughts have deprived us of good manual labor in our city slums and have substituted shoddy store-bought goods, clothes, and bread.

Poverty and manual labor — they go together. They are weapons of the spirit, and very practical ones, too. What would one think of a woman who refused to wash her clothes because she had no washing machine, or clean her house because she had no vacuum, or sew because she had no machine? In spite of the usefulness of the machine, and we are not denying it, there is still much to be done by hand. So much, one might say, that it is useless to multiply our tasks, go in for work for work's sake.

But we must believe in it for Christ's sake. We must believe in poverty and manual labor for love of Christ and for love of the poor. It is not true love if we do not know them, and we can only know them by living with them, and if we love with knowledge we will love with faith, hope, and charity.

On the one hand, there is the sadness of the world — and on the other hand, when I went to church today and the place was flooded with sunshine, and it was a clear, cold day outside, . . . suddenly my heart was so flooded with joy and thankfulness and so overwhelmed at the beauty and the glory and the majesty of our God that I could only think of St. Dionysius, "Concerning the Godhead":

> It is the Cause and Origin and Being and Life of all creation. And It is to them that fall away from It a Voice that doth recall them and a Power by which they rise; and to them that have stumbled into a corruption of the Divine Image within them, It is a Power of Renewal and Reform; and a Sacred Grounding to them that feel the shock of unholy assault, and a Security to them which stand; an upward Guidance to them that are being drawn unto It, and a Principle of Illumination to them that are being enlightened; a Principle of Perfection to them that are being perfected; a Principle of Deity to them that are being deified; and of Simplicity to them that are being brought into simplicity; and of Unity to them that are being brought into unity.

The immanence of God in all things! "In Him we live and move and have our being" (Acts 17:28). "He is not far from every one of us" (Acts 17:27).

> Hear, O Israel: the Lord our God is one Lord. Thou shalt love the Lord thy God with thy whole heart, and with thy whole soul, and with thy whole strength.
>
> And these words which I command thee this day shall be in thy heart. And thou shalt tell them to thy children. And thou shalt meditate upon them sitting in thy house, and walking on thy journey, sleeping and rising. And thou shalt bind them as a sign on thy hand; and they shall be and move [as frontlets] between thine eyes. And thou shalt write them in the entry, and on the doors of thy house. (Deut. 6:4-9)

The winter before Tamar was born, we lived in a little apartment on West Street looking out over the Hudson River docks which was as sun-filled as the chapel in which I meditated. And on the doors of that little apartment, down the street from St. Christopher's Church, in an apartment over a tavern, there were those holy words enclosed and tacked upon the doorpost inside that house. I was strangely moved when it was explained to me by a Russian Jew, a Communist, what it meant. I understand one can find many an apartment in New York, and doubtless in many of our cities with their large Jewish populations, with such small metal containers, hanging unnoticed by the door frame. I feel like going to one of the Hebrew stores on the East Side and purchasing one so that hereafter, always, it may hang on the door of my house. We need these reminders.

When the world is too much with us, how wonderful to think on these things, to let the mind rest on these things, to rejoice in these words: God is Light, Infinite Beauty, Goodness, "for there is no good save only God."

One very dreary, dark morning a year ago, when the dark, cold mist hung like a slime over the streets and tenements around Mott Street, I had been at Mass down at Transfiguration Church, where there was a mission going on. The priest gave a very good homily on the commandment "Thou shalt not take the name of the Lord thy God in vain." Each day he was talking on the commandments, one by one.

In his talk he said that any murmuring against God could be included in the violation of this commandment. He talked of "acceptance" of the will of God in whatever the day brought forth. His talk emphasized the virtue of abandonment to Divine Providence. He even brought in the weather.

And yet as I left the church and stopped to exchange some words with a neighbor, my first words were "Miserable weather, isn't it?" I was immediately conscious of my lapse and laughed at myself as I went down the street.

But it is true that most of our complaining can be construed as thoughtless complaining against God and His Providence. I remember reading once in Romain Rolland that we Western people have lost the beautiful quality of acceptance. Many writers on the East have talked of the philosophical calm and "acceptance" of the Eastern, the Oriental, in the face of heat and cold, disaster and suffering.

Cynically, our Westerner may say that is why they do nothing about poverty and filth and disease. Many of our soldiers were disgusted rather than pitiful at the poverty they saw everywhere, as though it came of choice and sloth. I have heard them express themselves so in regard to our own South. Certainly we Westerners have poverty, filth, and disease side by side with our wealth and comfort. I do not think much of that wealth and comfort, that shining civilization of gadgets and electric lights and skyscrapers, radio and movies. There was the ancient city of Ur out of which Abraham came. I like to turn my thoughts back to Memphis, that great city of Egypt, and Babylon, whose walls extended for forty miles in circumference. And there the Jews sat and wept when they remembered Zion, Jerusalem the golden, so many times razed to the ground.

"Praise the Lord, O my soul. Let all that is within me praise His holy name."

No matter what happens, it is possible to praise, and it is impossible to praise God without that swelling of joy within the breast.

And people! What about people — the evil that men do? I think of Sister Peter Claver and her saying that women's job is to love.

One summer Sister Peter Claver was rebuilding an old farmhouse over in Jersey which was going to be used as a retreat house for Negroes. The place was a wreck — it had not been used for years — and there was work to do in roofing it, painting it, [and] repairing it, and Sister had no money. She came to the Catholic Worker [house] and asked if anyone wanted to work for God. She had to beg for every scrap of paint, shingle, [and] lumber she put into it, getting what she needed week by week.

Two of our men volunteered. Both of them were men who drank, one steadily, the other periodically. John, who drank steadily, went out to Jersey for the summer and never touched a drop for the months he was there. Hugh went out and worked hard, but again and again was tempted and fell. In addition to his other work, he carved a huge beam which separated the sanctuary from the pews in the room they made into a chapel, and he made a crucifix. He had learned these crafts at the Catholic Worker [house].

Sister never became discouraged in her loving charity. She loved these men and brought out the best in them. I've been inclined to attribute that loving warmth of Sister Peter Claver to the fact that she is half-Jewish and half-Irish. It is in her nature to be warm and loving, to see the good in others, I argue to myself. But true it is, she forgives seventy times seven, she sees always the good in the other, she sees a man as made in the image and likeness of God, a temple of the Holy Ghost, the brother of Christ.

Oh, the joy there is in that warmth and love. Bernanos wrote, "Every particle of Christ's divine charity is today more precious for your security — for your security, I say — than all the specie in the vaults of the American government."

ADVENT IS a time of waiting, of expectation, of silence. Waiting for our Lord to be born. A pregnant woman is so happy, so content. She lives in such a garment of silence, and it is as though she were listening to hear the stir of life within her. One always hears that stirring compared to the rustling of a bird in the hand. But the intentness with which one awaits such stirring is like nothing so much as a blanket of silence.

Be still. Did I hear something?

Be still and see that I am God.

Zundel, in *Our Lady of Wisdom,* has some beautiful passages on silence:

> Do we understand at last that action must be born in silence, and abide in silence, and issue in silence, and that its power must be an emanation and the radiation of silence, since its sole aim is to make men capable of hearing the Word that silently reverberates in their souls?
>
> All speech and reasoning, all eloquence and science, all methods and all psychologies, all slogans and suggestions are not worth a minute of silence in which the soul, completely open, yields itself to the embrace of the Spirit.
>
> In solitude Christ speaks to the heart, as a modest lover who embraces not His beloved before all the world.

In silence we hear so much that is beautiful. The other day I saw a young mother who said, "The happiest hour of the day is that early morning hour when I lie and listen to the baby practicing sounds and words. She has such a gentle little voice."

St. James says, "If any man offend not in word, the same is a perfect man." And how much more women need this gift of silence. It is something to be prayed for. Our Lady certainly had it. How little of her there is in the Gospel, and yet all generations have called her blessed. [James says,]

> Behold, how small a fire, how great a forest it kindles. And the tongue is a fire, the very world of iniquity. The tongue is placed among our members, defiling the whole body, and setting on fire the course of our life, being itself set on fire by hell. For every kind of beast and bird and serpent and the rest is tamed and has been tamed by mankind. But the tongue no man can tame — it is a restless evil, full of deadly poison.
>
> With it we bless God the Father; and with it we curse men, who have been made after the likeness of God. [James 3:5-9]

To love with understanding and without understanding. To love blindly, and to folly. To see only what is lovable. To think only on these things. To see the best in everyone around, their virtues rather than their faults. To see Christ in them.

Many people think an examination of conscience is a morbid affair. Péguy has some verses which Donald Gallagher read to me once in the St. Louis House of Hospitality. (He and Cy Echele opened the house there.) They were about examination of conscience. There is a place for it, he said, at the beginning of the Mass. "I have sinned in thought, word, and deed, through my fault, through my fault, through my most grievous fault." But after you get done with it, don't go on brooding about it; don't keep thinking of it. You wipe your feet at the door of the church as you go in, and you do not keep contemplating your dirty feet.

Here is my examination at the beginning of Advent, at the beginning of a new year. Lack of charity, criticism of superiors, of neighbors, of friends and enemies. Idle talk, impatience, lack of self-control and mortification towards self, and of love towards others. Pride and presumption. (It is good to have visitors — one's faults stand out in the company of others.) Self-will, desire not to be corrected, to have one's own way. The desire in turn to correct others, impatience in thought and speech.

The remedy is recollection and silence. Meanness about giving time to others and wasting it myself. Constant desire for comfort. First impulse is always to make myself comfortable. If cold, to put on warmth; if hot, to become cool; if hungry, to eat; and what one likes — always the first thought is of one's own comfort. It is hard for a woman to be indifferent about little material things. She is a homemaker, a cook; she likes to do material things. So let her do them *for others,* always. Woman's job is to love. Enlarge Thou my heart, Lord, that Thou mayest enter in.

And now, with all this talk of silence, I finish this long account of the year. I send the book out with diffidence. It is the work of a journalist who writes because it is her talent; it has been her means of livelihood. And it is sent out with the hopes that it will *sell* so that the printing bill will be paid, and enough [will be] left over to bring out another book next year — perhaps the book about Peter Maurin as well as a book by another of the Catholic Worker editors. We write also to help support the work which we are doing, because we have a very big family, ranging in age from the infant twins at 115 Mott Street to an eighty-four-year-old woman who wandered in from the streets. It is written most personally because I am a woman who can write no other way. If it is preaching and didactic in parts, it is because I am preaching and teaching and encouraging myself on this narrow road we are treading.

"Life," said St. Teresa, "is but a night spent in an uncomfortable inn, crowded together with other wayfarers."

There are bills to pay at an inn, of course, and they are one of the reasons which led me to send this manuscript forth in the care of St. Joseph, patron of all families. May God bless it, and you who read it.